This edition published by Barnes & Noble, Inc.,
by arrangement with Hamlyn.

First published in Great Britain in 1999 by Hamlyn, a division of
Octopus Publishing Group Ltd

Copyright © Octopus Publishing Group Ltd 1999

2005 Barnes & Noble Books

M 10 9 8 7 6 5 4 3 2 1

ISBN 0-7607-7076-X

Printed and bound in China

Operations Director
Laura Bamford
Executive Editor
Jane McIntosh
Editor
Nicola Hodgson
Copy Editor and Proofreader
Mary Lambert
Veterinary Consultant (pp 142–157)
Aaron Hunt BVSc, MRCVS
Creative Director
Keith Martin
Senior Designer
Leigh Jones
Designer
Maggie Aldred
Illustrator
Kate Nardoni at MTG
Picture Researcher
Ellen Root
Production Controller
Sarah Scanlon

North American edition
Managing Editor JoAnn Padgett
Associate Editor Elizabeth McNulty

Encyclopedia of the
CAT

Angela Sayer and Howard Loxton

BARNES & NOBLE BOOKS
NEW YORK

Contents

INTRODUCTION

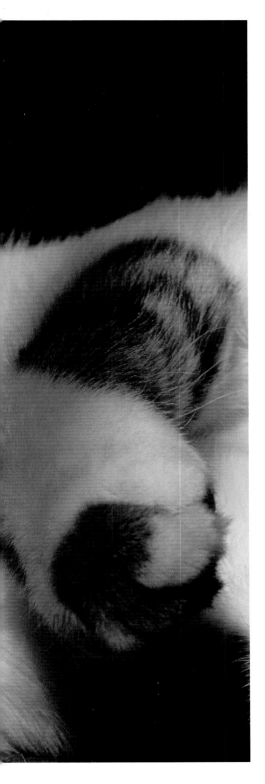

CATS ARE KEPT FOR A variety of reasons. Some are expected to earn their living, either as pest controllers or as breeding stock. Others are kept for prestige and are catered to, pampered, and groomed so that they can uphold the honor of their breed at cat shows. Most are kept just as pets, accepted for what they are: beautiful, graceful, and independent creatures. The cat is not only good company, it also imparts a sense of peace and tranquillity in a stressed, chaotic world. As with other pets, having a cat has been shown to have an advantageous effect in helping us recover from sickness and in keeping us alert and lively as we age.

The cat is an opportunist and has the best of two worlds. Free to slide through the shadows of twilight and dawn in pursuit of prey or romance, equally free to share the comforts of home, food, and a warm fire. Even after more than two thousand years of so-called domestication the cat still remains aloof—friendly and tame, but independent; politely tractable and clean, but living with us on its own terms. It is said that one household in every four throughout the developed world keeps one or more cats, and in Britain and the United States the cat now outnumbers the dog as the most popular pet. Yet, despite these loved cats in caring homes, there are still thousands of mistreated or abandoned pets and many feral animals living a precarious existence and acting as a reservoir for various cat diseases.

All cats should be wanted cats. Unchecked, the population multiplies rapidly and, unless the intention of the owner is to breed, all pet cats should be neutered. Animal welfare groups also have neutering programs for feral cats to control their numbers. Think before you own a cat. It will need a lot of care and attention, and food and veterinary bills have to be met. Be a responsible cat owner. This book will help you understand and care for cats. Enjoy them, and help every cat to have a healthy and happy life.

Detail from an Egyptian papyrus dating from around 1,000 B.C.

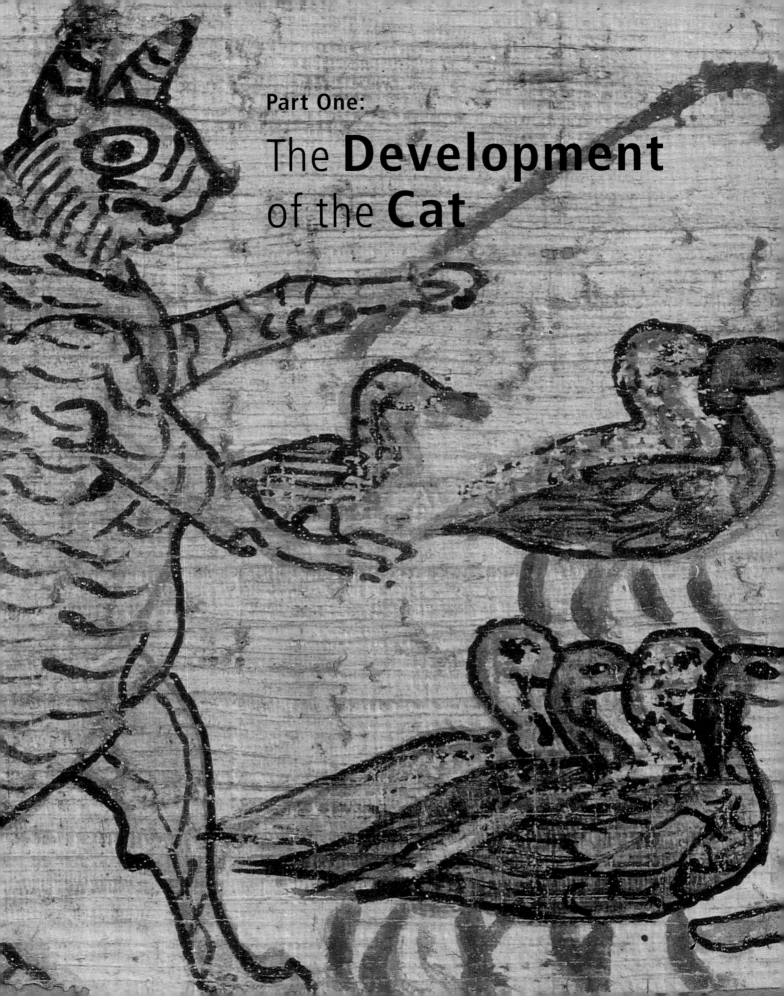

Part One:

The **Development**
of the **Cat**

WILD CATS AND EVOLUTION

right: Lynxes are the only wild members of the cat family to live in both the Old World and the New.

I N THE LONG HISTORY OF THE EARTH cats, like humans, are relatively recent arrivals, but cat-like animals were in evidence long before the earliest men and women stood up and began to walk on their hind legs. It is impossible to trace the full line of descent of the modern cat. Scientists have studied fossil bones and even done DNA tests to try to determine the relationships between different species, but they can only study what has been discovered to date, and many animals may have existed in the past unknown to modern science. As recently as 1964 a new species of wildcat was discovered on the tiny island of Iriomote, east of Taiwan. If living cats can still be discovered that have never before been recorded, what chance is there of finding those precursors of the modern cats that lived on Earth millions of years ago?

No one can be sure about the cat's precise ancestry, and scientists do not agree about the relationships between living cats, but we do know that about 60 million years ago, when mammals were becoming established, there lived creatures called Miacids who hunted and killed for food. They were tenacious little mammals, with short legs and a long, slender body, rather like a weasel in looks and in character. They were the ancestors of several groups of mammals known today, including the bear, the dog, the hyena, the mongoose, the raccoon, and all the members of the cat family.

Cat-like creatures

In the jungles of late Eocene North America, 40 million years ago, two early cat-like animals appeared. One group, including Hoplophoneus, were powerful animals with unusually developed skull structures. In fact, their powerful lower jaws were hinged in such a way that they could open almost at right angles to the upper jaw, and they also had very long, sharp, saber-like canine teeth. The other group included Dinictis, which lived in what is now South Dakota. They had cat-like ways and were somewhat like the modern serval. It used to be thought that this group was the main ancestor of the cat, but more recent research suggests that both groups belonged to the branch of animals that produced dogs. Another cat-like animal, Proailurus, lived in Europe a few million years later, although it seems to have been more like a modern Fossa. It is not until about 20 million years ago that evidence of a true cat, called Pseudaelurus, has been discovered. From this creature, and perhaps a related group of animals, the modern cat family has its origins.

above: Jaguars live in Central and South America. A jungle confrontation like this is echoed by domestic cats when they dispute rights to a territory.

From the Pseudaelurus group developed more saber-toothed animals, and a descendant was the Smilodon, the saber-toothed tiger, whose remains were found preserved in the tar pits of Los Angeles. Also, about 12 million years ago a lineage of creatures arose in Asia that crossed the Bering land bridge to the Americas and produced the ocelot and other smaller cats of South America. After about another two million years the wildcat line developed that was to produce the jungle cat, the African wildcat, and other small Old World cats. Another

part of human hunting and found a role as guards, there is no evidence of early domestication of the cat.

Domestication

When humans began to farm and store their harvests, cats may have come hunting mice attracted by the grain stores. That is only one scenario for their moving in with humans and there is no proof whether and when that happened. The domestic cat belongs to the same species as the wildcat of Europe and Africa. Wildcat bones were found in the city of Jericho when a layer was excavated dating back to 6700 B.C. More significant was the discovery of a wildcat jawbone, dating from about 6000 B.C. and found in Cyprus, which had no indigenous cats. There is no reason why anyone would import a wildcat into this area. It could have been brought from Egypt where pet cats were certainly known to be kept, even though the earliest firm evidence of their existence comes from some thousands of years later.

branch came about nearly four million years ago that produced the cheetah and the puma, while yet another one is today represented by the lynx and the marbled cat. Finally, the big cat members of the pantherine group were produced: the lion, tiger, snow leopard, leopard, and jaguar.

The modern cats

Some two-and-a-half million years ago, the Pleistocene age began. It was the era of the great Ice Age, which ensured that only the fittest and most adaptable forms of life survived on this planet. In those testing centuries the great lakes and fjords of the world were formed and land masses successively sank and rose again as ice sheets froze, then melted, over vast periods of time. Many mammals finally emerged as we know them today, including some 40 species of the cat family, which were highly tuned for survival under these most rigorous and changeable conditions. The upright apes developed greater brains and started to fashion stone implements to use as weapons and tools for killing and skinning other animals. Then about ten thousand years ago the Holocene period began, and climatic conditions improved on Earth as the last of the ice retreated to the Poles. The sea levels rose and great tracts of tundra were replaced by fertile zones, and forests of hardwood trees

sprang up. Humans developed at last from their ape-like predecessors and began to cultivate plants for food. They domesticated useful animals, drew symbols relating to their life on the walls of cave dwellings, and discovered how to make fire. None of the cave paintings found to date depict any animal vaguely resembling our domestic cats, so perhaps they did not feature among the animals that they hunted. It would make a charming picture to imagine the first timorous wild tabby slinking ever nearer to the warmth and comfort of the cooking fire at a cave mouth, of human children adopting kittens and turning them into pets. But while dogs began to become a

THE EGYPTIAN CAT

THE ANCIENT EGYPTIANS represented most of their gods in animal as well as human form, and kept some of these sacred animals in their temple precincts. Several gods and goddesses were shown as lions, or lion-headed. One of them, Bast or Bastet, a goddess of fertility, began to be represented with a cat's rather than a lion's head and the cat became her sacred animal. Cats were certainly kept in her temple at Bubastis in the Nile delta at a place now known as Tell Basta. Their behavior was carefully watched by Bast's priests for any signs they gave which could be interpreted as messages from the goddess. Bast was first shown with a lioness's head and assumed her cat-form in about 1500 B.C., but it is possible that cats were kept earlier at her temple to represent the lions who would have been more difficult to keep in the temple enclosure. Sekmet, a lion-headed daughter of the sun god Ra, was seen as the savage aspect of the hot desert sun, ready to destroy man for his faults. Bast, her sister, became identified with the sun's kindly, life-giving aspect. Great Ra himself was sometimes shown as a cat, especially when depicted overpowering the great snake which represented night, whom he had to vanquish every dawn. Some believed that it was in the eye of the cat that the sun's rays were held at night.

The first pet cats

Did the first domesticated cats originate as wildcats who had been caught, tamed and kept in temples? Were they animals attracted to Egyptian grain stores, did they become scavengers in Egyptian townships, or did they enter human habitations in some other way? Perhaps it happened in all these ways, but we have no sure way of knowing. Our best

left: A bronze and gold statuette of a cat representing the goddess Bastet, dating from about 664–610 B.C.

below: The mummy wrappings of Egyptian cats were sometimes woven into intricate patterns and their faces painted to suggest the animal. Many thousands of such mummies have been found in temple burials.

evidence of early domestication comes from wall paintings in ancient Egyptian tombs. There are several that depict cats apparently in homes, usually placed underneath a chair on which a woman is sitting, although in one case a tiny kitten is playing on the lap of a woman's husband who sits next to her. One cat is shown wearing an earring, one a collar and leash which it pulls at as it looks toward a bowl of food, one gnaws a bone, and another is eating fish. There are about a dozen pictures dating from about 2000 B.C. to 1200 B.C., some from the time when Bast was more usually given a lioness's head, which implies that the cat may have been kept in homes even before it found a place in temples. As well as these pictures of domestic settings, there are a number of paintings that show cats as part of hunting scenes, with human hunters throwing sticks to strike down fowl while the cats flush out the fallen birds and, it has been claimed,

act as retrievers, bringing them back to the hunter.

The ancient Egyptians are believed to have been very adept at handling and training animals and certainly today some pet cats enjoy playing retrieving games with their owners, so it is possible that in past times they could have been trained to help hunters in the marshes of the Nile Delta. However, these cat images may also have had a symbolic and magical function, because the cat also became an emblem of fertility for women and abundance for the hunter in the afterlife.

The temple at Bubastis

The temple of Bast was first erected in about 2500 B.C. at Bubastis by Cheops and Chephren, the pharaohs who built the Sphinx in front of their pyramids at Giza. The cat goddess had already been worshiped there for 15 centuries when a Libyan chieftain called Seshonq seized the throne of Egypt in 945 B.C. and made his capital at Bubastis. Bast then became the most important national goddess. Thousands upon thousands of people would leave their homes in late April and May to sail down the Nile to attend her great annual festival. She was a goddess of pleasure, of singing and dancing, so all the pilgrims brought flutes and cymbals and carried the sistrum, the rattle which statues of Bast often show her holding, which was shaken like maracas to beat out the rhythm of the dance and the rhythm of making love.

left: A wall painting from the tomb of sculptor Nebuman, c.1400 B.C., shows him hunting wild fowl with his wife and daughter in the marshes of the Nile delta. Is the cat helping him by flushing out the birds and retrieving them, or is he there as a symbol to bring fertility in life and success in the hunt?

below: Figures of cats and kittens appear to have been given as votive offerings at the temple of Egypt's cat goddess.

right: An Egyptian Mau is a modern breed originating in local Cairo cats and claims a direct link with ancient cats, whose appearance in ancient Egyptian paintings it resembles.

In the fifth century B.C. Herodotus, a Greek historian and traveler, described how 700,000 people arrived in a high-spirited holiday mood, singing and clapping if they had no instruments, and drinking more wine during this time than for the rest of the year. In his description of the temple he declared "other temples are larger and more magnificent but none more beautiful than this." It was a splendid construction, lower than the foundations of the encircling buildings, of red granite blocks to form an enormous square. On either side canals, one hundred feet wide, were fed by the waters of the Nile and in the center a grove of tall trees protected by a stone wall surrounded the shrine of the goddess. The interior walls were all richly decorated in relief with various scenes and inscriptions. One of these, inside the shrine, showed King Osorkon the Second presenting gifts to the cat goddess. The inscription says: "To thee I give every land in Obeisance. To thee I give all power like Ra"—so this is direct evidence of the cat's importance at the time.

Worshipers brought offerings to Bubastis and to other temples, such as the Bubastion at Saqqara and to the one erected to Pakhet, cat goddess of the middle Nile and a lesser goddess than Bast, at Beni Hassan. These offerings consisted of votive statuettes of Bast and of her sacred cats and of cats themselves: the remains of much loved pets, embalmed and mummified. Strangely, among these cat mummies, some (most of them young kittens) have been found with broken necks and appear to have been deliberately killed. There are others that are merely bundles of bones, not necessarily of cats, and are not really mummies at all. It seems possible that

some cats may have been ritually sacrificed or else bred especially to be mummified and sold to worshipers, in the same way you can buy candles to light in a Catholic church today. However, it seems that if the supply of cats ran out the vendors cheated the worshipers with fake mummies.

Household pets

Egyptian households valued their cats highly. Cats were certainly a feature of life in the homes of noblemen by 1500 B.C. and must soon have become a pet of the common people too. Their association with the goddess gave them protection as sacred animals, and anyone known to have deliberately killed a cat was severely punished. A visiting Roman was nearly lynched when he caused a cat's death in an accident. A Greek historian writing in the first century B.C. describes Egyptians as being so

scared of being blamed for a cat's death that if they came across a dead cat, they immediately began to mourn it.

When a household cat died, of illness or old age, the whole family went into a period of mourning and shaved off their eyebrows as a mark of respect for the dead animal. They would wail, chant, and pound their chests to show their grief, then beat death gongs. The cat would then be embalmed, in much the same way as a human mummy was embalmed. Some organs were removed and the body cavities filled with sand. Then, after a mixture of salts called natron had been rubbed into the body, it was arranged into a compact shape with the forelegs stretched down along the torso, the hind legs tucked up against the pelvis, and the tail curled between the feet. The body was then wrapped in bandages soaked in natron or treated with resin. Outer layers were sometimes

be interred at one of the other cat cemeteries.

Toward the end of the 1880s a cat cemetery discovered at Beni Hassan, near the temple of Pakhet, was found to contain more than 300,000 mummified cats, packed in layers 20 deep. Some were taken by local children and sold to foreign travelers. Local entrepreneurs sold the bones for tooth powder, while the wrappings were used for manure. Nearly 20 tons were loaded on a steamship to Liverpool, where they were sold as fertilizer. Fortunately a few were saved and, with others, provided evidence on the evolution of the cat species. More than a century later another cemetery was found at Saqqara and an undisturbed 66 yd. (60-meter)-long seam of mummified bodies at Pakhet's temple, which will give Egyptologists and zoologists more information about these ancient cats.

In the fifth century B.C. a Persian army led by Cambyses was able to exploit the Egyptians' regard for the welfare of their cats. When they marched on the port of Peluse, guarded by a garrison of Egyptian soldiers, Cambyses ordered his men to carry live cats in their front line as they attacked the city walls. Rather than risk killing any of the sacred animals, the Egyptians surrendered, and the Persians won a bloodless victory.

woven into elaborate patterns. Simple casings of colored straw provided a final covering for poorer families, while the wealthy often commissioned a mummy case specially carved in wood, or fashioned in metal or clay. Some cats were buried in box-shaped caskets, their lids decorated with tiny sculptures of cats and kittens. After the embalming and placement of the small body was completed, the bereaved family would take it to offer it to the goddess at Bubastis or to

right: Today's Egyptian cats are no longer revered as sacred animals but still live among the remains of ancient temples.

THE WORLDWIDE SPREAD OF CATS

EGYPTIAN LAW not only protected cats, it forbade cats being taken out of Egypt; but nevertheless they were exported. Cats appear on Greek vase paintings. In fact, one is carved, looking up at a bird cage on a young man's memorial stone from the fifth century. Another, on a leash, appears in a relief that shows it anxiously facing a playful looking dog. Travelers, such as Herodotus, had described the cat in Egypt and the Greeks knew it as an exotic animal and do not appear to have thought of it as a rodent catcher. For vermin control they relied on a kind of weasel, called a gali—confusingly, this word was also used later for cat. Nevertheless, by the third century a poet from the Greek colony in Sicily was writing "all cats like a cushioned couch," so by then the cat must have become familiar as a domestic pet.

The Roman world

When Julius Caesar conquered Egypt and took Cleopatra back to Rome, all things Egyptian became fashionable there. Temples were built to Isis and other Egyptian gods and, along with Egyptian cults, wealthy Romans imported cats. By the first century A.D., Pliny had written about cats in his *Natural History* and had clearly watched them hunting birds and catching mice. Then a century later, in a treatise on gardening, Palladius was recommending the use of cats for protection against moles and rats.

The Romans took their culture all across Europe, and in the wake of their legions of soldiers followed the rat. In Britain at least, there seem to have been no rats until the Roman period. Originally the black rat was a native of Asia Minor and the Orient, and the brown rat did not reach northern Europe for another thousand years. Cats also went with the Romans, both to hunt the rats and mice (who had arrived some centuries before Caesar's armies), and as domestic pets. A second century A.D. gravestone from western Gaul shows a child holding a pet cat, and cat bones and paw impressions left on wet tiles have been found at Romano-British sites. One cat bone found in Colchester, dated just before the Roman invasion, may be evidence that some cats had been taken to Britain by traders at an even earlier date.

The worth of a cat

At first the cat was probably an animal associated with Roman colonists and wealthy people, but eventually the cat would have become established in the farms and homesteads of the native populations of the Empire. In the unsettled times which followed the withdrawal of the Roman legions from the provinces and the disintegration of the Roman world, the cat probably became more

below: Cats appear in a few Greek vase paintings, on one memorial "stele," and on this panel of a statue base dating from c. 510 B.C. The dog has its head down and tail raised in a typical canine invitation to play, but the cat has arched its back and seems not to trust its potential friend.

of Horus and the eye of Ra, twin symbols of the sun and moon that appear in the talismanic uchat symbol that is often carved on Egyptian figures. Was "mau" originally an onomatopoeic rendering of the cat's voice, or is "meow" a buried memory of the Egyptian word? One version of Bast's name was "Pasht," and some people claim that to be the origin of our word "puss."

The English word "cat" may originate in the Nubian word "kadis," for in the early centuries A.D. a similar word traveled through the Baltic, Slavic, Mediterranean, and Atlantic countries, along the trade routes over which the increasingly popular cat was carried. The cat is called similar names in these countries, most of which have only minor differences in spelling or pronunciation.

HOLLAND AND DENMARK	KAT
SWEDEN	KATT
GERMANY	KATZE
POLAND	KOT
RUSSIA	KOTS
GREECE	GATTA
(but in classical Greek AILOUROS*)*	
PORTUGAL AND SPAIN	GATO
ITALY	GATTO
FRANCE	CHAT

Variations and other languages include the words: *catt, cath, catus, cattus, cait, katte, katti, kottr, kazza, kattos, kate, and kotu.*

The necessary cat

The early Christian Church associated the cat with paganism; not just the worship of Bast but goddesses which had many of her associations, such as the moon goddess Diana, or in northern religions Freya, whose chariot was drawn by cats. Diana also became identified with

valued for its usefulness than as a pampered pet. Its value was codified in laws enacted in 936 by the prince of southern Wales, Hywel the Good. One law decreed that the worth of a kitten from its birth until it had opened its eyes was put at one legal penny, from the time it opened its eyes until it was capable of killing mice it was worth two pence, and when it had reached hunting age it was worth four pence. The tiethi, or qualities, of a cat were to see, hear, and kill mice, to have sharp claws, and to rear kittens without devouring them. If anyone bought a cat and found it to be deficient in any one of these qualities, he was entitled, under Hywel's law, to have one

third of the purchase price returned. The law also covered the stealing and killing of cats. Recompense for the owner was determined by holding the cat by the tail tip so that the head just touched a clean and even floor, then threshed wheat was poured over the cat until the tip of the tail was covered, and the corn was said to be equal to the animal's value. If grain was not available, a milch ewe, her fleece, and her lamb was said to be equal to the value of the cat.

Names used for the cat

The Egyptian word for cat was Mau, a word which also means "to see," and the cat was linked with the concept of the eye

Hecate, originally a goddess but increasingly seen as a queen of witches with cats as part of her world. This did not stop some churchmen from loving cats, Pope Gregory the Great among them, and one of the most delightful poems about cats was written by an Irish monk about his pet Pangur Ban who sat up all night hunting mice as he sat up hunting words as he copied manuscripts. Cats were the only pets that nuns and abbesses of one monastic order were allowed, according to twelfth century regulations. The cat was accepted as a useful pet, and if peasants sometimes held on to some old beliefs about cats they did not seriously interfere with the practice of religion.

Things changed in the thirteenth century, when there was the development of the Albigensian and Waldensian sects in opposition to the established Church and a revival of pagan cults occurred, linked with Freya. Pope Gregory IX declared that heretics worshiped the devil in the form of a black cat, and a century later Pope Clement V, wanting to suppress the religious order of the Knights Templar, accused its members of similar practices. The Church also began to take seriously the idea of witchcraft, previously dismissed as a delusion, and associated cats with witches, leading to the persecution of thousands of harmless people and their pets and encouraging ceremonies in many places where cats were deliberately tortured and killed.

This persecution came at the very time that cats were most needed, to kill the rats that had been introduced to Europe by ships bringing crusaders home from the Holy Land. These rats spread the bubonic plague throughout Europe, and millions of people died. Cats continued to be viewed suspiciously up to the eighteenth century but practical considerations saw them return to favor as a necessity in a household, and the character of individual cats ensured their survival as much loved pets.

Cats in the eastern world

Trade links between the Mediterranean world and China flourished during the dominance of the Roman Empire and

that of the Han dynasty in the East. There is evidence of cats in China from about A.D. 400, but then nothing is recorded for nearly 600 years—except that in the sixth century A.D. some members of the Imperial family were banished to the perimeter of the Empire, accused of using "cat-specters" against the Empress. China also had what may have been a feline fertility god, a sort of divine ratter called Li Chou, and cats must have persisted in China because a cat from China was presented to Emperor Koko of Japan in 884. Cats must already have reached Japan by this time; a ghost story written in 705 describes a dead man appearing in cat form.

In 999, the Japanese Emperor Ichijo was presented with a cat from Korea. It gave birth to five kittens in the Imperial Palace in Kyoto, and Ichijo was so entranced when they were born on the tenth day of the fifth moon that he ordered special care and feeding arrangements for the family. He also instructed that they must be protected from all outside interference so that similar kittens could be bred in the future—this was the first record of a planned breeding program for domestic cats.

It is about this time that cats begin to appear in Chinese art, in particularly in portraits of the children of the nobility,

above: *This cat painted by Domenico Ghirlandino next to Judas in this fifteenth century fresco of the Last Supper represents evil Iscariot's perfidy.*

below: *In India both Hindu and Islamic traditions favored the cat and it appears as a pet in a number of court paintings.*

which was evidence of the prestige they had. In both China and Japan their practical value was also appreciated as a defense against the plagues of mice that attacked silkworm cocoons.

For a time Asian cats became so prized as pampered pets, rather than working cats, that pottery and painted cats were set up to frighten off the mice, sometimes with a candle set inside them. They were not effective. Granaries and food stores were plagued by vermin and the silk industry was seriously damaged. Eventually, although not until the seventeenth century, a law was passed in Japan which decreed that cats should not be kept on leashes and should not be bought and sold or even given as presents. They were free to behave as natural hunters and resume their role as working cats.

The cats of the Far East tend to have a slimmer form than those of northern Europe. Whether this is due to interbreeding with local wild cats or an adaptation of the original form to different climatic conditions is debatable. There have also been suggestions that the first

above: A banquet during the reign of the tenth century, fifth dynasty Tang Emperor, showing that the cat (lower left) was established at the Chinese Imperial Court by this time.

right: From China the cat was taken to Japan and became a pet of the Imperial Household and the nobility. Taiso Yoshitishi made this woodblock print of the beauty and her pet in the nineteenth century.

right: When this mid-nineteenth century Staffordshire pottery ornament was made the cat was already well-established and a popular fireside pet.

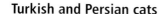

longhaired varieties may have developed under the controlled conditions in which cats were kept in both homes and temples. This would have enabled a mutant kitten, treasured for its appearance, to produce more longhaired kittens. Scroll paintings attributed to a fifteenth century Chinese emperor depict longhaired cats, and traditionally it has been claimed that longhaired cats with pointed patterns like the Siamese were kept in Buddhist temples in southeast Asia. This has been questioned by those who believe the modern Birman cat was more likely a twentieth century European creation. However, in 1960 two cats of this kind were discovered in Tibet.

The Siamese cat, and several other cats with different markings, including the blue Korat, were known long ago in Thailand. In fact, they appear in an ancient scroll that may date from as early as the fourteenth century, and in Japan a breed with a short tail, often curled back to look like a rabbit's tail, became established. All developed, perhaps, because of the prestigious revered position that cats once held in Asian countries.

Turkish and Persian cats

Unlike the Christian church, Islam approved of the cat. Traditionally it was believed that the prophet Mohammed had cut off the sleeve of a garment rather than disturb his cat Muezza, who was sleeping upon it, and that he used water for purifying himself despite the fact that a cat had been drinking from the same source. One of his close followers was so fond of cats that Mohammed gave him a new name, Abu-Kurairha, which means "father of cats."

It was from the Islamic world that the first longhaired cats were brought to western Europe in the sixteenth century, although their origins may have been in colder northern lands. They came from

left: August Renoir loved to include a cat in his paintings of women. When he painted this one in 1875, the cat was already beginning to attract enthusiasts, and longhairs like this were soon to dominate the early cat shows.

Turkey and were described as being "beautiful to behold, ash-colored, dun and speckled." These cats had long silky fur, long heads, and pointed ears—we now know them as Angora Cats. A slightly later arrival was the Persian cat, which had much thicker fur, a broad head, and a long bushy tail. The new arrivals were treated as exotic pets rather than working cats.

Ships' cats

Nowhere was the cat more highly valued than aboard ship, especially after the brown rat joined the black rat in Europe from the sixteenth century. The holds of ships often teemed with rats, and the cat was the only way of keeping them under control. Ships' cats were a law unto themselves. They came aboard and went ashore at will, although they were usually loyal to their own ship. Kittens were often born at sea, and, when independent, might disembark to start a new life in a port far from the land of their conception. In this way not just cats, but cats of new shapes and colors, were carried around the world.

Brown rats colonized everywhere. They thrived in conditions unsuitable for black rats, and soon a cat became a necessary addition to the staff of offices, shops, warehouses, government buildings, and royal palaces. Every farm, bakery, food store, and shop had its cats and they became an acceptable part of the home and workshop in most countries of the world, accepted on their own terms. Despite its independence, the cat has insinuated itself into the lives and hearts of many, eventually establishing itself firmly and irrevocably, first as a fireside pet, and later still as an object of acquisition as specific breeds developed.

below: Feral cats on the Greek islands keep an eye open for an opportunity to steal or beg a fish from the day's catch or demand food from tourists.

CATS OF MYTH AND MAGIC

CATS HAVE BEEN ASSOCIATED with many superstitions, religious ceremonies, and magical rites since the earliest days of their domestication. Bast and Freya were both cat-linked fertility goddesses and as the cat is such a fecund creature it is not surprising that the cat features in fertility rituals. A reversal of such pagan associations can account for the Christian world associating cats with demonic powers. In the Eastern world they are not the only animal with shape-changing occult associations, but perhaps the nocturnal life of cats and their ability to arrive from nowhere and to disappear suddenly encouraged such ideas. Today, pharmaceutical preparations involving cats seem more like witch's spells than real remedies, but an element of superstition still survives: a black cat is often seen as an omen, a good luck charm, or a vestige of the idea that cats "suck breath" from babies.

right: When German artist Hans Baldung made this woodcut of a witches' sabbath in 1510 he saw a cat as an essential component of the witches' gathering.

below left: The medieval church associated the cat with darkness and the powers of evil. Coupled with a demonic bat on this church seat, it reminded monks that they should be watchful for the devil.

Cat rituals

The sacrifice of the king-priest or of a sacred animal to ensure the renewal of the seasons and the earth was part of ancient belief, echoed even in Christ's crucifixion. In France and Germany cats were richly fed, garlanded with flowers, then ritually eaten on the first day of harvest. In Eastern Europe a cat was buried alive to ensure a field gave a good harvest. Elsewhere, a cat was bound within the last sheaf of corn and then beaten to death with the flails used for threshing. Later the cat was spared but the final sheaf that was cut and tied was called the "cat's tail." In Silesia the man who cut it was given a tail of stalks to wear and called Tom Cat. A second reaper was chosen as She Cat, and together the two would chase the other harvesters, beating them ritualistically.

Remnants of old beliefs passed down the generations, and children of rural areas were warned against trampling the growing corn for fear that the corn cat would get them. Cats were adorned with flowers, ribbons, and ears of corn at the start of the harvest in Briançon, France, and were the center of celebrations until the crop was safely gathered in, when the decorations were ritualistically removed. Any reaper cutting himself with a scythe during the harvesting would have the wound licked clean by the cat.

Farmers in southeast Asia used cats in rain-making rituals. In Malaya they prayed and played instruments as a cat was repeatedly immersed in a large earthenware pan of water and almost drowned. In Java cats were repeatedly dipped in pools, and in the Celebes the cat, tied securely in a sedan chair, was carried three times around a parched field before being doused with water to bring the rain. Sumatran ceremonies required a black cat so that the sky would darken with rain clouds. The cat was carried into the river, then released to swim ashore, while being chased and splashed before it could make its escape.

In Aix-en-Provence in France, a cat sacrifice was turned into a strange

Christian celebration. On the feast of Corpus Christi a fine tomcat was caught, swaddled in linen, then placed in a beautifully appointed shrine for public worship. Incense was burned and prayers chanted; then, at the close of the day, the bound cat was put in a wicker basket and thrown alive into the heart of a bonfire in the city square while priests walked up and down and sang anthems.

At least as late as the eighteenth century cats were used in a building sacrifice, replacing what was once a human offering, and in more recent years has become a burial of coins or other objects with foundation stones. Several cats have been discovered in London. One, found in Southwark, held a rat in its jaws and had another pinned beneath its forefeet. At Hay Hill a very well preserved cat with a small bird was discovered, dating back to the fourteenth century. Such cats were were thought to give protection from vermin or from witchcraft.

Cat medicine

Many superstitions arose concerning the healing powers of the cat. The Roman writer Pliny considered cats' feces to be effective when they were mixed with: mustard to cure ulcers of the head, with resin and oil of roses to cure problems of the uterus, and mixed into a paste with wine to draw out thorns. Centuries later, Edward Topsell, in *The History of Four Footed Beastes*, recommended dried powdered cat's liver as a cure for bladder stones, rendered cat fat to cure gout, and for eye pains and blindness gave instructions to burn the head of a black cat, make a powder from it and blow it through a quill into the affected eye. In 1693 William Salmon was still repeating such recipes in his *Compleate English Physician*.

Folk beliefs ranged from rubbing the eye with a black cat's tail to cure a sty to curing whitlows by winding the tail of a black cat in an intricate pattern through the fingers of the affected hand, on each of three successive days. Three drops of blood from a cat's tail were thought to provide a cure for the "falling sickness," or epilepsy, and in Mark Twain's

Adventures of Tom Sawyer, Huckleberry Finn explains how to cure warts by taking a cat to a graveyard in the middle of the night when "...Devil follow corpse, cat follow Devil, wart follow cat, that will fetch any wart."

Cat's fur was used to relieve the pain of Londoners burned in the Great Fire of 1666. Dead cats were skinned and their soft fur placed against people's burns, insulating the wound against the air. In Holland and elsewhere dead cats' skins were used to treat sore throats and severe skin infections, and in Japan a live black cat was placed across the stomach to treat severe gastric troubles and epilepsy.

Sea cats and weather lore

The cat became such an invaluable part of a ship's crew that it was inevitable that nautical traditions developed around it. It was widely believed to bring good luck, and to the Japanese a mi-ke cat (tortoiseshell or patched white, red, and black) was thought particularly lucky. It was usually treated well by sailors; to treat cats badly was unlucky, and to throw one

overboard, especially a black cat, was considered a certain way to invoke a violent storm.

Cats were seen as a guide to forthcoming weather—and certainly, like a barometer, they are extremely sensitive to air pressure and become restless and nervous of sudden noises a few hours before a storm breaks. There have been some conflicting ideas about how their behavior should be read: a cat washing its face has been seen as a sign of good weather, but also interpreted as a sign of coming rain. The mi-ke cat not only could tell when storms were coming, but if sent up the mast was thought to be able to scare away storm demons. Cats were also thought to be able to raise a wind when a ship was becalmed, but first an iron pot had to be brought on deck, turned upside down, and the cat placed beneath it.

On shore too, cats were guides to weather. In China, they were said to wink when rain was coming. Washing behind their ears was said to predict rain, and if they sat with their backs to

left: A Russian woodcut representing the cat, from the eighteenth century.

the hearth, a hard frost was expected. In Scotland a cat scratching at a table leg foretold gale force winds, while elsewhere cats wildly scampering about and mewing presaged severe storms. A Slav myth claimed that cats' bodies were inhabited by demons during thunderstorms and that the thunderclaps brought forth angels' prayers, while the cat devils mocked them. Lightning was aimed by the angels at the cats to cast out the demons, so when there was a storm cats had to be chased from the house to prevent it from being struck by lightning.

Demons and witches

It was not only to his worshipers that the Devil appeared in cat form. Sightings of the Devil in the form of a black cat have been frequently linked with various disasters ranging from a city-wide outbreak of St. Vitus' Dance in Metz (now in France) for which 13 cats were burned each year thereafter for four centuries, to an appearance in Salem, Massachusetts, where 150 people were accused of witchcraft in 1692. At Salem, Robert Downer testified that a She-Devil in cat-form

leapt through his window and attacked him on his bed. Public cat burnings took place at other places too: in Paris, for instance, on St. John's Day. In Ypres live cats were thrown down from a tower, a custom revived today with stuffed fabric cats as part of a festival which celebrates cat history and legends.

One Japanese demon in cat form murdered the beautiful lover of a prince, then took her shape to share the prince's bed and suck his blood. Witches were also thought to be able to alter shape, and one Scotswoman accused of witchcraft in 1662 was made to reveal her spell for changing into a cat. A sixteenth-century book claimed that witches could only take cat form nine times. There are many stories of witches being identified because someone managed to injure them while in their cat form and later, when they changed back to human shape, they still bore the same wounds.

Japanese witches were often attended by "nekomata," or demon cats. They could often, but not always, be recognized because they had a tail that split in two. Sometimes people cut off kittens

above left: A twentieth-century artist's interpretation of the famous seventeenth-century Witch Trials in Salem, Massachusetts, shows the most famous American example of witchcraft charges. Here a male witch protests his innocence.

above right: A nineteenth century woodblock print by Taisho Yoshitoshi shows sorcerers with their animal demons. Japanese witches, like European ones, could change their shape into cats.

left: Puss-in-Boots, hero of the famous fairy tale, is typical of the French "matagot," or luck-bringing cat, that ensured that those who treated them properly had good fortune. This is one of Gustave Dore's illustrations of the story.

above: Maneki-neko, "Beckoning Cat" figures, are a good luck talisman in homes and often used to welcome customers to Japanese shops and restaurants.

tails to stop them from developing into nekomata. In Britain, more strongly than in continental Europe, there was a strong belief in witches having demon servants, known as familiars, in return for their pact with the Devil. These could take many forms, usually small animals, but Edmund Topsell claimed in 1609 that they "most ordinarily appear in the shape of cats, which is an argument that the beast is dangerous to soul and body." It is easy to see how in olden days someone, especially a woman living alone, making a fuss over her cat and perhaps letting it sleep on her bed, could be accused of being a witch and consorting with the devil. Such accusations brought death to thousands of people and their cats, for the persecution continued for many years. The last witch trial in Britain was in 1712, and as late as 1749 a Bavarian nun was beheaded after confessing that three cats she kept and talked to were really devils.

Lucky cats

Today, witches' cats have been consigned to fiction but people still have supersti-tions about cats. Strangely there are often quite contradictory beliefs in different places. Black cats are lucky in Britain, but are often thought unlucky in the U.S.A., where white cats bring good luck—except at night when they too are considered unlucky. In the French region of Brittany it used to be believed that all black cats had at least one white hair and, if you could find it and pull it out, that would bring you both wealth and luck in love.

In the Far East, Buddhists consider all cats lucky, but in Japan there is an espe-cially lucky one, the Maneki-neko, or Beckoning Cat. This was the cat of an impoverished Buddhist shrine who one day attracted the attention of passing samurai by raising a paw to them and encouraging them to visit. While resting there and hearing the resident monk speak on spiritual matters they escaped a violent storm. Their lord was very impressed when he heard what had hap-pened and took an interest in the temple, which over the years became well estab-lished with his support. Today, it is a shrine where people come to pray for their cats and make offerings, often of fig-ures of the maneko-neko with his arm raised in greeting. The figure of the beck-oning cat has now become a good luck talisman for people who do not even know its story.

Scandinavians have their own good luck cat, the Butter Cat, for whom some people put out cream, but it was in south-ern France that a belief in lucky cats was strongest. These were known as "matagots," and if you treated them properly they were thought to bring good fortune—the most famous matagot being the one that featured in the fairy tale of Puss-in-Boots.

rt Two:
he **Breeds** of the **World**

COAT COLORS AND PATTERNS

CATS VARY IN THEIR SHAPE AND SIZE but are broadly classified by the length and color of their fur. The hair color depends upon pigment granules containing melanin in the cells of the epidermis, the outer layer of the skin. Melanin takes two forms, one giving rise to black and brown (eumelanin), the other to red or yellow (phaenomelanin).

right: Oriental Cinnamon

Tabbies, solid coats, and pointed patterns

The original wildcat coat, with both these forms present, has black hairs banded (ticked) or tipped with yellow and is called agouti. In the ancestors of the domestic cat this formed a variety of patterns of spots and stripes against paler ticked backgrounds and the variations known as tabby patterns, the oldest and most dominant markings in the domestic cat.

There are four basic tabby patterns: the ticked type, as found in the Abyssinian breed; the vertically striped mackerel; the clearly defined spotted; and the intricately marked classic, blotched with whorls or "oyster" marks on the sides of the body. It seems likely that the first color mutation was a simple non-agouti gene giving rise to black cats; this was probably the first solid- or self-color coat. The same mutation can be seen in other cat species, with black (or melanistic) forms fairly common in wild populations.

Another mutation produced a series of alternate genes or alleles, known as the albino series, which reduce the level of pigmentation. These have produced the restriction of pigmentation found in breeds such as the Burmese, or more extremely the Siamese, in which the color is removed from most of the body and diluted in intensity on the extremities; and finally also albino cats. White can also be the result of a dominant gene that prevents the spread of pigment carrying melanocytes through the body, and a similar gene is thought to produce white markings.

Coat colors

All the various colors now found in the cat are mutations from the original black and yellow. One mutant gene occurred that has the effect of reducing the normal black pigmentation to brown, or chocolate, while on yellow it produces an auburn effect.

A dilution of black to blue was brought about by a simple mutant gene, inherited as a recessive. The pigment granules within the hair shafts are arranged in such a way that the animal appears to be slate gray in color. This dilution gene also works on yellow pigmentation, changing it to cream, and on chocolate, changing it to lilac or lavender.

The mutation that gave rise to orange or red coloring in the cat is particularly interesting, as the gene is linked to the X chromosome and the coloration it produces is therefore sex-linked. This gene is independent of other color and pattern genes, and so can be inherited along with them, giving rise to many beautiful and variable coat patterns, particularly in the female.

The gene for silver takes out most of the yellow, especially in any agouti areas, but leaves the black. The gene for Burmese takes out even more yellow and modifies the black areas to dark brown.

Eye colors

Eye color in the cat is very variable and is also due to the distribution of melanin. Some genes that influence coat color also affect the color of the eyes—all Siamese or Himalayan patterned cats, for example, have blue eyes, whatever the color of their points. The requirements for pedigree cats often stipulate that cats should have an eye color appropriate to breed or coat color.

far left: *Persian Cameo Tabby*
left: *British Red Spotted Shorthair*

right: British Cream Shorthair

Color and pattern terms

Most of the varieties of cat are known by their descriptive names or colors. Some of the basic colors of the cat are simple to interpret—black, white, cream, and silver for instance, but others are more obscure.

Blue refers to any shade of cold-toned gray, from the palest to the darkest shade of slate.

Lilac is a very pale warm-toned gray.

Brown can refer to any shade of dark brown, except in the brown tabby, when it refers to a cat that is genetically black, having black markings on an agouti background.

Sable is used in some cases, especially in the U.S.A., for brown cats that are genetically black.

Chocolate refers to a rich warm brown coloration.

Cinnamon is a lighter shade of chocolate.

Red refers to all shades of ginger, although the deeper coppery tones are most sought after.

Ruddy is the modification of the black in the Abyssinian to reddish brown and burnt sienna.

Sorrel is the modification of the red in the Abyssinian to brownish orange to light brown.

Mink is a range of colors in the Tonkinese.

Champagne is a buff-cream color, especially in the Burmese, with warm honey beige shading to pale gold tan.

Platinum is pale silvery gray with pale fawn undertones.

Bronze is warm coppery brown that lightens to buff.

Bicolor is a white coat with dark patches.

Harlequin is a bicolor coat with white 50–75%, color 50–25%.

Tortoiseshell is the name given to a cat with two colors in the coat, patches of black and red. This is often shortened to Tortie, or if it has white patches and is tri-colored, it is called a Tortie-and-White.

Calico is the term used in the U.S.A. for Tortoiseshell-and-White

Blue-Cream is the dilute version of Tortoiseshell, with a mingled or patched coat of palest gray and cream. There are Chocolate-Cream and Lilac-Cream varieties of some breeds as well.

Particolor covers both bicolors and tortoiseshells.

Patched is a two-tone tabby coat with darker and lighter patches, mingling tabby and tortoiseshell.

Tortie is an alternative name for patched.

Smoke cats often look plain colored, but when the fur is parted, the undercoat is white, each hair being white at the roots and colored at the ends. Tipped coats are when hairs are colored only at the very tips, creating a sparkling effect.

Chinchilla is a white coat that has colored tips.

Cameo is white fur with red tips.

above: British Blue, Tortie and White Shorthair
below: British Silver Classic Tabby

Shorthaired Breeds

SHORTHAIRED BREEDS

I N THE WILD ALL CATS have short hair, so this can be considered the natural coat of the domestic cat and variations as mutations from it. The cats of ancient Egypt and those found today around the Mediterranean are generally rather slender animals, while the breeds known as Shorthairs are chunkier cats. This is because they are derived largely from the northern European type, which may have been influenced by some interbreeding with the European wildcat and belongs to the same species as the African wildcat. The slimmer cat is more like those generally thought of as Orientals or Foreign Type—although they may be neither Oriental or even foreign in origin. Those listed under Shorthairs here include cats that were developed from the cobby shorthair stock even though their appearance does not conform to that type.

Until comparatively recently little distinction was made between the British and European shorthairs, and they were often treated as the same breed. So too was the Chartreux, which many considered to be another name for the British Blue Shorthair type. Characteristics that occur through chance mutation, such as changes of hair type to curly Rex fur or the dropped ears of the Scottish Fold, did not meet approval from many cat breeders when they were first developed into breeds. Therefore they were not immediately recognized, and in some cases are still not recognized by some cat associations.

Shorthaired cats can make delightful pets and do not require elaborate grooming.

CHARTREUX

T HE CHARTREUX IS THOUGHT to be an old French breed that may go back hundreds of years, although the modern show breed was not developed until the end of the 1920s. A French Dictionary of 1723 contains the first known reference to Carthusian monks being linked with this cat and it is sometimes claimed that in the seventeenth century it was imported from the Cape of Good Hope in South Africa by Carthusian monks—although there has never been a Carthusian foundation there. The same dictionary provides another possible explanation of the cat's name as it describes a fine wool cloth known as Pile de Chartreux—and the Chartreux cat is renowned for its short, glossy, dense coat with a slightly woolly undercoat that makes the hair stand out. The Carthusian identification stuck and the breed is known in Italy as the Certosino, in Germany as the Karthäuser, and in Holland as the Karthuizer.

The breed had to be almost completely recreated after World War Two and French breeders made use of other shorthair and non-pedigree cats with suitable coats until the distinctive plush blue coat had been achieved. These cats were very like the British Blue Shorthair and consequently there was resistance to considering a different breed. It is still not accepted by the British Governing Council. However, the Chartreux should be a more massive cat with broad shoulders and a deep chest set on medium-length legs with round feet. In Europe large feet are expected, but in the U.S.A. they are much more dainty. The tail is long, can taper, and should have an oval tip. The head is rounded and broad with a flat narrow space between the ears, big jowls in males, and a broad straight nose, all set on a short, thick-set neck.

The highly placed ears are medium large and flaring. The eyes are large and rounded in the U.S.A., but in Europe the outer edge should be turned slightly upward. They should be deep yellow to copper, with an intense orange preferred.

This is considered a friendly and gentle cat and is often described as lazy until the appearance of a mouse, when it turns into a fierce predator.

Color

This is a one color cat. All shades of blue are permissible, but the plush coat must be even in tone. In the U.S.A. a bright blue is preferred; in Europe a pale, gray blue.

right: Chartreux
previous page: British Blue Shorthair

BRITISH SHORTHAIR

THIS STURDY, MUSCULAR CAT had its origins in the household working cat that was first introduced to Britain by the Romans, but must now conform to strict breed standards. It is heavier and stockier than most ordinary domestic pet cats. The British Shorthair was developed when competitive cat shows began to be held from 1871. It almost disappeared at the end of the century but was revived by the creation of the Shorthaired Cat Society in 1901.

The British Shorthair has a low-lying body with a level back, deep broad chest, massive at the shoulders and rump, set on short legs with rounded paws—a conformation usually described as "cobby." The thick tail is medium-long, thicker at the base and tapering slightly to a rounded tip. The round, massive head is apple-shaped with full cheeks and has a broad, short, straight nose with a not very prominent break, a level bite and a firm chin on the same plane as the nose tip. The ears are small, with rounded tips and set well apart. The eyes are large, round, and are also set well apart.

The fur is short and dense but not woolly or forming a double coat. It rarely tangles, making grooming a simple process; hand-grooming will remove most of the old hairs, although daily brushing is desirable to keep the coat in good condition. The blue variety of this breed has long had the reputation of having the plushest fur of all the shorthaired cats, combined with good conformation and a very gentle nature.

The eyes should be gold, orange, or copper with most coat colors; these or blue or odd-eyed with white; green or hazel with silver; and green with gold-tipped fur. British Shorthairs have retained their hunting skills and make friendly domestic companions.

The breed is recognized in the U.S.A. as distinct from the American Shorthair but at present in fewer color varieties than have been accepted in Britain.

Colors
GCCF
Self or Solid Colors: White, Black, Chocolate, Lilac, Red, Blue, Cream.

Tabby (classic and mackerel): Red, Brown, Blue, Chocolate, Lilac, Cream, Silver, Blue Silver, Chocolate Silver, Lilac Silver, Red Silver, Cream Silver.

Spotted: Brown, Blue, Chocolate, Lilac, Red, Cream, Silver, Blue Silver, Chocolate Silver, Lilac Silver, Red Silver, Cream Silver.

Tortie Tabby: Tortie, Tortie Silver, Tortie Spotted, Tortie Silver Spotted.

Tortoiseshell: Tortie, Blue-Cream, Chocolate Tortie, Lilac Tortie.

Tortoiseshell and White: Tortie and White, Blue Tortie and White, Chocolate Tortie and White, Lilac Tortie and White.

Bicolor: Black and White, Blue and White, Chocolate and White, Lilac and White, Red and White, Cream and White.

Smoke: Black, Blue, Chocolate, Lilac, Red, Cream, Tortie, Blue Tortie, Chocolate Tortie, Lilac Tortie.

Tipped: Black, Blue, Chocolate, Lilac, Red, Cream, Black Tortie, Blue Tortie, Chocolate Tortie, Lilac Tortie, Golden.

Colorpointed: Seal, Blue, Chocolate, Lilac, Red, Cream, Seal Tortie, Blue-Cream; Tabby, Silver Tabby, and Smoke versions of these colors.

CFA
Any color and pattern other than those involving chocolate, lavender, or colorpoint (Himalayan) pattern.

above: Black Smoke British Shorthair

right: Cream Tabby British Shorthair

AMERICAN SHORTHAIR

right: Red Tabby American Shorthair
far right: Silver and Red Tabby European Shorthairs
below: Silver Tabby American Shorthair

THE AMERICAN SHORTHAIR, which until 1966 was known as the "Domestic Shorthair," is now quite distinct from British and European Shorthairs. The breed originated in the working cats that were imported into America long ago. The first registered under the name Shorthair in the U.S.A. was a red tabby called Belle—despite being a tom-cat—that arrived from Britain at the beginning of the twentieth century.

This breed is a medium-large cat with a compact, muscular, and heavy body and a short, rounded face. The body length from breastbone to rear should be slightly longer than the height from the ground to the shoulderblades. The head is usually large and full-cheeked and slightly longer than wide with a continuous curve from the forehead over the top of the head and a medium-long nose. Mature males should have a definite jowl. The ears are slightly rounded and the eyes are large and wide set, the upper lid having an almond-shaped curve and the lower fully rounded. The legs are medium-long, slightly longer than the British Shorthair,

and the medium-long tail tapers to an abrupt blunt end.

The coat is short, thick, and hard in texture, not resilient like that of the British Shorthair, but more dense.

The eyes should be brilliant gold with most coats, except for white which may also be blue or odd-eyed, and for silvers which should be green, hazel in tabbies, and green or blue-green with cats with tipped coats.

American Shorthairs are character-ized as robust, friendly, intelligent, and independent. They are good hunters and excellent working cats, while their placid nature makes them ideal companions.

Colors
CFA
Solid Colors: White, Black, Blue, Red, Cream.

Shaded and Silver: Chinchilla Silver, Shaded Silver, Shell and Shaded Cameo, and Blue and Cream versions of these.

Tabby (Classic and Mackerel patterns): Silver, Red, Brown, Blue, Cream, Blue Silver (Pewter), Cameo, Cream Cameo, Blue Silver (Pewter).

Patched Tabby (Tortie Tabby): Brown, Blue, Silver, Blue Silver (Pewter).

Tabby and White: White with Tabby in Brown, Blue, Red, Cream, Silver, Cameo; with Patched Brown, Blue and Silver; and with Van, Blue Cream.

Smoke: Black, Blue, Cameo (Red), Tortoiseshell, Blue Cream.

Smoke and White: As for smoke but with both Shell and Shaded Cameo.

Bicolors: White with Red, Blue, Cream, Calico, Dilute Calico, and Van versions of these colors.

Particolor: Tortie, Calico (Tortie and White), Dilute Calico (Blue Cream), Van Calico, Van Dilute Calico and Shaded versions of Tortie, Dilute Tortie, Chinchilla Tortie and Dilute Chinchilla Tortie.

EUROPEAN SHORTHAIR

I N 1982 THIS BREED was established on the European Continent as distinctly separate from the British Shorthair and it is also recognized as such by the Cat Association of Britain, although the Governing Council of the Cat Fancy does not yet recognize it as a separate breed. It is very like the British Shorthair and has its origins in similar domestic working and pet cats, but its differences have become more marked since it was given separate breed status. It is a muscular cat with a stocky body of medium length set on strong, thick legs that are slightly longer than those of the British cat, and with rounded paws. It does not have the same cobby look. Its medium-long tail can reach back to between the base of the rib cage and the shoulder. It has a rounded head with a muzzle slightly longer than in the British cat, making it a little longer than it is wide, and in profile there is a slight indentation at eye level. Its ears are rounded, larger than in the British cat, and set well apart, as are its large, round eyes.

The fur of the European Shorthair is short, very thick, and firm to the touch.

The eyes should be blue, orange, or one of each with white cats; green or hazel with silver coats; green with gold-tipped fur; and gold, orange, or copper with other coat colors.

The European Shorthair has been described as being intelligent, having a good temperament, being adaptable, and a quiet and lively cat.

Colors
All solid colors, bicolors, and tabby patterns and in theory the same color range as the British Shorthair. Some countries also recognize an albino variety (as distinct from the normal white coat) with pale blue eyes.

MANX

THE MANX IS A TAILLESS CAT that takes its name from the Isle of Man in the Irish Sea midway between England and Ireland, with which it has become closely associated and where a government cattery ensures the maintenance of the breed. There are many different legends to explain the existence of the Manx cat, such as that it was the last animal into the Ark and as Noah shut the door its tail was trapped and cut off. The taillessness is, of course, a genetic mutation. Sadly, the mutation is one that not only affects the tail but can cause fusion in the spinal vertebrae and other problems; when two completely tailless Manx are mated the kittens die before birth or shortly afterward. If the Manx was introduced today as a new breed it would probably not be permitted because of these problems, but it does exist and breeders have worked hard to ensure that healthy kittens are born by careful breeding programs that mate full Manx with partially and fully tailed cats.

The body of the Manx is solid, compact, and as short as possible, with a broad chest, deep flanks, and the back rising to a high, round rump, all set on strong legs. The longer, very muscular hind legs raise the rump higher than the shoulders, and the paws are neat and round. The head is round with prominent cheeks, a broad nose, and a strong muzzle that is set on a short thick neck. The CFA specifies heavy jowls and very large whisker pads. The ears have rounded tips, are wide with an open base, and are set so that they are angled slightly outward. The eyes are large and round and the CFA standard asks for the outer corners to be higher than the inner corners. Eye color specifications conform to those for the coats of other shorthaired cats.

above: Tortoiseshell and White Manx
below: Red and White Bicolor Manx

The coat is double with a close, thick undercoat and a slightly longer topcoat that gives a well-padded feeling, considered much more important than color or markings.

Manx litters can produce tailless cats (known as "Rumpies"), vestigially tailed cats ("Rumpy-risers"), cats with a short stump ("Stumpies") and fully tailed cats. All these variants should have the full Manx conformation and their existence is essential to the continuation of the breed, but the GCCF standard demands true taillessness with a decided hollow at the end of the spine. The CFA allows a rise of bone provided that it does not stop the judges' hand moving smoothly over the rump or spoil the appearance of taillessness.

Colors

The Manx can be all colors and patterns except for the pointed pattern of the Siamese and, in the case of the CFA, not chocolate or lavender or those involving the Himalayan pattern.

SCOTTISH FOLD

below: *Cream Tabby Scottish Fold*
bottom: *Black and White Bicolor
Scottish Fold*

THIS BREED IS THE RESULT of a mutation that appeared in 1961 among a litter of farm cats in Scotland. Instead of the ears being perkily erect, as with almost all other cats, they fold down. This is not immediately apparent when they are born but develops at about 25 days old when the cartilage in a kitten's ears would normally start to harden—in the Scottish Fold this does not occur. Sometimes this is a single fold, sometimes a double one, in which case the tips of the ears fold over to almost touch the fur of the head.

The original drop-eared cat had two kittens before she was killed in a road accident. From them all Scottish Folds are descended. They were bred to British Shorthairs which determined the general conformation, but skeletal abnormalities appearing in some kittens made the GCCF refuse to accept the breed and much of the breeding stock was exported to the U.S.A., where it received more of a welcome. Now the breed is not only healthy but has developed a reputation for being disease resistant and, since the creation of the Cat Association of Britain in 1983, has found a place in their shows.

The Scottish Fold's body should be of medium size, rounded and even from shoulder to pelvic girdle, with no sign of thickening in the legs and tail, and neat well-rounded toes. Long tapering tails are preferred. The head is well-rounded with prominent cheeks, well-rounded whisker pads, a short nose with a gentle curve, and a firm chin and jaw. The ears have rounded tips and are set in a cap-

like fashion to expose a rounded cranium. They fold forward and downward, and small tightly folded ears are preferred to loosely folded ones.

The fur of this breed is soft, dense, and plush. It should be so thick that it stands away from the body. The eyes are large and well rounded, set far apart with a sweet expression. Their color should be appropriate to the coat.

Their unusual appearance gives Scottish Folds an added interest but they also make excellent pets and good working cats.

Colors

Any coat color and pattern is permissible except for chocolate and lavender and those with the darker points of the Siamese.

EXOTIC SHORTHAIR

DURING THE DEVELOPMENT of the American Shorthair, Persian-type cats were used in the breeding program to strengthen quality and some intermediate types resulted. These were used to create a shorthaired version of the Persian, which by 1966 had become known as the Exotic. It is in fact slightly more like the British Shorthair than the American in appearance. When British breeders sought to create a similar cat they naturally used British Shorthairs crossed with Persian longhairs. Although they have ended up as similar cats they have different ancestries.

The Exotic has a cobby, heavily boned body of large or medium size that is set low on short thick legs with large round paws, and has a short tail in proportion to its body length. The head is usually round and massive with full cheeks and a short, broad, snub nose with a definite break, a firm chin, and small round-tipped ears set wide apart and low on the head.

below: *Red Tabby Exotic Shorthair*   **bottom:** *Shaded Golden Exotic Shorthair*

The coat is plush, soft, and full of life. Its density makes it stand out from the body. It is slightly longer than other shorthairs but not long enough to flow. The eyes are large and round, set well apart but not deep set. They should be of a brilliant color to match the color of the coat. Despite the length of its fur, the GCCF classes this cat with the longhairs, because its conformation is that of the Persian cat.

Exotics are usually sweet-natured and undemanding pets.

Colors

Almost all colors and patterns known in Shorthairs and Persians are found in this breed.

AMERICAN WIREHAIR

This breed had its origin in a red-and-white male kitten called Adam that had strange wiry fur and was born near Vernon in New York State in 1966. He was mated to a normal-coated female from the same litter, and by 1969 true breeding cats were produced that had hairs that were crimped, bent, or hooked, giving a harsh, dense, springy coat. The breed was recognized by the CFA in 1977.

The Wirehair is otherwise similar to an American Shorthair. It has a medium to large body with a level back and well rounded rump set on medium long, well-muscled legs with compact oval paws. The tail tapers to a well-rounded tip, neither pointed nor blunt. The head has prominent cheekbones, a gently curved nose, well-developed muzzle and chin, and a slight whisker break. The medium-size ears have rounded tips and are wide set. The large, round eyes are set well apart and the aperture has a slight upward tilt. Eye color should be appropriate to that of the fur. Some cats have curly whiskers as well as wiry fur.

The personality of this cat has variously been described as quiet and reserved and also as "ruling its home and other cats."

above: Tabby and White American Wirehair
below: White American Wirehair Kittens

Colors
All recognized colors are permissible except for chocolate, lavender, and pointed patterned coats.

AMERICAN CURL

below left: Brown Tabby
American Curl (longhaired)

below: Red Tabby
American Curl

A STRAY KITTEN WITH strangely shaped ears who turned up on a doorstep in Lakewood, California in 1981 was the origin of this breed. Named Shulamith, she passed this feature on to some of her kittens and within a few years the breed was established and gaining recognition with American Cat Societies, being adopted by the CFA in 1986. The moderately large ears are wide at the base and curve back in a smooth arc revealing luxuriant tufts

of hair. The ears feel rigid and stiff to the touch and are caused by a dominant gene that results in 50% of curled ears when Curls are mated with plain-eared cats. At birth the ears are straight but within two to three days they curl up tightly and in the months that follow relax to the adult condition.

The body of this breed is a semi-foreign shape, length one and a half times shoulder height, set on straight legs, when seen from the front, with round feet and a tail that tapers from a wide base. The head forms a gently curved, modified wedge with a straight nose that has a slight rise from the bottom of the eyes to the forehead. The eyes are quite large and walnut shaped, one eye-width apart, and set on a slight bias centered between the base of the ear and the tip of the nose. There are no color rules for the coat except that pointed patterned cats must have blue eyes.

The coat of the American Curl may be short or long. Shorthairs have short fur with a minimal undercoat and tail fur the same length as on the body. Longhairs have semi-long, silky fur, minimal undercoat, and a long plumed tail.

Colors
All colors and patterns are acceptable, including those with points.

AMERICAN BOBTAIL

THIS AMERICAN BREED derives from a tabby male found in the 1960s near an Indian reservation in Arizona. The name refers to the short tail, not to any connections with the American wildcat called the bobtail. This is a stocky, longhaired cat with a broad, round head, wide ears, large eyes, and a short tail. The tail has a good plume of hair and can be either straight or slightly curled. The undercoat has two lengths: long, and medium. It is described as having "a scratchy little rambling voice."

This breed is not currently recognized by the CFA, British, or European bodies.

There appears to have been an earlier form of Bobtail, that also went by the name of Rabbit Cat, in the eastern seaboard of the United States, but it does not seem to have survived.

above: Brown Tabby American Bobtail kitten

left: Brown Tabby American Bobtail

Colors
All colors are acceptable.

JAPANESE BOBTAIL

THIS IS AN ANCIENT Asian breed that, though now associated with Japan, seems once to have been more widely known in the Far East. It is often seen in Japanese paintings, porcelain, and wood-block prints, but it was not until Americans, who were in Japan after World War Two, became aware of it that it attracted the attention of the Cat Fancy in the West. A pair was sent to the United States in 1968, and by 1970 enthusiasts had formed a breed club. The CFA gave it full recognition in 1978. Its characteristic bobtail, although looking somewhat like a "stumpy" Manx, is caused by a quite different gene and produces none of the physiological problems that occur in the Manx.

It is not a standardized shape but the effect is like a rabbit's tail with the fur fanning out to create a pompon appearance that hides the underlying structure.

This is a strong, muscular cat with a long and elegant torso, set on slender legs with oval paws that should not be dainty or fragile looking. Its hind legs are longer then the forelegs, but are bent when the cat is relaxed so that the back is carried level. The tail is carried upright and should not extend further than 3 in. (7.5 cm) from the body, although straightened it might be up to twice that length. The head is long and forms an equilateral triangle with gently curving lines and high cheeks, giving a chiseled appearance. The nose is long and the muzzle broad, rounding into the whisker break. The ears are large, upright, and set well apart at right angles to the head. The large, oval eyes have a definite slant and may be any color that is appropriate to the coat.

The fur of the Japanese Bobtail is medium-long, soft, and silky with no noticeable undercoat. The CFA now also recognizes a longhaired version.

Japanese Bobtails tend to be playful, inquisitive, and affectionate.

above: Tortoiseshell and White Japanese Bobtail

below: Red and White and Tortoiseshell and White Japanese Bobtails

Colors

Most colors are recognized, with preference given to those with dramatically marked coats (not in Siamese pointed patterns). Tricolored cats, known as Mi-Ke (*Mee-Kay*) in Japanese, are the most sought after, or, since they are all females, bicolors in males.

GERMAN REX

IN 1946 A CAT FOUND WANDERING in the grounds of a hospital in ruined East Berlin was rescued by Dr. Ruth Scheuer-Karpin, who gave her the name Lammchen (Lambkin). She had no guard hairs and unusually short awn hairs and undercoat, giving a curly coat; the first well-recorded example of a cat with the fur type now known as Rex. It was not until ten years later, when mated with one of her own sons, that Lammchen produced kittens with rex fur. The German Rex is recognized as a distinctive breed by cat associations belonging to the Fédération Internationale Feline.

The body of the German Rex is of medium size and length with a strong chest, rounded in profile, set on medium-long, fine legs with rounded feet. The medium-long tail tapers from a substantial base to a rounded tip. The head is round with a strong chin, well-developed cheeks, and a slight indentation at the base of the nose. The wide-based ears have slightly rounded tips and are spaced well apart. The eyes are of medium size, well opened. and of a color that harmonizes with the coat.

The German Rex has the same rex gene as the Cornish Rex (see right), but its awn hairs are a little thicker than those of the undercoat, giving a woollier look, and its body form is closer to that of the European Shorthair.

Colors
All colors and patterns are permissible in this breed.

below: Black and White Cornish Rex. The GCCF places this in their Foreign group.

CORNISH REX

THE ORIGIN OF THIS BREED was a male red tabby born in a farmhouse on Bodmin Moor, Cornwall, England in 1950 with what is now known as rex fur. This fur is both finer and shorter than other cat coats, there are no guard hairs, and awn hairs are so reduced and look so like down hairs that it has often been said that they too are missing. Mating the red tabby back to its mother produced more kittens and began the establishment of the new breed, the name being taken from that of the curly haired Rex (originally Castorex) rabbit. In 1957 a pregnant descendant of these cats was sent to San Diego and her litter of four kittens established the breed in the United States.

The Cornish Rex has a hard, muscular body with a long slender torso and long straight legs with oval paws. Its long slender tail tapers toward the tip and is extremely flexible. The head is small and narrow, forming a medium wedge with a rounded muzzle and a small chin. The profile curves gently at the forehead and continues in a straight line to the nose tip. Its large ears are set high, wide at the base, and taper to rounded tips. The medium-sized eyes are oval and may be any color.

The coat is short and plushy with a silken texture, and must have a wave or ripple, especially on the back and tail. Whiskers and eyebrows should be crinkled and be of a good length.

This breed has been described as intelligent, playful, and affectionate. Cornish Rex tend to stand with their backs arched and the underside "tucked up." which seems to be linked with a facility to leap.

Colors
All colors and patterns are permissible in this breed.

DEVON REX

SELKIRK REX

THE DEVON REX appeared after the Cornish Rex, in Devon, when a stray tom was seen living in a disused tin mine with the unusual Rex coat. He mated with another stray, one of whose kittens, another male, was born curly coated. He was reared by a local resident and given the name Kirlee. It was assumed at first that it was another occurrence of the same mutation as the Cornish Rex, but mating Kirlee with Cornish Rex produced only normal coats. Only inbreeding reproduced the curly fur; his coat was the result of a different gene. So the Devon Rex was developed as a different breed. In Britain it was recognized by the GCCF in 1967 but not in the United States until 1979.

The Devon Rex is a slender cat with a hard, muscular body and a broad chest, carried high on slim legs with small oval paws, the hind legs being somewhat longer than the forelegs. The neck is slender, the tail long, fine and tapering. The head is wedge shaped with full cheeks, a short muzzle, strong chin, and whisker break. There is a well defined stop and the forehead curves back to a flat skull.

Its large ears are very wide at the base, set low and wide apart, tapering to rounded tops. The CFA standard describes three distinct curves when the head is seen from the front: the outer edge of the ears, the cheekbones, and the whisker pads. The oval eyes are large and wide set, sloping toward the outer edges of the ears, and may be any color.

The coat is very short, fine, wavy, curly, and soft, can appear rippled, and is slightly harsher to the touch than the other Rex. Some guard hairs are acceptable, and tufts and muffs on the ears are acceptable. Whiskers and eyebrows should be crinkled, rather coarse, and medium length.

Devon Rex are friendly, extroverted, and playful. They need a warm place to sleep. Because they have little hair they are attractive to those allergic to cat fur.

Colors
All colors and patterns are permissible in this breed.

THIS BREED BEGAN WITH a curly-coated dilute calico kitten born into a straight-haired litter in Wyoming in 1987 and is named after the Selkirk Mountains of Wyoming. It is a large, heavily-boned cat, much bulkier than the other Rex breeds, with large round feet and a medium-length tail. Its head is round and full-cheeked with a short muzzle, broad-based tapering ears, and a nose stop.

The coat comes in two lengths: short and long. On shorthairs the tail hair is as long as on the body at between 1–2 in. (2.5 and 5 cm) and on the longhair the tail curls are plumy, and the ruff that frames the face is longer and more noticeable. It is dense and stands out from the body with obvious curl.

left: *Fawn Devon Rex*
above: *Smoke Selkirk Rex*

Colors
In the CFA all colors and patterns are acceptable, including Mink, Champagne Mink, Blue Mink, Platinum Mink, these versions of Sepia, and pointed coats.

SPHYNX

THE SPHYNX IS A "HAIRLESS" CAT. In fact it does have some hair, a thin covering of down that is perceptible only on the ears, muzzle, tail, and on the testicles of males. Mutations creating hairlessness have occurred on a number of occasions—one pair in New Mexico at the beginning of the century was claimed to be the last of an ancient Aztec breed—but the Sphynx itself began with a hairless male kitten called Prune, born in Toronto, Canada, in 1966. When Prune was mated back to his mother more hairless kittens were produced, and by 1971 the breed had attained Championship status.

However, there was considerable opposition to the breed because of the problems encountered in rearing kittens and its status was revoked. European enthusiasts helped to ensure that the breed did not die out and it is now recognized by the International Cat Association but not by the GCCF, CFA, or CA of Britain.

The gene that produces hairlessness also seems to have affected the conformation of the Sphynx which, though Prune's mother was of "ordinary" cat shape, seems very long and angular. The body is long and muscular with a barrel-like chest and long slender neck, the legs long and slim with dainty paws, and the tail is long and tapering. The head is slightly longer than it is wide with a whisker break and in profile has a clear stop or change of angle. The ears are very large and the eyes are large and round with the outer corners slightly higher than the inner.

The skin should be taut and free of wrinkles, except on the head. It should "look like velvet and feel like moss." There are no eyebrows or whiskers. This suede-like covering gives no protection against extremes of temperature so it must always be kept in comfortably warm conditions.

Colors
All colors are acceptable in this breed.

above: *Red Sphynx kitten*
left: *Sphynx*

SNOWSHOE

THE SNOWSHOE, OR "SILVER LACES" as it has sometimes been called, is a breed created in the United States by crossing a bicolored American Shorthair with a Siamese. In the 1960s one breeder thought of trying to base a breed on white spotted cats that appeared in Siamese litters but there was opposition from other Siamese breeders. One breeder, Vikki Olander, however, persisted and the breed gained Cat Fanciers Federation recognition in 1982. After seeing Snowshoes in a New York show in 1986, British breeder Pat Turner decided to form a British breed club.

They have the solid bulk of the American Shorthair with the length of the Oriental cats; the body forming a rectangle with the legs, which are of medium bone, with compact oval paws and a thick-based, medium to long, slightly tapering tail. The head is triangular in shape with high cheekbones and large, broad-based, pointed ears. It is longer than a Birman head but shorter than the Siamese. The large eyes are ovoid, rather like a walnut in shape, and slanted toward the base of the ears. They should always be a sparkling blue.

The medium-short coat is close lying and glossy but not fine textured. The pattern is pointed, like that of the Siamese but with white "gloves" and "shoes" on the paws as in the Birman cat—although there are no Birmans in the breeding. These markings should be ankle high on the front paws and to just below the hock joints on the rear legs.

The Snowshoe is said by those who own one to have an affectionate and "unflappable" personality.

Colors
All of the colors that are accepted for Siamese cats are recognized by those associations that accept the Snowshoe.

above: Sealpoint Snowshoe

below: Bluepoint Snowshoe

CALIFORNIA SPANGLED CAT

MUNCHKIN

MOVIE WRITER PAUL CASEY was so horrified by the destruction of leopards he had seen in Africa in 1971, that he created a domestic breed that would be a reminder of the big cat. He says it was only ever his intention to breed a small number as a way of drawing attention to the plight of the wild cats worldwide and the need for conservation policies. Eight different types of domestic cat contributed to his creation: an American Shorthair, a British Shorthair, an Abyssinian-domestic cross, an angora-like silver spotted tabby, a spotted Manx, a Siamese, a house-cat from Malaysia, and a feral cat from the streets of Cairo in Egypt. After eleven generations of breeding, the required look was achieved—a spotted cat that, incidentally, might appeal to people who have a yearning to keep one of the wild spotted species. The breed was presented to the world through the 1986 Christmas Catalog of the Los Angeles branch of Neiman-Marcus at $1,400 each. This created a strong reaction from people who felt that a cat was being sold as just a piece of expensive decor "in any color clients may desire." However, this did not affect their appeal to the wealthy; a decade later the price was $3,600 and a there was a long waiting list of would-be owners. It has now been recognized by the International Cat Association.

The California Spangled is a long-bodied, well-muscled cat that carries itself low. The medium-long tail is of even width with a blunt, dark tip the color of the spots. It has large ears, set high on the rounded head, which tapers to the muzzle with pronounced whisker pads. In profile there are two clear slopes for the forehead and nose. The eyes are round and set well apart.

This is said to be a good-tempered and intelligent cat.

Colors
Black, Blue, Bronze, Charcoal, Gold, Red, Silver, White,

right: *Tabby and White Munchkin*

NAMED AFTER THE CHARACTERS in *The Wizard of Oz*, the Munchkin is also known as the Dachshund Cat, the Weiner Cat, and the Minicat—all reflecting the fact that it has very short legs. A mutant stray discovered in the U.S.A. in 1983 became the foundation of the breed in Louisiana. The breed was presented at a show in 1991. The main characteristic of this breed is its short legs, of which the front legs should not be more than 3 in. (7.5 cm), and the hind legs a little longer.

Virginia breeder Penny Squires, who has been responsible for developing the Munchkin, suggests that their short legs are suitable for house pets because they are unable to "jump onto kitchen counters."

Colors
No color range appears to have been designated.

left: *Blue California Spangled Cat and Bronze Kitten*

LONGHAIRED BREEDS

THERE ARE NO TRULY LONGHAIRED CATS among the wild cat species; it would be difficult for such a cat to keep long fur in good condition, but some of those species living in colder regions have longer, thicker fur. Northern subspecies of the wildcat (*Felis silvestris silvestris*) are bulkier with longer fur than the African Wildcat (*Felis silvestris lybica*) and, although it is the African cat from which the domestic cat derives, either matings with the northern forms or adaptation among the domestic cats themselves could account for longer fur. Another suggestion has been that the Manul, or Pallas's Cat (*Felis manul*), which has longer and thicker fur than other Felis, may have been the origin of the longhaired domestic cats. Peter Pallas, who discovered it, claimed that it liked to mate with domestic cats, although there is no zoological record of kittens being born and such cross-species hybrids are usually sterile.

Norway and Russia have indigenous breeds with quite long fur and in the nineteenth century writers mention Indian and Chinese longhaired cats—the Chinese one having pendulous ears. The last two have disappeared, if they ever existed. Much earlier there were cats in Turkey and Iran with long hair, that began to appear in western Europe in the sixteenth century when some were taken to France by the naturalist Nicholas-Claude Fabri de Peirsec. Both types were seen in early cat shows, but the Persian Cat became more popular and the Angora (Turkish) Cat disappeared from the show bench. This beautiful cat did, however, survive in Turkey and is now back on the international cat scene (see page 59).

Longhaired cats require much more attention than shorthairs and should be groomed daily.

PERSIAN

WE CANNOT BE SURE what the first Persian cats taken to Europe looked like and how they differed from the Angoras, but by the end of the nineteenth century they were very solid cats of a rounded shape with long, thick fur. The Persian cat's face has a flattened look that has become more extreme over the years.

It has a muscular, cobby body, set low on the legs, with a deep, broad chest, massive shoulders and rump, and a short tail. The CFA describes the tail as carried without a curve and at an angle lower than the back. The legs are short and thick with large round paws. The head is round and massive with good breadth and set on a short, thick neck. The short, broad snub nose is of even width with a stop or break centered between the eyes. The forehead is rounded, the cheeks full, and the ears are small, round-tipped and set wide apart and low on the head to fit its rounded contour. The CFA standard specifies that they should tilt forward.

left: *Cream Persian*
previous page: *Chinchilla*

left: Blue Colorpoint Himalayan Persian

right: Tortoiseshell Persian

The eyes are large, round, full, and bold, far apart, not deep set; giving, says the CFA, "a sweet expression to the face."

The coat of the Persian is its glory. Long, thick, and standing from the body, it is fine textured and has an immense ruff which continues in a deep frill between the front legs. There are long ear and toe hairs and the tail is bushy.

This is usually an extremely gentle and affectionate cat—a measure of the effect that selective breeding can have on character as well as on appearance. Indeed, when Persians first appeared at British cat shows they seemed to be bad-tempered, even savage, compared with shorthaired cats. The modern Persian makes a placid pet but is demanding in that it needs regular daily grooming to keep the coat in good condition.

Colors

GCCF

Self or Solid Color: Black, White, Blue, Red, Cream, Chocolate, Lilac.

Smoke: Black, Blue, Chocolate, Lilac, Red, Tortie, Cream, Blue-Cream, Chocolate Tortie, Lilac Tortie.

Chinchilla and Shaded: Chinchilla, Golden, Shaded Silver, Cameo, Pewter.

Tabby: Silver, Brown, Blue, Chocolate, Lilac, Red, Tortie, Blue Tortie, Chocolate Tortie, Lilac Tortie.

Tortoiseshell and Tortoiseshell and White: Tortoiseshell, Blue-Cream, Chocolate, Lilac-Cream, Tortie and White, Blue Tortie and White, Chocolate Tortie and White, Lilac Tortie and White, Tortie Tabby and White, Blue Tortie Tabby and White, Chocolate Tortie Tabby and White, Lilac Tortie Tabby and White.

Bicolors: Black and White, Blue and White, Chocolate and White, Lilac and White, Red and White, Cream and White, Brown Tabby and White, Blue Tabby and White, Chocolate Tabby and White, Lilac Tabby and White, Red Tabby and White, Cream Tabby and White.

Colorpoint: Seal, Blue, Chocolate, Lilac, Red, Cream, Seal Tortie, Blue-Cream, Chocolate Tortie, Lilac-Cream, Seal Tabby, Blue Tabby, Chocolate Tabby, Lilac Tabby, Red Tabby, Cream Tabby, Seal Tortie Tabby, Blue-Cream Tabby, Chocolate Tortie Tabby, Lilac-Cream Tabby.

CFA

Solid or Self Color: White, Blue, Black, Red, Peke-faced Red (see below), Cream, Chocolate, Lilac.

Silver and Golden: Chinchilla Silver, Shaded Silver, Chinchilla Golden, Shaded Golden.

Shaded and Smoke: Shell Cameo, Shaded Cameo, Shell Cream, Shaded Cream, Shell Tortoiseshell, Shaded Tortoiseshell, Shell Blue-Cream, Shaded Blue-Cream, Black Smoke, Blue Smoke, Cream Smoke, Red Smoke, Tortoiseshell Smoke, Blue-Cream Smoke.

Tabby (Mackerel and Classic patterns): Silver, Silver Patched, Blue-Silver, Blue-Silver Patched, Red, Peke-faced Red (see below), Brown, Brown Patched, Blue, Blue Patched, Cream, Cameo, Cream Cameo.

Particolor: Tortoiseshell, Blue-Cream, Chocolate Tortoiseshell, Lilac-Cream.

Calico and Bicolor: Calico, Van Calico, Dilute Calico, Chocolate Calico, Van Chocolate Calico, Lilac Calico, Van Lilac Calico; Bicolor White with Black, Blue, Red, Cream, Chocolate or Lilac; Van Bi-color White with Black, Blue, Red, Cream, Chocolate and Lilac; Smoke and White, Van Smoke and White, Calico Smoke, Dilute Calico Smoke, Chocolate Calico Smoke, Lilac Calico Smoke, Tabby and White in tabby colors above, Van Tabby and White in tabby colors above.

Himalayan: Chocolate, Seal, Lilac, Blue, Flame (Red), Cream, Tortie, Blue-Cream, Chocolate Tortie, Lilac-Cream and Lynx (Tabby) in the same colors.

PEKE-FACED PERSIAN

THE PEKE-FACED PERSIAN is the extreme form of the Persian breed in which the aim has been to emulate the snub nose, flattened face, and bulging eyes of the Pekinese dog. Such cats were already being seen in America in the 1930s where they attracted attention as the ultimate in the Persian look. The Peke-face met much opposition, however, because, as with all such brachycephalic exaggeration, this physiognomy brings an increased danger of problems such as blocked tear ducts, breathing difficulties caused by constriction of the nasal passages, and a poor bite when the mouth is closed. These are problems that can also become more aggravated as the cat gets older. The British and European bodies do not recognize this as a breed but it is accepted in the U.S.A. where the CFA now places it as a variety within the Persian breed but with its own specific requirements.

In recent years, even in Britain and Europe, the Persian cats appearing on the show bench seem to have become increasingly exaggerated and the lay person may have difficulty in seeing any difference between them and the Peke-faced. However, the Peke-faced should have a bone structure beneath its fur that differs from that of the standard Persian and results in a very round head with a strong chin.

The CFA standard specifies a short nose that is depressed and indented between the eyes, which should be large, round, and set wide apart. The muzzle should be wrinkled. The horizontal break, located between the usual nose break and the top dome of the head, runs straight across the front of the head, creating half-moon boning above the eyes and an additional indentation located in the center of the forehead bone structure. The ears are placed slightly higher than in other Persians to conform to the underlying bone structure.

Colors

Only Solid Red and Red Tabby are recognized in this variety.

AMERICAN CURL

Treated by the CFA as one breed with the shorthaired form, this is identical to it in all except coat length, which is longer and on the tail should be a fine plume. (See American Curl, page 40.)

HIMALAYAN

THIS IS ANOTHER NAME for the color-pointed variety of the Persian Cat that, when first recognized by the United States registries in the late 1950s and early 1960s, was not accepted as a Persian but was given this name. The first efforts to apply this coat to a Persian took place in Sweden in the 1920s, followed by breeders in Massachusetts in the 1930s, but it was in California that the breed was finally developed under the name Himalayan. British breeders were also working on this variety in the 1930s and it is their stock from which the Canadian and European lines are descended.

Himalayan and Colorpoint Persians follow the same standards as other Persians, but with the pointed pattern and blue eyes they inherit from the Siamese. As in Britain and Europe the CFA now class them as varieties of Persian.

above: Seal Point
Himalayan

Colors
All colors accepted for the Siamese.

left: Red Point Himalayan
with a Blue Point kitten

CYMRIC

THE CYMRIC IS THE NAME for the long-haired version of the Manx. Its name comes from the Welsh ("Cymru" meaning Wales in that language) and was chosen because of the proximity of Wales to the Isle of Man, after which the Manx is named. Some cat bodies, including the CFA, simply call it the Longhaired Manx. Longhaired cats had appeared in Manx litters over the years but it was not until the 1960s, when Canadian breeders became interested in them, that they were developed, exhibited, and given their name.

Cymric are like the Manx (see page 36) in every way except for their coat, which should be double, dense, and well padded over the main body, then lengthening on the shoulders and the rump. It has a soft and silky texture, falling smoothly over the body, but plush due to its double nature. Britches, abdomen, and the neck ruff, which extends from the shoulders to a bib over the chest, are longer than the main body and the cheeks are thick and full. The rest of the fur on the head and legs below the hocks should be shorter, but still dense and full. Ear and toe tufts are desirable.

Colors
All colors and patterns are permissible except for chocolate and lilac and those with points.

right: *Red and White Bicolor Cymric*

LONGHAIR FOLD

THIS CAT, VARIOUSLY KNOWN as the Longhair Fold, the Highland Fold, the Scottish Fold Longhair, and in Britain as the Coupari, is the longhaired version of the Scottish Fold (page 37), and comes from the same stock. It was first recognized by the International Cat Association and received championship status from the CFA in the United States in 1991.

It is the same as the Scottish Fold in all respects except for fur length. The ears are set in a cap-like fashion to expose a rounded cranium; they fold forward and down.

The coat is medium long to long with a full coat on the face and body, but short hair is permissible on the face and legs. Britches, tail plume, toe tufts, and ear tufts should be clearly visible and a ruff is desirable.

Colors

Any color or pattern is acceptable except for chocolate and lilac and pointed patterns.

above: Silver Tabby
Longhair Fold
left: Brown Tabby
Longhair Fold

CHANTILLY

THE CHANTILLY, OR TIFFANY as it was formerly called, has often been described as the longhaired version of the Burmese Cat, but that is not strictly true. The most usual variety of the Chantilly has coloring like the Burmese, but this is believed to be due to a different gene. This American breed had its origin in a pair of cats acquired by New York breeder Jennie Robinson in 1967, that were golden-eyed, chocolate colored longhairs. They produced a litter of chocolate kittens that was registered with the American Cat Association as Foreign Longhairs. The Burmese look made people think they must be from Burmese stock, a misunderstanding reinforced when Sigyn Lund, well-known as a Burmese breeder, bought some and began to develop the breed, using the name Tiffany. A similar-looking pregnant cat walked into a Canadian home in 1973 and produced identical kittens. In neither case is the origin of the founding cat or her mate known, but from these the breed has been established. Because a new English breed of Oriental longhair has been developed under the name Tiffanie (see page 69), the name Chantilly was proposed to avoid confusion between the two, but not everyone has adopted it and this breed is still known as Tiffany by some.

This is a medium-sized cat with a long, silky coat with a full neck ruff and a plumed tail.

Chantilly/Tiffany are said to be affectionate cats with quiet voices. They are quite distinct from the British Tiffanie.

Colors

The traditional color for this breed is solid rich brown color but various dilutions have been bred including blue, cinnamon, lilac, fawn, and tabby forms of all these colors.

JAVANESE

THE NAME JAVANESE CAT has been applied to several forms of cat. All have been of Oriental type but they are not the same breed, which leads to considerable confusion. American cat societies use the name Javanese for colors and patterns in the longhaired Siamese that Europeans include with the Balinese, since in the U.S.A. only solid color points are accepted in that breed. Associations that are members of the FIFe use the name for non-pointed forms of the Balinese. In New Zealand all the point patterns are accepted as Balinese, but Javanese is used for similar cats with all-over solid color or cats with spotted coats without the points. In Britain long-haired Orientals created by the breeding program designed to recreate the Angora (see page 58) were given the name Javanese by the Cat Association.

A cat of British Angora/Javanese type that was taken to Holland was assigned a new breed name, Mandarin, and this name has now become popular as an alternative to Javanese in Germany.

below: A solid colored
Seal, called Javanese in
New Zealand

above right: Javanese

Colors
CFA
Solid Point: Red, Cream.
Lynx Point: Seal, Chocolate, Blue, Lilac, Red, Cream.
Tortie: Seal Tortie, Chocolate Tortie, Blue-Cream, Lilac-Cream, and Lynx versions of all these.
For colors accepted by other associations, see main text.

ORIENTAL LONGHAIR

THE ORIENTAL LONGHAIR is a fairly recent development as a longhaired version of the Oriental Shorthair, first recognized by the International Cat Association, and now by the CFA and other bodies. The British Angora is the parallel British breed, but has its own standards. These are cats of the same conformation as the Siamese but with long fur that lacks the pointed Siamese pattern.

The standard for these cats is the same as that for the Oriental Shorthair and for the Siamese itself in most particulars. The body is long and svelte but muscular, with the hips never wider than the shoulders, and the abdomen tight, forming a sleek tube set on long, slim legs, with the hind legs higher than the front. There are small, dainty oval paws and a long tail that tapers from a thin base to a pointed tip. The head is a long tapering wedge flaring from the nose in straight lines to the pointed tips of the ears, which are strikingly large and wide at the base. The nose is long and straight continuing the forehead without a break. The eyes are of medium size, almond shaped, and slanted toward the nose. They are green in color except for those with white fur, which may be blue, green, or odd-eyed.

Colors

CFA

Solid: Blue, Chestnut, Cinnamon, Cream, Ebony, Fawn, Lavender, Red, White.

Shaded: Blue Silver, Chestnut Silver, Cinnamon Silver, Cream Silver, Ebony Silver, Fawn Silver, Lavender Silver, Red Silver and Particolor Silver (of Black, Chestnut, Cinnamon with red patching or intermingled and of Blue, Fawn or Lavender with cream).

Smoke: Red, Chestnut, Cinnamon, Cream, Ebony, Fawn, Lavender and Particolor (as for Solid).

Tabby (Classic, Mackerel, Spotted, or Ticked): Blue, Red, Cream, Cinnamon, Chestnut, Ebony, Fawn, Lavender, and Silver forms in all these colors.

Bicolor: As for the varieties above with the addition of White.

Particolors: Blue-Cream, Cinnamon Tortoiseshell, Chestnut Tortoiseshell, Fawn-Cream, Lavender-Cream, Ebony Tortoiseshell.

The Oriental Longhair's fine, silky coat is of medium length, without a downy undercoat, and lies close to the body, which may make it look shorter than it is. The tail hair is the longest and should spread out like a plume.

This is a cat of a lively, intelligent, affectionate, and sometimes mischievous personality.

RAGDOLL

below: *Sealpoint Ragdoll*

THIS BREED, ORIGINATING in America from a mating between a Birman male and a white longhaired female called Josephine, gets its name from the tendency of the breed to relax when handled, floppy like a rag doll. Ann Baker, the original breeder, attributed this quality to injuries, including a broken pelvis, that Josephine suffered in a car accident. This could not, in fact, have made any difference to the genetic inheritance of the kittens. She also claimed that these cats showed no fear and felt no pain; a lack of sensitivity that would have made them vulnerable to both danger and abuse and put cat lovers against the breed. Fortunately these claims were false, although Baker does appear to have combined the docility inherent in Persian and Birman stock to produce a relaxed breed that readily accepts handling. Other breeders, especially the Daytons in California, reversed these misconceptions and the breed was recognized first by the National Cat Fanciers Association in 1965. Some of the Dayton's cats were taken to Britain in 1981 and the breed is now accepted there.

This is a large heavy-set cat with a long, muscular body and a broad, rectangular chest. It is set on sturdy legs with large round paws, hind legs higher than the forelegs, a long tail that tapers toward the tip and which should reach back at least to the shoulder. The short, heavy-set neck carries a large triangular-shaped head, the distance between the outside base of the ears matched by the length to the gently rounded muzzle. There is no dome, but a flat plane between the ears; cheeks are well developed but in line with the wedge. The nose is of medium length with a gentle dip and a slightly retroussé tip. the medium-sized ears are wide-set, wide-based, have rounded tips and tilt slightly forward. The eyes are large and slightly oblique (the CFA standards specifies oval) and should be vivid blue.

The medium-length coat has a soft and silky texture with a minimal woolly undercoat and abundant guard hairs. It is short on the face and shortish on the shoulderblades, lengthening toward the fully plumed tail, and preferably has a ruff and knickers. Ears should be well furnished with fur, and paws tufted. Full coat does not develop until the cat is mature. All Ragdolls have pointed patterned coats. In bicolors and Van-patterned cats this is overlaid with white, but they must conform to very strict color distribution.

The Ragdoll is indeed a very docile, relaxed cat and an undemanding indoor pet. Its fur should be naturally non-matting but it will still need some grooming. Ann Baker considered the cats bred in Britain not sufficiently floppy to be considered true Ragdolls, but not carrying the characteristic to extremes is considered by many cat-lovers to be an advantage. The GCCF classifies this breed as a semi longhair.

Colors

GCCF

Seal, Blue, Chocolate, Lilac. These are permitted in Colorpoint (like the Siamese), Mitted or Bicolor patterns. Mitted have white paw pads like the Birman (see p.65). Bicolors must have markings modifying the color-point pattern as follows: A white inverted V starts on the forehead and extends downward covering nose, whisker pads, and chin but not beyond the outer aperture of the eye. Bib and chest should be white, front legs all white, and back legs preferably white to the level of the underbody.

CFA

Colorpoint: Seal, Chocolate, Blue, Lilac, Cinnamon, Fawn, Red, Cream, and in Lynx (Tabby) Point versions of all these colors, and all these in Tortie and Tortie-Tabby combinations.

Bicolor: As for Colorpoint but with markings as described above.
Van Pattern (as in Turkish Van): As for the Colorpoint but with color restricted to tail, ears, and upper part of the mask.

Smoke: As for Colorpoint.

Shaded: As for Colorpoint.

RAGAMUFFIN (U.S.A.)—color versions of Ragdoll

The Ragdoll was not originally accepted as a show cat and its originator, Anne Baker, attempted to rigidly control development of the breed. A rival group of breeders banded together in 1994 to establish the Ragamuffin that, in effect, is a Ragdoll with a wide range of colors. It has been recognized by the United Feline Organization and can be registered with the American Cat Fanciers Association, though not yet shown with them. It is a large cat of the same conformation as the Ragdoll and with luxuriant fur.

Colors

Pointed, mitted and particolor varieties are accepted. **Colorpoint:** All pointed colors including Lynx and Tortie forms.
Solid color: All Persian cat colors plus Mink and Sepia. **Particolor:** All Persian cat colors plus Mink and Sepia.

CHERUBIM

This breed is a development from the Ragdoll that has still to find acceptance (see page 58).

HONEYBEAR

This breed is a development from the Ragdoll that has still to find acceptance (see page 58).

left: Ragamuffin

above: Turkish Angora

TURKISH ANGORA

ANGORA IS THE OLD spelling of Ankara, the modern capital of Turkey, and it was the zoo at Ankara that ensured the survival of the breed by setting up a breeding program. Angoras from the zoo were taken to America in the 1960s and became the foundation for the breed there, where it was accepted by the CFA in 1970 as the Turkish Angora.

The Angora is a medium-sized, fine-boned cat with a long, slender body, long legs (that are slightly longer at the rear), small round paws, and a long tapering tail. The head is set on a rather long, slim neck and is proportionally small to medium, forming a medium-long, smooth wedge with a flat top meeting the line of the nose at an angle slightly above the eyes and without a nose break. The muzzle continues these smooth lines to a gently rounded chin. The ears are large, pointed, wide at the base, and set high on the head. The eyes are large and almond-shaped, slanting slightly upward. They can be any shade of green, gold, green-gold, copper, blue, or odd-eyed.

The fur of the Angora is single coated and of variable length but it has long, finely textured hair on the tail and ruff and britches on the hind legs. Tufts between the toes are desirable.

These are personable cats that are said to make affectionate pets.

Note that the cat which the GCCF in Britain calls the Angora (see page 60) is a completely different breed.

Colors

Ankara Zoo bred only white cats, and this was at first a one-color breed, but all colors and patterns are now acceptable except for chocolate, lavender, and those showing a pointed pattern.

BRITISH ANGORA

THIS IS A BRITISH BREED that was developed in the 1960s in an attempt to recreate the Angora. Even if Turkish cats had been available, British regulations meant putting cats introduced from abroad through six months in quarantine. Hence, Angora-looking types were selected from long-haired Oriental cats that were closer to the original's elegant look than the more cobby Persians. This resulted in a more distinctly Oriental-looking cat than the Turkish Angora. The GCCF standard requires a cat with a long, svelte, and muscular body on long slim legs with small oval paws, the rear legs being higher than the front legs, and the tail long and tapering. The head is long, narrowing in straight lines to a fine muzzle with no break or whisker pinch. It should be neither round nor pointed and should avoid an exaggerated look. The nose needs to be straight, without a stop or dip, the chin strong, with the ears large, wide at the base and continuing the lines of the face. The eyes are Oriental in shape and slant toward the nose, with good width in between. They should be green in all colors except blue-eyed and odd-eyed whites.

The coat is medium-long, fine, and silky, with no woolly undercoat. The tail should be plume-like and the neck, chin, underside, and tail may tend to frill.

This graceful cat is said to be an excellent indoor pet. It frequently retains the more vocal personality of the Oriental from which it was developed. Despite superficial similarities it has no connection with the Turkish Angora, which is not recognized by the GCCF. The GCCF classes this breed as Oriental.

above: Chocolate Angora
left: Blue Cream British Angora
with Tortoiseshell kittens

Colors
Self colors only: White, Black, Blue, Chocolate, Lilac, Red, Cream, Cinnamon, Caramel, Fawn.

TURKISH VAN

THE TURKISH VAN COMES from the Lake Van area of northern Turkey. The breed known in Europe and the U.S.A. is descended from cats taken back to Britain by British photographers Laura Lushington and Sonia Halliday in 1955. They were given a male and a female kitten: Van Atilla and Van Guzelli Iskenderun. Despite the problems of quarantine they imported further cats and in 1969 they were recognized as a breed by the GCCF, and eventually reached the U.S.A. in 1982.

The Turkish Van is very like the Turkish Angora in type, but the standard specifies a large muscular body with great breadth to the chest. The British standard describes neat, well-rounded feet; the American one requires them to be rounded and moderately large. The head forms a broad wedge with a medium-long nose, prominent cheekbones, and a slight dip between the eyes, barely perceptible but marked by a change in the lay of the fur. The ears are large and set high. The CFA asks for them with slightly rounded tips, the GCCF close together. The eyes are large and the CFA specifies a rounded aperture drawn out at the corners and set at a slant. Eyes should be amber, blue, or odd-eyed, and the GCCF requires pink rims.

The Turkish Van cat's fur should be semi-long with no woolly undercoat, with longer, thicker fur in winter and a short summer coat. There should be a full brush on the tail, well-feathered ears, tufted toes, and a frontal ruff. The breed does not achieve full maturity until three years old and the ruff and tail brush become more pronounced with age.

In their homeland white is considered the only color for a true Van Cat

above and below:
Turkish Van

and odd-eyed cats are preferred, but the Halliday/Lushington cats had auburn tails and head markings and these markings are now considered essential for the breed. Faint rings on the tail are allowed and tail color may extend part way up the back. The CFA permits color on body and legs provided it is not more than 20 percent and does not distract from the basic Van pattern.

Turkish Van cats make loveable and affectionate pets. In Turkey they are considered to have a long life span. In their homeland they seem happy to dabble in streams and pools, and have earned the name "swimming cat."

Colors
GCCF: White with Auburn or Cream Van pattern markings only.
CFA: White with Van pattern markings in Red, Cream, Black, Blue, and in Tabby versions of these colors, Tortoiseshell, Dilute Tortie, Blue and Brown Patched Tabby, other colors and white excluding chocolate, lilac, and point restricted patterns.

MAINE COON

THIS IS A TRULY AMERICAN breed that developed from the working cats of the state of Maine on the eastern seaboard of the United States. It was already established a century ago; one took the Best in Show award at Madison Square Garden in 1895, and for 30 years before that there had been a competition at the Skowhegan Fair for Maine State Champion Coon Cat. Interest in the breed then declined, until in 1953 the Central Maine Coon Club was set up and began to re-establish it. Stories that the breed originates in matings between farm cats and raccoons are totally unfounded. It may be linked with similar cats of northern Europe, such as the Norsk Skogcatt, that might have been taken to America by Viking sailors. It is more likely that its origin is in house cats who became feral and developed a heavier body and thicker coat as protection against Maine winters.

The Maine Coon is a rugged, muscular, medium to large cat, one of the largest of the domestic breeds, with a broad chest and long back giving a rectangular appearance. The GCCF standard describes it as of semi-Oriental type. The legs are substantial and medium-long with large round paws; the tail long, wide at the base, and tapering. The medium-long neck is particularly muscular in mature males. The head is medium-long, the width slightly less then the length, with a square muzzle, high cheekbones, and a firm chin in line with the nose and upper lip. The medium-long nose should be of uniform width with a slight concavity at the nasal bridge when seen in profile but no sharp break or stop. The ears are large, tall, and set high, wide based and tapering to the tip. The eyes are full and round, with a slightly oblique aperture, set with the slant toward the outward base of the ear. They may be green, gold, and copper, or in white cats, blue or odd eyes.

The coat of the Maine Coon is heavy and shaggy but silky in texture and falling smoothly. It is waterproof and virtually self maintaining, with the undercoat covered by a more substantial glossy topcoat. It is shorter on the head, neck, and shoulders, but longer on the stomach with full britches and frontal ruff beginning below the ears. The ears are well feathered and there are tufted toes and a profuse and flowing tail.

The Maine Coon takes up to four years to reach maturity. It has an amiable disposition and a soft voice but remains an alert and capable hunter. It requires less arduous grooming than other cats with such a full coat.

above: Silver Tabby Maine Coon
right: Brown Tabby Maine Coon

Colors
Most coat colors and patterns are acceptable but not those involving chocolate, lilac, all-over agouti (like the ticked coat of the Abyssinian) or pointed patterns.

NORWEGIAN FOREST CAT

THE NORWEGIAN FOREST CAT (Norsk Skogcatt) is a large but elegant breed that developed from the working farm cats of Norway. It was not until the early twentieth century that it was first mentioned as a distinct type, but in the 1930s it attracted interest in its homeland and a breed club was formed. After the interruption of World War II it reappeared as a show cat in the 1970s, becoming a FIFe championship breed in 1977 and going on to gain international recognition as the Norwegian Forest Cat. In Norway it is often affectionately known as the "Wegie." There are similar cats in Denmark and Sweden that go under the names Racekatte and Rugkatt.

This is a big, strongly built, muscular cat with a solid bone structure. It has a broad chest and longish body and considerable girth without being fat. Thighs are heavily muscled and the hind legs longer than the front, raising the rump above the shoulders. Paws are round. The long tail should ideally reach back to the short and heavily muscled neck. The head is triangular, the width between the outside of the ears equaling that of the strong, gently rounded chin. Whisker pads are pronounced and the profile is straight without a break, the flat forehead continuing into a gentle curved skull and neck. The ears are high and open, wide at the base and set to the side with their line following that of the face. The eyes are large and almond-shaped, set with the outer corner angled higher. They can be any colors regardless of coat color.

The coat of the "Wegie" is double with a dense woolly undercoat covered by a smooth, water-repellent outer coat. There are full britches on the hind legs and a ruff in three sections: side mutton chops, a short collar at the neck, and a full shirt front. The toes are tufted and the ears are well furnished; lynx-like tufts at the tips of the ears are considered to be desirable.

The Norwegian Forest Cat takes four years to reach full development. Kittens are born with short, soft fur. Tough guard hairs develop as the cat matures. It retains the vigor of the farm working cat, is said to be a skillful tree-climber, and is not a cat that should be confined indoors.

above: *Black and White Bicolor Norwegian Forest Cat*
left: *Blue Norwegian Forest Cat*

Colors
All colors and patterns are allowed except for chocolate, lilac, and pointed patterns. Areas of white on other colors are also allowable, such as white paws, blaze, locket, and chest.

SIBERIAN FOREST CAT

below: Silver Tortie Forest Cat

below left: Tabby and White Silver Forest Cat

THIS TYPE OF LONGHAIRED CAT, which is very similar to the Norsk Skogcatt, seems to have been long established in northern Russia. It may be the ancestor of the Norwegian or even the Middle Eastern Longhairs. Some of these cats, then known as Russian Longhaired Cats, appeared in nineteenth-century British cat shows and one was owned by Harrison Weir, who mounted the first show at Crystal Palace in 1871. However, it was not until 1987, when a pair found in St. Petersburg was taken to Germany and became the foundation of a new breeding program, that they reappeared on the international scene under the Siberian name. In 1990 they were introduced to the U.S.A., where a breed club now exists.

The Siberian Forest Cat is a strong and sturdy cat with a fairly long body set on strong legs and a tail that can reach back to the shoulders. The head has a broad skull and is rounder than in the Maine Coon and the Norsk Skagkatt. The equilateral triangle of the face is softened by rounded contours but has a straight profile. The ears are wide-based and high-set. The large eyes are not quite round but slightly oblique and their color is in keeping with the coat.

The fur is made up of a thick insulating undercoat and a long and glossy top coat with a full ruff, britches, and bushy tail. Kittens are born with short fur, the glossy guard hairs of the topcoat appearing when they are three months old.

Reports of their personality range from docile to active and shrewd.

Colors

Russian breeders are now developing a variety of colors, but the most usual is a golden tabby with black patterning over a golden agouti. The cats often have a white ruff and paws.

BIRMAN

below left: Seal Tabby Point Birman

below: Chocolate Point Birman

THERE IS AN UNSUBSTANTIATED story that the Birman cat had for centuries been the cat of temples in Burma (now officially known as Myanmar), together with a delightful legend of how it obtained its pattern and colors on the death of a revered monk. A female called Sita is said to have been sent to France where she produced kittens, including one called Poupée, who was mated with either a Siamese or Persian cat to found the western breed. What is certainly true is that the breed became established in France where it was recognized in 1925 under the name Sacred Cat of Burma.

This is a cat with a long, massive, muscular body, unlike that of either the Persians or Siamese. It has thickset, medium-long legs with large round paws, and a medium-long tail. The head is broad and round with a strong skull; a medium-long, Roman-shaped nose with no stop, only a slight dip in profile; full cheeks and a strong, slightly tapering chin. The ears are tall, round-tipped with bases almost as wide as their height, and set well apart. The eyes are almost round, tilted very slightly upward and always blue, a deep blue being preferred.

The coat is medium-long to long, silken in texture, slightly curly on the stomach, with a full ruff at the neck and a bush tail. Its markings are distinctive: the body is even with subtle shading allowed in seal and blue, with the dark color following the Siamese pointed pattern on ears and face mask. This mask is connected to the ears by tracings in the mature cat, tail and legs. The feet are not the point color but pure white. On the front paws the white area ends in a line across the paw, not extending beyond the angle formed by paw and leg; the CFA standard specifies to the metacarpal (dew) pad. White covers the entire rear paws and extends up the back of the leg, tapering to finish just below the point of the hock. Ideally, markings on left and right legs match. Birmans are usually gentle and affectionate cats. They have soft voices and are not very vocal.

Colors

GCCF

Solid Point: Blue, Chocolate, Lilac, Red, Cream.

Tortie Point: Seal, Blue, Chocolate, Lilac.

Tabby Point: Seal, Blue, Chocolate, Lilac, Red, Cream.

Tortie Tabby: Seal, Blue, Chocolate, Lilac.

CFA

Solid Point only: Seal, Blue, Chocolate, Lilac.

SEYCHELLOIS (LONGHAIRED)

THIS IS A BREED created by British breeder Pat Turner after she heard reports of local cats in the Seychelles Islands in the Indian Ocean. It is not a cat from those islands, but was bred from Tortie and White Persians, Siamese, and other Orientals to produce a cat with white fur patterned with small splashes of color and a fully colored tail similar to that of the endemic cat. The first examples to achieve this satisfactorily were exhibited at a British show in 1988. It has since been produced in both longhaired and shorthaired forms.

The Seychellois is of Oriental conformation with a slim, elegant body that is set on long legs with oval paws and with a long neck and tail. The head is wedge-shaped with large, wide-set, pointed ears and large almond-shaped eyes, brilliant blue in color.

The fur in this longhaired version is long, fine, and silky, lying close to the body but with a slightly longer ruff. The ears are well feathered and the tail is plumed.

There are three recognized patterns for color distribution: Septième, Huitième, and Neuvième. Septième has large splashes of color on flanks, legs, and head; Huitième has smaller patches with a similar distribution, and the Neuvième has splashes of color on the head and legs but not on the body. All have dark tails. Kittens are born white, as in the Siamese, and color markings develop slowly.

These cats draw on both calm Persian and inquisitive Siamese traits in their ancestry and their personalities have been described as scatterbrained, attention-seeking, demanding, and demonstrative.

Colors
White with any color or combination of colors except black.

below: Blue Somali kitten

SOMALI

THE SOMALI IS A LONGHAIRED version of the Abyssinian cat (see page 74). The breed had its origin in longhaired cats turning up occasionally in Abyssinian litters, which some breeders found attractive. A longhaired Abyssinian was first exhibited in Australia in 1965 and Somalis are now as popular there as the shorthaired breed. New Jersey breeder Evelyn Mague named the breed Somali, not because the cat has any connection with Somalia but because that country is close to Ethiopia (formerly Abyssinia). She began her breeding program with a male called George who was born in 1967. The CFA gave the breed Championship status in 1978, FIFE in 1982, and it is now also recognized by British societies.

The Somali follows the conformation of the Abyssinian Cat with a medium-sized, long, and graceful body of foreign type, long legs with oval feet, a long, broad-based, tapering tail and head with a slightly rounded wedge with a slight rise from the bridge of the nose to the forehead and a slight break in profile. The chin is firm and the muzzle shows no foxiness or whisker pinch. The large ears are broad and cupped at the base, set well apart, and moderately pointed. The eyes are large and almond shaped, set obliquely, and accentuated by dark lid skin encircled by a light-colored area. The CFA standard specifies a rounded rib cage and a slightly arched back "giving the appearance of a cat about to spring."

The coat is double and dense with a very soft texture, flat along the spine and shorter over the shoulders but medium length elsewhere. There is a full brush tail, and ruff and full britches are preferred, ears well furnished, with tufts between the toes. Ear agouti hair is ticked with at least three bands, making six color sections from base to tip. Chest, belly, below tail, and inside of legs and britches are the color of the unmarked base hair, which should be clear and bright. There are dark lines extending from the upper eyelid, upward from the inner end and from the outer point toward the ear; cheekbone shading and dots and shading on whisker pads are also desirable.

Somalis are intelligent and active and should be given freedom.

Colors
GCCF
On an apricot base: Usual (black ticking), Rich gold brown, formed from apricot ticked black, Sorrel (apricot ticked cinnamon), Chocolate (apricot ticked dark chocolate), Blue (oatmeal/mushroom ticked blue), Lilac (oatmeal/mushroom ticked lilac), Fawn (oatmeal/mushroom ticked fawn), Red (bright red ticking), Cream (rich cream ticking).
CFA
Ruddy (black or dark brown ticking on burnt sienna base), Red (red ticked chocolate brown), Blue, Fawn.
Some associations also recognize tortie and silver variations of these colors.

SNOW CAT / ALASKAN SNOW CAT
This is a new experimental breed developed in the United States by crossing Somalis and Silver Persians. It is the intention to produce a round-headed, heavily-boned cat rather like the Siberian Forest Cat. The fur is thick and silver colored.

SUQUTRANESE
This is a dazzling white, unticked version of the Somali which has been developed in Britain, where it was first publicly seen at a Cat Association show in 1990.

below: Somali

BALINESE

left: Chocolate Point Balinese

below: Cream Balinese

THE BALINESE IS THE longhaired version of the Siamese cat. Its origin was in longhaired kittens born in Siamese litters. These may have been accidental mutations, but it has been suggested that during the 1920s some Angora blood had been introduced into some Siamese lines in Britain. California breeder Marion Dorset appears to have been the first to plan a breeding program, followed in the 1960s by New York breeder Helen Smith, who suggested the name Balinese instead of Longhair Siamese. By the end of the 1960s the Balinese had gained acceptance with the American cat societies. It was more than a decade, however, before the breed was recognized in Europe. In Australia it is also known as the Oriental Longhair, but it should not be confused with the breed known more generally by that name (see page 57).

The Balinese has the conformation of the Siamese: a graceful, long body set on long slim legs with small oval feet and a long tapering tail. Its elegant neck carries a wedge-shaped head, narrowing in straight lines to a fine muzzle, the tips of the large, pointed ears continuing the triangle. A straight line should be felt from the top of the head to the tip of the nose with no bulge over the eyes or dip in the nose. The eyes are almond shaped, slanting slightly toward the nose, with at least an eye's width between them. They must be a bright, clear blue color.

The coat is fine, silky, and of medium length with no woolly undercoat. It softens the line of the cat so that it looks less extreme than in the shorthaired Siamese. A tendency to a neck frill and some ear tufting are permitted, but ideally should not be present. The body should be an even color with subtle shading, if any, on the back and sides. Point color is restricted to the tail, feet, and ears. The mask, which covers the face including whisker pads, is connected to the ears by tracings but should not cover the top of the head. Kittens are born with short coats and no markings. Although color appears in the first few weeks, the full coat may not develop until they are adult.

The Balinese has the lively, intelligent, and inquisitive character of the Siamese and can be equally vocal.

Colors

GCCF

Solid Points: Seal, Blue, Chocolate, Lilac, Red, Cream (in Red and Cream, barring and striping of the points are permissible).

Tortie Points: Seal Tortie, Blue Tortie, Chocolate Tortie, Lilac Tortie, Cream.

Tabby Points: Seal, Blue, Chocolate, Lilac, Red, Cream, Tortie.

CFA

Solid Points only: Seal, Chocolate, Blue, Lilac.

TIFFANIE

left: Lilac Smoke Tiffanie

THIS BRITISH BREED IS A semi-long-haired version of the Burmese that was developed during the breeding program which created the Burmilla in the 1980s. It is part of what is known as the Asian Group that shares general GCCF standards for type. It was named the Tiffany when it was erroneously thought that the American Tiffany (page 56) came from the same Burmese origins—the spelling having to be changed because Tiffany was already being used as a cattery's prefix for registration purposes and an overlap of names is not permitted by the GCCF.

This is a cat of medium foreign type with a medium-long body, firmly muscled, with a generous chest and a straight back from shoulder to rump, although the hind legs are slightly longer than the forelegs. The paws tend to be oval. The elegant, proudly carried tail is medium to long and of medium thickness, tapering slightly to a rounded tip. The head, carried on a medium neck, should be a short wedge shape from the front, wide at the jaw hinge, and tapering to a blunt finish

below: Shaded Silver Tiffanie

at the muzzle, with a distinct nose break in profile that is gently rounded on top. The ears are medium to large with a rounded tip, set wide apart and continuing the angle of the upper face to produce a butterfly-wing outline from the front. The eyes are full and expressive but, although slightly Oriental, should be neither almond nor round. They are set wide apart and any color from yellow through chartreuse to green is permissible, depending on the variety. In Silvers, green is preferred; in the Selfs, gold is allowed.

The coat of the Tiffanie is semi-long, fine, and silky in texture. It should be noticeably longer on the tail and have a distinct ruff around the neck. The furnishings from inside the ears should form "streamers," and tufts at the ear tips are acceptable.

This is an affectionate and elegant cat, although some owners have suggested that it can be rather bossy, with quite a strident voice when it wants attention.

The GCCF classes the Tiffanie with the Foreign Cats.

Colors
Black, Blue, Lilac, Red, Caramel, Apricot, Black Tortie, Cream, Blue Tortie, Chocolate Tortie, Lilac Tortie, Caramel Tortie, the Burmese color restriction of these colors or their silver varieties, and all these colors in Smokes, Classic, Spotted, Mackerel and Ticked Tabbies and Tipped Agouti (like the shorthaired Burmilla), although not all these have been produced.

Foreign Breeds

FOREIGN BREEDS

FOREIGN IN THIS CONTEXT DOES NOT necessarily mean breeds that originated overseas, but indicates that they are cats with long elegant lines and fine bones of the type associated with the Siamese and other cats often called Orientals (though, again, Oriental is a description of type and not of origin). Their conformation ranges from the extreme type of the contemporary Siamese to the unique structure of the beautiful Korat. Both breeds came to the West by chance from Thailand, where they had been long established, although it is impossible to establish where they originated.

The Foreign Shorthairs have diversified, each breed having developed its own special characteristics. Considerable variation can be seen even in breeds that have developed from the same roots, although at the same time the ways in which the cat associations of the world have responded to new types and colors does mean that in some cats the differences lie in their color varieties. This is not quite so odd as it appears, for new colors are introduced by crossbreeding with other types of cat and inevitably this brings the possibility of altering the basic type of the breed.

An interesting example of the way in which different characteristics develop is the Havana Brown of the United States. Descended from cats imported from Britain in 1954, the breed has now developed so that it looks totally different from today's British Havana, which would be classed as an Oriental Chestnut in the United States. The Burmese is another case where there has been divergence between types on opposite sides of the Atlantic leading to different requirements in the show standards.

EGYPTIAN MAU

IN 1953 A pair of spotted cats attracted the interest of a Russian emigrée, because they reminded her of the cats in ancient Egyptian paintings and sculptures. The female had been spayed, but a similar cat was obtained from Cairo, a spotted silver, that was mated to a smoke male from Rome. Of the two kittens produced, one died, but the other was mated back to his mother, producing a female. The surviving kittens were exhibited at the Rome International Cat Show in 1955 and at the end of the following year their owner moved to the United States. The new breed gained Championship status with the Cat Fanciers Federation in 1968 and was soon accepted by other cat societies.

In 1960, a British breeder, co-author Angela Sayer, also sought to resurrect the ancient Egyptian type. These cats are now known as Oriental Spotted Tabby, Oriental Shorthair Tabby, or Spotted Oriental.

The Egyptian Mau of Egyptian stock has a stocky build midway between that of the Orientals and the American and British Shorthair type with a graceful but muscular medium-long body. The CFA standard refers to a loose skin flap extending from flank to hind leg knee.

The hind legs are longer than the forelegs. The feet are small, dainty, and slightly oval, the tail medium-long with a thick base tapering slightly to the tip, and should be able to reach back to the shoulders. The head is a slightly rounded wedge, not full cheeked and with a gently contoured profile showing a slight rise from the bridge of the nose to the forehead. The nose is even in width, the chin is firm, and the alert ears medium to large, broad based and slightly flaring to a moderate point. The eyes are large and almond shaped with a slight slant toward the ears. They are a light gooseberry green, but may show some amber tones when young.

The coat is of medium length with a high sheen and varies in texture according to color: silky and fine with smoke, dense and resilient in silver and bronze. Each hair accommodates two or more bands of ticking, striated by lighter bands. Ears may be tufted.

This is a lively and easily trained breed, more likely to adapt to a leash than many cats. Affectionate with owners, it tends to be shy with strangers.

left: Silver Egyptian Mau

Colors
Silver, Bronze, Smoke, all with black spotted pattern.

RUSSIAN BLUE

THE RUSSIAN BLUE IS A BREED that has been known for a long time. One tradition claims that these cats were taken to Britain by sailors trading with the Russian port of Archangel as long ago as the reign of Elizabeth I in the sixteenth century. They were certainly around in the early days of British cat shows when they were often in competition with British Blue Shorthairs, and sometimes penalized for the thickness of their coats until given their own class in 1912. In the U.S.A., where the breed was also known by the turn of the century, there was similar confusion. For a time it was known as the Foreign Blue, but was reinstated as Russian in 1939. World War II drastically reduced the numbers of the breed in Britain and Europe, and as breeders tried to rebuild them, Siamese blood was introduced with a consequent change to type. This led to a rewriting of the standard in 1950 to accommodate the change. Interest in the breed in the U.S.A. had declined, but when these more Siamese-type cats began to arrive

there it became re-established.

By the mid 1960s breeders in Britain sought a return to the original type of Russian Blue and began breeding to achieve it. Hence, as occurs in several breeds, differences developed between expectations for the breed on either side of the Atlantic with minor variations in standards worldwide.

This is a cat with a long graceful body, long legs, and small feet that are oval in the GCCF standard and round in the CFA standards. The tail is long and tapers from a moderately thick base. The head forms a short wedge from nose to eyes with the distance from eyes to ears the same or slightly longer. The top of the head appears flat between the large pointed ears, which are wide at the base and set vertically, continuing the outer line of the face. The ears should be scantily furnished with hair and the CFA standard particularly asks for the cat's skin to be thin and translucent. In Britain prominent whiskers pads are required, giving a blunt end to the head and, though there should be no stop or break on the nose, the profile from the top of the head down the nose should have a shallow concave curve from the level of the upper edge of the almond shaped eyes. The American standard requires no whisker pads and a straight line at a downward angle from the top of the nose, and for the eye apertures to be round. Both require the eye color to be vivid green.

The plush double coat is fine, short, and soft, the undercoat very dense so that it stands out from the body. The British standard defines its texture as different from any other breed and one of the main criteria for judging the cat. Its color should be a bright blue throughout. In the U.S.A. lighter shades are preferred; in Britain, medium tones. A silvery tipping to the guard hairs is required by the CFA but this is a fault in Britain, although some absence of pigment at the hair tip is permitted.

Russian Blues are shy cats with strangers, but can be very affectionate to people and other cats they know.

Colors
Blue is the only color permitted in the U.S.A. and Britain, although White, Black, and Red are known in some countries. In Britain there are White and Black forms known as Russian Shorthairs.

RUSSIAN SHORTHAIRS
These are essentially color varieties of the Russian Blue as recognized by the GCCF in Britain. Both require the coat color to be solid with no variation, dark marks, or rustiness in the black.

Colors
Solid Black and Solid White.

ABYSSINIAN

below left: Sorrel silver Abyssinian　　*right: Ruddy or Usual Abyssinian*

THE ABYSSINIAN IS A long-established breed said to have been introduced to Britain with a cat called Zula from Ethiopia in 1868. Its conformation is much like that of ancient Egyptian cat figures and it has been suggested as a direct successor to the pharaonic cats. Others have seen the breed as having been created by British breeders in the latter half of the nineteenth century. The agouti fur type of the Abyssinian with its ticked hairs can be seen in some recently recognized breeds that have their origin in Singapore and Ceylon (see below). Genetic studies suggest that the gene concerned mutated in the region of Ceylon and the Bay of Bengal, an area crossed by regular trade routes between the Horn of Africa and Malaysia, and this could have accounted for its distribution.

The Abyssinian has a lean, muscular body, between the extremes of the cobby and the svelte Siamese. It has long slim legs and small oval feet, with the tail thick at the base, but tapering and long enough to reach back to the shoulders. The head, set on an elegant neck that should arch in an unbroken line from the shoulders to the top of the head, is gently rounded, especially from the brow to the top of the head, and forms a slightly rounded wedge without flat planes, with brow cheek and profile all showing a gentle contour. The CFA describes the muzzle as gently rounded and there is a slight rise from the bridge of the nose to the forehead. For the GCCF a slight nose break is essential and the line from nose tip to chin should be very straight. The ears are large, alert, broad at the base, and well cupped with their line following the shape of the head wedge. The CFA describes them as moderately pointed. The large eyes, which the CFA specifies to be a gold or green color and almond-shaped, and the GCCF states amber, hazel, or green and rounded almond, are set well apart. They are accentuated by an encircling dark line surrounded by an area of lighter color.

The coat is fine and close-lying, resilient to the touch, and not soft. It is comparatively short but long enough to accommodate two or three dark bands of ticking—the GCCF specifies at least four bands of color with the roots the base color and the tips dark.

WILD ABYSSINIAN

This is a domestic breed, developed from cats discovered in Singapore in the 1980s. It is a return to the style of Abyssinian known over a century ago. The Wild Abyssinian has a larger body than the Abyssinians of the modern breed and is slightly larger overall. There are dark rings on the tail, dark bars on the legs, dark rings on the neck, and a dark M-shaped frown on the forehead. The agouti coat is otherwise like that of the Abyssinian.

Colors
GCCF
All-over colors: Usual (golden brown ticked black), Sorrel (copper ticked chocolate), Blue (soft blue ticked deeper blue-gray), Chocolate (copper brown ticked dark chocolate), Lilac (dove-gray ticked deeper gray), Fawn (ticked deeper fawn), Red (apricot ticked red), Cream (ticked deeper cream).

Tortoiseshell: Usual (brown areas ticked black, red areas ticked red), Sorrel (bright apricot and reddish apricot ticked chocolate and red), Blue (pinkish mushroom and cream ticked blue-gray and cream), Chocolate (rich apricot and reddish apricot ticked dark chocolate and red), Lilac (pinkish cream and cream ticked pinkish dove gray and cream), Fawn Tortie (fawnish cream and cream ticked mixture of fawn and cream).

Silver: All the above all-over and tortoiseshell colors with silver versions of the ground color.

CFA
All-over colors only: Ruddy (equivalent to the British Usual—burnt-sienna ticked with shades of dark brown and black), Red (equivalent to British Sorrel—red ticked with chocolate brown), Blue (beige ticked with shades of slate blue), Fawn (rose-beige ticked with light brown).

Colors
Only the original Ruddy coloring is bred.

KORAT

THE KORAT IS AN ANCIENT breed from Thailand where it has been highly regarded for centuries and is thought to bring good luck to its owners. Korat, (or Koraj, the "j" pronounced like a western soft "t") the name of a province of Thailand, is a comparatively recent name. Its more traditional name was *Si Sawat* which means "the color of the Sawat seed." In Thailand these cats were never sold but given as symbolic presents, as a wedding gift, for instance. An English traveler received one and shortly after his return from Thailand exhibited it at a London cat show in 1896, where it was judged as a Siamese and thought a poor example. Korats did not reappear in the West until a pair was presented to the American ambassador in Bangkok in 1959. They were sent to the United States to breeder Jean Johnson, who became interested in the breed after seeing it in Thailand. This pair was later joined by others, enabling a breeding program to be started. The Korat became a recognized Western breed in 1966.

The Korat is a medium-sized, muscular cat with a semi-cobby body, neither compact nor svelte, with a broad chest. The paws are oval and front legs are slightly shorter than hind legs. The CFA specifies height to base of the tail to be equal to the distance from base of tail to the neck. The tail is medium-long, heavier at the base, and tapering to a rounded tip. The head is heart-shaped when viewed frontally, with breadth between and across the eyes, the eyebrow ridges forming the upper curves of the heart, curving from a large flat forehead down to a well-developed but neither square not sharp-pointed muzzle. The nose is short and curves slightly downward and the GCCF standard specifies a slight stop between forehead and nose. The large, round-tipped ears are set high with a large flare at the base. The eyes are large and prominent. The aperture appears well-rounded when fully open but has an Asian slant when closed or partly closed. They are bright and luminous and preferably a brilliant green, although an amber cast is permitted. Young cats have amber or yellow eyes, not achieving their full color until two to four years old.

The coat is special to the Korat. It has only a single coat of short, glossy hair (short to medium in the GCCF standard) that lies close to the body. Over the spinal area it is inclined to break as the cat moves. The fur is blue with silver tipping, the more tipping the better. Each hair is usually lighter at the roots, darkening to just before the tips, enhancing the silver effect. Tipping develops through kittenhood and adolescence to reach full intensity at about two years old. There should be no shading or markings. An ancient manuscript illustrating the types of Siamese cats described the Korat as having hair "with roots like clouds and tips like silver," the eyes "shining like dew drops on a lotus leaf."

The Korat is a playful and intelligent cat with a gentle voice, but can be very defensive of its territory.

above: Korat

Color

There is one color only and a major characteristic feature of the Korat: blue with silver tips.

SIAMESE

THE SIAMESE IS A BREED that has been in Thailand for many centuries. Known there as the Vichien Mat, it seems to have been a pet of royalty and nobility. A tradition tells how one of these cats was placed in the tomb of deceased Emperors and that, when it emerged through a hole specially left, it was thought to have carried the soul of the dead from the grave on the first stage of its journey to the next life.

Although Siamese cats were already in the West and seen at early British cat shows, they may not have had the clear pointed pattern with which the breed is now identified. Indeed, cats with coats darker at the extremities had been reported elsewhere in the world long before. The first well-authenticated example to be sent from Thailand was a gift sent to the wife of America's President Hayes in 1878. Sadly, she did not long survive her arrival in Washington. A British Consul who acquired a pair sent the cats to England in 1884, and there his sister, Lilian Velvey, proceeded to breed them. She later imported more, probably from a cattery that her brother established in Bangkok. Since then breeders have created an elegant Siamese cat that has become more exaggeratedly slim and angular (see page 87).

The modern Siamese is lithe and muscular with a graceful, svelte body of medium size, its hips never wider than the shoulders, to give sleek tubular lines. The legs are long and slim, the hind legs higher than the front, with small oval paws. The tail is long and tapers to a point. The elegant neck carries a long head with width between the ears, narrowing in a tapering wedge with perfectly straight lines to a fine muzzle, with straight profile. It also has a strong chin and a level bite. The ears are large, pointed, wide at the base and continue the lines of the head. The eyes are almond shaped and slant toward the nose, but with width in between. They are always a vivid blue, the deeper the better.

The glossy coat of the Siamese is short, fine in texture, and close lying. It should be an even color on the body, with subtle shading, if any, on the back and sides. The darker areas, the points and mask so characteristic of the breed, should be clearly defined but restricted to the tail, feet, ears, and face. The mask should cover the face, including the whisker pads, and be connected to the ears by tracings, but should not cover the top of the head. The gene that produces the pointed restriction also dilutes the color of the points, and the first Siamese cats, although the color was known as Seal, were a dilute form of black. Seal was the only color recognized until the 1930s, when blue became

left: *Cream Point Siamese*
above: *Seal Point Siamese*

Colors
GCCF
Solid Point: Seal, Blue, Chocolate, Lilac, Cinnamon, Caramel, Fawn, Red, Cream.
Tabby Point: Seal, Blue, Chocolate, Lilac, Red, Cream, Cinnamon, Caramel, Fawn, and Tortie versions of these colors except for Red.

Tortie Point: Seal Tortie, Blue Tortie, Chocolate Tortie, Cinnamon Tortie, Fawn Tortie, Caramel Tortie, Lilac Tortie.
CFA
Solid Point only: Seal, Chocolate, Blue, Lilac. For other colors see Colorpoint Shorthair.

accepted. In the 1950s Chocolate was acknowledged to be a different color, and then Lilac (or Frost Point, as it was first called in the U.S.A.) was accepted. Now a whole range of colors and patterned points have been produced, recognized by the GCCF in Britain as Siamese, but classed separately by some cat societies. There are also unpointed versions that are seen as different breeds.

Siamese are affectionate and demanding of attention. They can be decidedly vocal, even conversational, and sometimes have a raucous voice.

COLORPOINT SHORTHAIR

Cats of Siamese type and pattern, not in the four traditional Siamese colors. The GCCF includes them with the Siamese.

Colors

CFA recognize points in Red, Cream, Seal Tortie, Chocolate Tortie, Blue-Cream Lilac, Lilac Cream, and Lynx (Tabby) versions of these.

ORIENTAL SHORTHAIRS

below left: Apricot
Oriental Shorthair

THE ORIENTAL SHORTHAIRS are of Siamese type, but with a wide range of coats that do not have the Siamese color limitation. In the 1920s, when only Seal Point Siamese were considered acceptable on the show bench, British breeders began to call these cats Foreign Shorthairs; a name that continued to be used. In the U.S.A. they then became known as Orientals, and in the 1990s the GCCF adopted the name Oriental Shorthair (excepting the Foreign White, see page 78).

In the 1950s, black and chocolate solid-colored cats were produced. At first the black was largely ignored but the brown was developed into the Havana. Havanas exported to the U.S.A. developed differently and became the Havana Brown (see page 78), but in Britain it remained entirely Siamese in type and was renamed the Chestnut Brown until the 1970s when the old name was re-established for the color, ignoring any confusion in name with the differing American breed. Since then several new colors have been added and tabby and other patterns developed. Cat societies differ in those they recognize.

The standards are those of the Siamese cat in conformation and coat quality but, except for those cats carrying white in the coat, the eye color should always be green. In the Whites and Bicolors recognized by the CFA they can be blue, green, or odd-eyed.

Oriental Shorthairs share the character of the Siamese and it is claimed that they are more adaptable than most cats in training to walk on a leash.

Colors

GCCF
Self: Havana (Rich warm chestnut brown), Lilac, Black, Blue, Red, Cream, Apricot, Cinnamon, Fawn.

Non-Selfs (excluding Tabbies): Tortie (Black), Blue Tortie, Chocolate Tortie, Lilac Tortie, Cinnamon Tortie, Caramel Tortie, Fawn Tortie, Smoke, Shaded.

Tabby (Classic, Mackerel, Spotted or Ticked): Brown, Blue, Chocolate, Lilac, Red, Cream, Apricot, Cinnamon, Fawn, Tortie, Blue Tortie, Chocolate Tortie, Lilac Tortie, Cinnamon Tortie, Caramel Tortie, Fawn Tortie.

Silver Tabby (Classic, Mackerel, Spotted or Ticked): Black, Blue, Chocolate, Lilac, Red, Cream, Apricot, Cinnamon, Caramel, Fawn, Tortie, Blue Tortie, Chocolate Tortie, Lilac Tortie, Cinnamon Tortie, Caramel Tortie, Fawn Tortie (all with silver tipping on the ground color).

CFA
Solid: Blue, Chestnut, Cinnamon, Cream, Ebony, Fawn, Lavender, Red, White.

Shaded: Blue Silver, Chestnut Silver, Cinnamon Silver, Cream Silver, Ebony Silver, Fawn Silver, Lavender Silver, Red Silver, and Particolor Silver (of Black, Chestnut, Cinnamon with red patching or intermingled, and of Blue, Fawn, or Lavender with cream).

Smoke: Red, Chestnut, Cinnamon, Cream, Ebony, Fawn, Lavender, and Particolor (as for Solid).

Tabby (Classic, Mackerel, Spotted or Ticked): Blue, Red, Cream, Cinnamon, Chestnut, Ebony, Fawn, Lavender, and Silver forms in all these colors.

Bicolor: As for the varieties above with the addition of White.

Particolors: Blue-Cream, Cinnamon Tortoiseshell, Chestnut Tortoiseshell, Fawn Cream, Lavender Cream, Ebony Tortoiseshell.

FOREIGN WHITE

HAVANA BROWN

below: Havana Brown
below left: Foreign White

THE FOREIGN WHITE IS a white, unpointed version of the Siamese, but it did not originate in the unpointed cats found in Thailand alongside pointed-patterned coats. British breeders deliberately set about the creation of this blue-eyed white of Siamese type by crossing Siamese with white Shorthairs.

It has the same conformation as the Siamese and the Oriental Shorthairs, and in the U.S.A. would be classified as an Oriental cat. In Britain it was allowed to retain the name under which it was first recognized before the many other Oriental colors had been created, and is still classed as a separate breed.

Although it is a pure white cat with vivid blue eyes, the Foreign White does not suffer from the usual linkage of deafness with this combination.

It shares the character of its other Oriental relations.

Color
This is a single color breed.

THE HAVANA BROWN, NAMED for its cigar-brown color, began with the British-bred cat now known as the Havana Oriental Shorthair, that was created in 1952 by the crossing of Siamese with black shorthairs. This was variously called the Oriental Chocolate Cat, Havana, and Chestnut Brown Foreign, and it was exported to the U.S.A. The first show standard followed the type for Russian blue, but in Britain breeders decided to maintain the Siamese conformation and continued breeding to Siamese, resulting in their modern breed. In the U.S.A. the original standard was followed, although it has now developed with its own characteristics and is different from both the Russian and the Siamese.

The Havana Brown is a medium-sized cat with a conformation midway between the thickset and svelte breeds. Its muscular torso is of medium length, as are its neck and tapering tail. It stands high on relatively long straight feet with compact oval paws. Hind legs are slightly longer than forelegs. The head is longer than it is wide and narrows to a rounded muzzle with a pronounced break on both sides behind the whisker pads. In profile there is a distinct stop at the eyes, and the muzzle appears almost square ended, with the tip of the nose and chin forming an almost perpendicular line. Its large ears are round tipped, cupped at the base but not flaring, and they are tilted forward, giving the cat an alert appearance. The medium-size eyes are set wide apart, the aperture oval, and the color a vivid and level shade of green, the deeper the better.

The coat of the Havana Brown is short to medium in length, smooth, and lustrous and brown is the only color.

This is a seemingly intelligent breed that likes human attention and company.

Color
This is a single color cat and should be a rich and even shade of brown throughout, tending toward red-brown (mahogany) rather than black-brown.

OCICAT

below: Cinnamon (left)
and Chocolate Ocicats

THE FIRST OCICAT APPEARED in 1964, the result of a mating between a Chocolate Point Siamese and a hybrid female with an Abyssinian mother and a Seal Point Siamese father. This kitten, Dalai Tonga, did not fit breeder Virginia Daly's breeding program to produce an Abyssinian-pointed Siamese and was neutered and sold as a pet. Later Mrs. Daly's interest in spotted cats grew and she repeated the mating to create the foundation stock for the breed. Its resemblance to the spotted ocelot suggest the name; half ocelot, half cat. Outcrosses to American Shorthairs added size and the silver color range to the breed, which consequently does not have the elongated look typical of the Oriental cats. Recognition was given to the breed in the U.S.A. in 1986 and it is now accepted by some European clubs. The GCCF gave it preliminary status in Britain in 1987.

The Ocicat is a medium to large cat with an athletic appearance but surprisingly heavy for its size. The chest is fairly deep and the ribs well sprung, the back level to slightly higher in the rear, with a fairly long, medium-slim tail with only a slight taper. The powerful legs are medium long with compact oval feet. The head is a modified wedge shape on an arched neck. There is a slight curve from muzzle to cheek and a gentle rise from nose bridge to brow. The broad muzzle is squarish and in profile shows good length, the chin is strong, the jaw square and there is a moderate whisker pinch. The ears are alert, moderately large and set at an angle of 45 degrees to an imaginary line across the brow. The eyes are large and almond shaped, angling slightly upward toward the ears and with at least an eye's width between them. All eye colors except blue are allowed and they need have no correspondence with the coat color.

The coat is short, smooth, and satiny in texture with a lustrous sheen and must be correctly marked. It should be tight and close lying but long enough for each hair to carry the necessary bands of color. The entire fur is agouti banded, except for the tip of the tail; markings are tipped with a darker color and the ground color has a lighter tip. Chin, jaw, and around the eyes are usually a lighter color with the tip of the tail the darkest. Spotting must be clearly defined with good contrast, though this will be less in the pale colors. A row of spots should run along the spine from shoulder blades to tail, which should have horizontal brush strokes along the top, ideally alternating with spots, and a dark tip. Thumbprint-shaped spots should be well distributed on the sides of the torso with a subtle suggestion of the classic tabby pattern, a spot circled by spots in place of the bull's eye or whorl, and the belly should be well spotted and spots scattered across shoulders and hindquarters, extending as far as possible down the legs. There are broken bracelets and necklaces on the lower legs and throat, the more broken the better. There is an intricate tabby M mark on the forehead and markings extend up over the head between the ears before breaking into spots on the lower neck. There are mascara markings around the eyes and on the cheeks, the eyes being rimmed with the darkest color and surrounded by the lightest color. The color of the tail tip is used to identify the color of the cat.

Ocicats make affectionate companions but may not be happy to share a household with several other cats.

Colors

CFA

Tawny (Brown Spotted Tabby), Chocolate, Cinnamon, Blue, Lavender, Fawn, Silver, Chocolate Silver, Cinnamon Silver, Blue Silver, Lavender Silver, Fawn Silver, with other varieties permissible but not reds, creams, or torties (patched/tortie tabbies).

BURMESE

left: Blue Burmese

below left: Brown Burmese
below right: Black Bombay

ALL-BROWN CATS OF Burmese type have been reported from various places in the Far East, and a similar cat is painted along with the Siamese and Korat in the ancient Thai Cat Poems scroll, so this may be a long-established Oriental type. There were certainly dark-brown cats among those exhibited at early cat shows in Britain. The modern breed, however, has its origins in a single cat called Wong Mau who was imported into the United States by Dr. Joseph Thompson, a psychiatrist from San Francisco, in 1930. Thompson kept Siamese and at first thought Wong to be a dark form of Siamese, but with the help of other breeders and geneticists established that she was a cross between a Siamese and an unknown dark-coated cat. When she herself was bred with a Siamese and then back-crossed to her male kitten she produced Siamese with normal points, very dark Siamese like herself, and all-brown kittens. These kittens became the foundation stock for the breed. In 1942 three more cats reached the United States

from Burma and one of them brought fresh blood to the breeding program.

The breed was first recognized in the United States in 1936 but the introduction of fresh Siamese genes led to the suspension of registration for a time until 1953, when type had been re-established. Burmese were first sent to Britain in 1949 and when the GCCF granted recognition there, in 1952, it was for a breed with a more Siamese look than in the U.S.A., a divergence that still persists. There was further divergence when British breeders began to develop new color varieties while American breeders concentrated on eliminating barred markings and darker points on the sable brown. A much smaller range of colors is accepted in the U.S.A. Some societies still only accept brown, and call other varieties Malayan cat.

The Burmese is a medium-sized, muscular cat that presents a compact appearance. The chest is strong and rounded in profile and the back straight from shoulder to rump, the tail straight and medium length; the GCCF standard specifies a medium-thick base tapering to a rounded tip that if brought gently around the side of the body should reach the shoulder. Legs are in proportion to the body (slender in the GCCF standard) with round paws in the U.S.A. and oval ones for the GCCF.

Standards differ for the head. The CFA describe it as "pleasingly rounded without flat planes," full-faced with breadth between the eyes and a broad, well-developed muzzle, a visible nose break, and a rounded chin. The GCCF requires it to form a short wedge when viewed frontally, wide at the cheekbones and tapering to a blunt muzzle, and slightly rounded between the ears, the brow slightly rounded and a distinct nose break followed by a straight nose and a good depth of chin. Both require medium-size ears, set well apart, broad at the base, rounded at the tip and tilting slightly forward. Large round yellow to gold eyes are specified by the CFA, but for the GCCF they may be from yellow to amber. Their lower line should be rounded and the top line show a slant toward the nose. Both the GCCF and the CFA prefer a deep and brilliant gold.

A distinctive feature of the Burmese is its glossy coat, which is short, fine, satin-like, and very close-lying. The aim is an even-colored cat but the underparts tend to be lighter than the back, though the shading should be gradual.

Colors

GCCF

Solid: Brown, Blue, Chocolate, Lilac, Red, Cream.

Tortoiseshell: Brown Tortie, Blue Tortie, Chocolate Tortie, Lilac Tortie.

CFA

Sable (brown), Champagne (honey beige shading to pale gold tan), Blue (with warm fawn undertones), Platinum (silvery gray with pale fawn undertones).

BOMBAY

IN 1958 KENTUCKY breeder Nikki Horner mated Sable Burmese to Black American Shorthairs, aiming at what she called "a copper-eyed mini-panther with patent-leather fur," choosing the name Bombay to suggest the Indian homeland of the real black leopard. At first these cats shared characteristics of both breeds, but selection for Burmese type created the breed as it is today. It was granted Championship status in the United States in 1976. British breeders used similar matings between Burmese and British Shorthairs to develop their version of the Bombay, and consequently the cats differ between the two sides of the Atlantic in the same ways as the types of Burmese differ. In Britain it is classed as a variety of the Asian Shorthair.

The Bombay has a medium-sized, muscular body, neither compact nor rangy, a straight tail, and legs in proportion. The head is rounded with no sharp angles, the face full with a considerably well-developed muzzle that maintains the rounded contours of the head. In profile there is a moderate stop, merely a slight indentation, between the eyes, providing a change in direction from the rounded head to the medium-rounded muzzle, with no suggestion of a pug-like look, the end of the nose being slightly rounded to complete the roundness of the head. The ears are set well apart, broad based, round tipped, and tilting slightly forward. The eyes are round, set far apart, and can range in color from gold to copper, the deeper and more brilliant the better.

The close-lying coat is short, fine, and satin-like in texture with a shimmering patent-leather sheen.

The Bombay is friendly, alert, and outgoing, with a strong voice.

Color

A one color breed: Black, which should be jet black to the roots.

SEYCHELLOIS SHORTHAIR

THE SEYCHELLOIS SHORTHAIR was developed from the same breeding program as that which produced the longhaired version (see page 66) when British breeders Pat Turner and Julie Smith began their attempt to meet the former's aspirations to create a breed with the colored tail and white body with color patches of cats reported in the Seychelles.

This is a long-bodied and elegant cat of Oriental conformation, having long legs with oval paws and with a long, whippy tail. The head, set on a long neck, is wedge-shaped with large wide-set, pointed ears and large, slanting, almond-shaped eyes of brilliant blue.

The fur is short and fine, lying close to the body.

As in the Longhair, there are three recognized patterns for color distribution: Septième, Huitième, and Neuvième. Septième has large splashes of color on flanks, legs, and head; Huitième has smaller patches with a similar distribution, and the Neuvième has splashes of color on the head and legs but not on the body. All have dark tails. Kittens are born white, as in the Siamese, and color markings develop slowly.

These cats are very athletic but inherit both the calmness of the Persian and the inquisitive traits in their Siamese ancestry, which can also make them attention-demanding and demonstrative.

Colors

White with any color or combination of colors except black.

ASIAN SHORTHAIRS

"**A**SIAN" HAS BECOME A TERM used to describe those cats of Burmese type in colors not accepted for the Burmese breed. Far from being of Asian origin, however, they are all British creations (except for the Bombay, which was developed independently in the United States). Three of these Asians, the Bombay, Burmilla, and Burmoire (now more correctly know as the Asian Smoke), became well established under their own names, but the GCCF now classes them all as Asian Group, along with others with self-colored coats, tabbies and the longhaired Tiffanie (see page 69).

The Asian Group cats are all of medium foreign type; any tendency to Siamese type or to the cobbiness of the British Shorthair is not permissible. Females are smaller and much daintier than males. The body is medium long, firmly muscled, with a generous chest and the back straight from shoulder to rump. Legs are of medium length with hind legs slightly longer than forelegs. Paws tend to be oval. The elegant, proudly carried tail is medium to long and of medium thickness, tapering slightly to a rounded tip. The head, carried on a medium neck, should be a short wedge shape from the front, wide at the jaw hinge, and tapering to a blunt finish at the muzzle, with a distinct nose break in profile and gently rounded on top. Ears are medium to large with a rounded tip, set wide apart and continuing the angle of the upper face to produce a butterfly-wing outline from the front. Eyes are full and expressive but, although slightly Oriental, should be neither almond nor round. They are set wide apart and any color from yellow through chartreuse to green is permissible, depending on variety. In Silvers green is preferred; in the Selfs, gold is allowed.

The coat should be short, fine, and close-lying to the body (except for the semi-long hair of the Tiffanie).

The Asian Selfs should all have solid color throughout, except for red, in which some shading to paler underneath is allowable and even slight tabby markings would not penalize an otherwise good cat. This is also allowable in those that show the Burmese color restriction: Caramel, Apricot, and Caramel Tortie. The GCCF does not allow the latter three to compete in shows, although they are permitted in breeding programs. They are permitted in the Burmilla, Smokes, and Tabbies. The Caramel has a cool-toned brownish-lilac color, shading to honey on the body, with lilac overtones. The apricot has a cool dusty cast over pinkish cream, shading to paler, warmer tones on the body, and may have denser pigmentation on mask and ears. The caramel Tortie may also have a denser pigmentation on mask and ears.

The Burmilla and Burmoire (now Smoke) varieties were originally treated as separate breeds and have separate entries below. The Tiffanie appears with the longhairs.

All the Asian Group cats are said to have appealing temperaments, although they have been called "bombastic" and "bossy" by one owner. They can be quite vocal, usually only moderately so, but when hungry or thwarted they can be quite noisy.

Colors

Self: Bombay (see above), Blue, Chocolate, Lilac, Red, Cream, Caramel, Apricot.

Tortoiseshells: Black Tortie, Blue Tortie, Chocolate Tortie, Lilac Tortie, Caramel Tortie.

Tabby (Classic, Mackerel, or Spotted): Black, Blue, Chocolate, Lilac, Red, Caramel, Apricot, Cream, Black Tortie, Blue Tortie, Chocolate Tortie, and Burmese color restriction of these colors.

Smoke: See Burmoire below.

Burmilla: See below.

Tiffanie: See page 69.

BURMOIRE

BURMOIRE WAS THE NAME first given to what is now officially known as the Asian Smoke, being the Smoke version of the Asian Shorthair, with the same conformation as the other Asian Shorthairs.

It was created as a continuation of the Burmilla mating program to produce a non-agouti cat with a silvery-white or near-white undercoat. This should be approximately one third to one half of the total hair length in adults, with ghost tabby markings giving the impression of watered silk on the body, silvery frown marks on the forehead, and silvery rings around the eyes.

The Asian Smoke shares the temperament of the other Asian Shorthairs.

Colors

Black, Blue, Chocolate, Lilac, Red, Caramel, Apricot, Black Tortie, Chocolate Tortie, Lilac Tortie, Caramel Tortie, or any of the Burmese restriction of these colors.

below: Burmoire or Asian Smoke

left: Blue Burmilla

BURMILLA

THE BURMILLA WAS THE second of the Asian Group to be created, more than two decades after the Bombay. It came about through an accidental mating between a male Chinchilla Persian and a female Burmese who belonged to breeder Baroness Miranda von Kirchberg. Faberge, the Burmese, was briefly shut away in the breeder's study while she went out. Sanquist, the Chinchilla, was meowing outside the door and an unthinking member of the household let him in. The Baroness returned and took Faberge off to a Burmese stud for an "official" mating. It was some surprise when nine weeks later, instead of the expected kittens, Faberge produced four kittens of good Burmese type but with black-tipped silver fur. Their paternity was obvious, and Sanquist himself was very protective toward them, even helping to groom them. Their attractive appearance and excellent temperament encouraged the Baroness to create a breeding program to produce more such cats and she decided to call them Burmillas, linking the names of their parent's breeds. They were officially recognized as a new breed by the GCCF in 1990.

The Burmilla conforms to the Asian Shorthair standard but is an agouti cat, either standard or silver, shaded or tipped with color. The undercoat should be as pale as possible in the standard coat and nearly white in the silver. There is a dense concentration of color along the spine, extending down the tail, dispersing gradually over the flanks to become as light as possible on the underparts. Shading may vary from tipping to medium-heavy shading, evenness and symmetry being more important than depth, provided a cat is not so lightly tipped that it appears white. A denser concentration of color should extend from the feet up the back of the leg to the hock. Ideally, there should be no tabby markings on the body, but the forehead should be marked with an M and lines should be penciled on the cheeks and run from the outer edge of the eye, with the eye rim emphasized in the base color. Paws should be lightly barred, and the tail marked with incomplete rings and a solid color tip. All the Burmese colors are accepted.

The Burmilla shares the temperament of the other Asian Shorthairs.

Colors

Tipping: Black, Blue, Chocolate, Lilac, Red, Caramel, Apricot, Black Tortie, Cream, Blue Tortie, Chocolate Tortie, Lilac Tortie, Caramel Tortie, or with Burmese restriction of any of these colors. All silver varieties of these colors.

SINGAPURA

SINGAPURA IS THE Malay name for Singapore, and since 1993 a type of cat found there has been the official symbol of Singapore with the name "Kucinta, the Love Cat." This same cat also used to be known as the Drain Cat or River Cat. Tommy and Hal Meadow, the American couple who developed the breed in the West, say that their first Singapuras were ships' cats that Hal sent back to Texas in 1971. These returned to Singapore when Mrs. Meadow went out there in 1974 and were brought back with others in 1975. The return to Asia by Mrs. Meadow led to rumors that the breed was the result of a cross between Burmese and Abyssinians, both of which Tommy Meadows had owned. These rumors were fanned by the fact that "for security reasons" the Meadows originally suppressed mention of the re-importation— but it seems more likely that the type had been long established on its island homeland.

above: Singapura

The Singapura does have an appearance similar to a Burmese-Abyssinian cross, although much smaller and well-muscled. It used to be featured in the *Guinness Book of Records* as the smallest breed but now on average weighs 4–5 lbs. (2 kg) for females and 6–7 lbs.(3 kg) for males. It has a rounded head, narrowing to a definite whisker break, with a shortish, broad muzzle and a blunt nose. Ears are large, wide-based, and deeply cupped, and the large wide-open eyes show a slight slant when closed. The compact body has a long slender tail, just short of the shoulder when laid along the body, with a blunt tip, and the legs taper to small oval feet.

The coat, which is short and silky, has agouti fur with ticked guard hairs along the back, head, legs, and tail. The tail has a dark line running along the top and a dark tip. The inside front legs and rear knees are barred and there are dark spurs on the lower back of the hind legs. The appealing Singapura face has dark outlining of the nose and eyes and "cheetah" lines from the inner corner of the eye to just behind the whisker pad.

The eyes should be hazel-green or yellow.

Singapura are lively cats with the affectionate character of the Oriental, but they have quiet, gentle voices. They are often inquisitive cats who like to have a good view of the world, not staying on ground level. Many seem to be happy sitting on their owner's shoulder.

TONKINESE

above: *Tonkinese mother and kittens.*

THIS INTERMEDIATE BETWEEN Siamese and Burmese was developed by American breeder Milan Greer in the 1950s. It was another breeder, Edith Lux, who proposed the name Tonkinese, the proximity of the Gulf of Tonkin to both Burma and Thailand suggesting the closeness of this to the Burmese and Siamese breeds. It was first recognized in Canada and soon accepted by American cat societies, being recognized by the GCCF in Britain in 1991.

The Tonkinese is described by the CFA as of intermediate type, neither cobby nor svelte, but the GCCF describe it as of foreign type, reflecting their differences in the Burmese. American and British standards are otherwise very similar. The torso is medium to long, firm and muscular, with a slightly rounded chest, set on slim legs, hind legs slightly longer than forelegs and with paws more oval than round, fully oval for the GCCF. The tail is neither thick nor whippy, preferably reaching back to the shoulder, and the CFA specifies it as tapering. The head is gently rounded to form a modified wedge of medium proportions, slightly longer than wide, the muzzle neither pointed nor square for the GCCF but blunt for the CFA. There is a slight whisker break or pinch and a slight nose break at eye level. There is a gentle contour with a slight rise from the nose stop to the forehead, which rounds gently to the top of the head. The ears are medium size, slightly taller than wide, and pricked forward for the GCCF, broad based and oval tipped. The eyes are more open than Oriental and should be aquamarine.

The coat is short and close-lying, fine, soft, and silky. The coat pattern requires the points to be distinctly darker than the body color but merging gently into the body color. The body color itself is slightly paler on the lower parts.

Tonkinese are lively, inquisitive, and friendly cats.

Color

Singapura are only recognized in one color: sepia agouti, a golden ivory with brown tipping. Each tipped hair should be light next to the skin and have at least two bands of sepia ticking separated by light bands and a dark tip. Muzzle, chest, stomach, and inner legs are untipped. The CFA specifies dark lines from the brows and outside corner of the eyes and extending downward along the nose from the inner corner of the eyes.

Colors

GCCF

Solids: Brown, Blue, Chocolate, Lilac, Red, Cream.

Tortoiseshells: Brown Tortie, Blue Tortie, Chocolate Tortie, Lilac Tortie.

Tabbies: Brown, Blue, Chocolate, Lilac, Red, Cream, Brown Tortie, Blue Tortie, Chocolate Tortie, Lilac Tortie.

CFA

Mink: Natural Mink (medium brown with ruddy highlights acceptable, dark brown points), Champagne Mink (buff cream to beige with reddish highlights acceptable, medium brown points), Blue Mink (soft blue gray with warm overtones, slate-blue points), Platinum Mink (pale silver gray with warm overtones and darker frosty gray points).

Solid and Pointed: Darker and lighter versions respectively of each of the Mink colors. These are all classed as "Any Other Variety."

BENGAL

THE BENGAL CAT DEVELOPED from a hybrid produced by mating domestic cats to the Asian Leopard Cat, *Felis bengalensis*. It was first known as the Leopardette, but Bengal was later adopted as the official name to link it with the scientific name for the Leopard Cat. There have been many attempts to breed domestic cats with wild species. However, cross-species breeding usually produces hybrids which are infertile. The Leopard Cat is a different species so it is surprising that fertile kittens should have resulted. It appears that the male chromosomes do not match so closely as in the female and in early generations only females are fertile. All male crosses are sterile in the first generation, about 2% are fertile in the second, and increasingly more in subsequent generations.

In the 1970s, Dr. William Centerwell of the University of California was conducting research with Asian Leopard Cats that appeared to be immune to feline leukemia, though the immunity was not passed beyond the first generation of hybrids. This research was abandoned with the advent of a vaccine, but eight out of the female outcrosses were obtained by Jean Sugden-Mill, who had herself bred such hybrids two decades earlier until circumstances made her stop the program. She mated them to a brown spotted tabby rescued by a Los Angeles cat shelter and a red feral cat found living in the rhinoceros enclosure of Delhi Zoo.

Other breeders also became involved, and crosses used included Egyptian Mau, Ocicat, Abyssinian, Bombay, and British Shorthairs. In 1983 The International Cat Association (TICA) gave the new breed recognition, and in 1991 it achieved Championship Status. It reached Britain in the early 1990s and was granted Preliminary Status by the GCCF in 1996.

The Bengal is a large cat with a long, sleek, muscular body, high hindquarters, a medium-long tail that is carried low, and large rounded feet. Its head, rather

left: Marbled Patterned Bengal

small in proportion to the body, is a broad medium wedge with rounded contours, the profile gently curving from the forehead to the bridge of the nose, which is wider that in most domestic breeds as it has more oscillating membranes (for smelling), and puffed whisker pads due to widely spaced canine teeth. The chin is firm and slightly rounded and the ears medium in size, rounded, and wide-based. Eyes are oval, slightly almond shaped, gold, green, or hazel with brown tabbies, blue with snow, which carry Siamese coat color restriction, and gold, green, or blue-green with those that have Tonkinese or Burmese restriction.

The coat is short, thick, and plush with a luminous sheen. It is unique in having a phenomenon known as "glitter," which gives the appearance of gold dusting to Black/Brown Bengals and of pearl dusting to Snows. Spots may be random or in horizontal bands, some-times showing rosettes like those of leopards. In diluted the coat may be randomly marbled. The legs are barred, the tail ringed with a dark tip and the face marked with lines from the eyes across the cheekbones and over the top of the head, sometimes with an "M" mark on the forehead. Kittens go through a fuzzy stage at about two months; this disguised wild kittens from predators.

Bengals are intelligent and loving, and are bred partly for their delightful temperament.

Colors
Brown/Black Spotted, Brown/Black Marbled: background color ranging from rufus (rich orange) to pale gray. Snow Spotted, Snow Marbled: background color ranging from creamy white or ivory to a very pale tan.

RECENT BREEDS

IN ADDITION TO THE breeds and varieties already described, there are a number of others that are known only in a few places or that are in development and not yet fully recognized. There are also variations of coat and color or of modifications to conformation that are still to be created. Whether they are will depend on whether breeders find them attractive and desirable, and whether the cat societies are prepared to support them. The following are not yet established and are awaiting acceptance by the world's cat societies.

Spotted Mist

The first breed to be developed entirely in Australia was created by a breeding program begun in 1976 through which Dr. Truda Straede set out to produce a new spotted cat using no fewer than 30 foundation cats to ensure a wide gene pool. They were chosen to produce a cat with the temperament, conformation, and color dilution of the Burmese (who made up half the foundation stock), the intelligence, color and ticking of the Abyssinian (who made up a further quarter), and the health, vitality, and reproductive abundance of the domestic tabbies (who formed the remainder). Ten years later the Royal Agricultural Society Cat Control of New South Wales accepted the breed for registration.

The Spotted Mist is a muscular, medium-sized cat of moderately foreign type with a broad chest, strong legs with neat oval paws, and a long thick tail with minimum taper. The broad head has a firm chin, well-developed whisker pads, and large, wide-based ears, set well apart and tilted slightly forward. The large, lustrous eyes are any shade of green from chartreuse to ultramarine. Its short, fine, and close-lying coat, easy to keep in good condition, is clearly and delicately spotted against the ground color, the legs and tail ringed, and the face lined as in other tabby varieties. Five colors are currently recognized: Brown (Seal markings on creamy fawn), Blue (blue-gray on silvery cream), Chocolate (chocolate on creamy fawn), Lilac (dove gray on pinkish gray), Gold (old gold on rich cream), and Peach (salmon pink on pinkish cream).

This is said to be a particularly affectionate cat.

Sokoke Forest Cat

This breed, which is being developed by Jeni Slater in Denmark, originates in the Sokoke region of eastern Kenya where a litter of kittens with unusual markings was discovered during land clearance on the edge of forest in 1977. It is variously suggested that these were a local species of wild cat, an accidental mutation in a domestic cat, or a cross between a local domestic cat and a wild cat. No more of these cats have been found and they proved remarkably easy to tame, which suggests that probably they were descended from domestic cats.

The Sokoke Forest Cat has an elegant, slender body and a long tail that tapers to a point. In most respects its short coat is like that of other tabbies; the main difference is the shape of the blotches or "oyster" marks on its sides, that carry what has been described as a "wood-grain" pattern.

Celonese or Ceylonese

The Celonese is from Sri Lanka and is also known as the Ceylon Cat. It is a local form of domestic cat that was found feral by Italian veterinarian Paolo Pellegata and taken back to Italy in 1984. They were shown at the Como Cat Show that year and a breeding program was begun. The cat was submitted to the Fédération Internationale Feline (FIFe) in 1984 for recognition.

This is an agouti cat that looks much like an early Abyssinian, of the kind now being recreated as the Wild Abyssinian.

above: Reverting to a less extreme type for the Siamese is producing cats variously known as Opal Cats and Apple-Headed Siamese.

right: Ceylon Cat, developed in Italy.
far right: York Chocolate Cat, a chocolate-patched white.

The original coloring is known as Manila (black markings on a sandy-golden ground), but Blue, Red, Cream, and Tortoiseshell varieties have now joined it.

Poodle Cat

The Poodle Cat, or Pudelkatzen, was created in Germany by Dr. Rosemarie Wolf by crossing a Devon Rex with a Scottish Fold to produce a cat with both a Rex coat and folded ears.

Thai

A new British breed that is in its early stages and is a longhaired form of the Korat, identical in all ways to that breed except for the length of its fur.

York Chocolate Cat

An American breed that dates from 1983 when two farm cats, a longhaired black male and a longhaired black-and-white female, produced offspring with a dark chocolate brown coat. Their ancestry is unknown, although appearances suggest a trace of Siamese, which has made the cat societies reluctant to register the breed. They take their name from the original color and from the location of owner Janet Chiefari's farm in New York State. Some have predominantly brown coats, others have white fur patched in chocolate brown in various ways.

La Perm Cat /Alpaca Cat

A new curly-coated breed originating in The Dalles, Oregon, and should more properly be called The Dalles La Perm Cat. It originated with a litter of farm cats found by Linda Koehl in 1986, one of which was bald. After two months it began to grow a curly coat, and when mature this brown tabby, now called Curly, became the foundation for the new breed. It has been developed as both a shorthair with what has been described as an "Afro" look, and as a longhair with tight ringlets. It was recognized by the International Cat Association in 1995 and all colors are permissible.

American Lynx

A new breed developed in America by Robert Mock of Seattle, Washington, and Joe Childers of North Carolina. It is a stump-tailed cat and has been produced in both shorthaired and longhaired varieties and in a variety of coat colors, including two tabby variants that they have called Leopard and Tawny.

Ojos Azules

Ojos Azules is the Spanish for "Blue Eyes," and is an extremely rare new American breed originating from a tortoiseshell female with vivid blue eyes discovered in New Mexico in 1984. The blue has proved to be controlled by a dominant gene and, it is claimed, unlike the usual blue color it is not linked with deafness when it appears with pure white coats.

Nebelung Cat

The Nebelung Cat is an American breed that is a long-haired version of the Russian Blue. It was developed in the 1980s by breeder Cora Cobb and was bred from a female who appeared to carry Angora genes. She was mated to a Russian Blue male and a pair of her kittens formed the foundation stock used by breeder Cobb to firmly establish the breed. It was given recognition by the International Cat Association in 1987. The name Nebelung comes from those foundation cats who were called Siegfried and Brunhilde, names of leading characters in the Ring of the Nibelungs.

The Nebelung is identical to the Russian Cat except in length of coat. It is recognized in two colors: Blue (light blue-gray with a silvery sheen), and White (pure white).

Apple-Headed Siamese

Apple-Headed Siamese, also known as Opal Cat, is a return to the early type of Siamese, being developed by breeders who prefer it to the extreme type favored in the modern Siamese.

left: The blue-eyed Ojos Azules.
above: La Perm Cat.
right: Nebelung Cat, another American creation.

Part Three:
Physiology and Behavior

THE CAT'S BODY

LIKE EVERY OTHER MAMMAL, the cat has a body skeleton that shelters its internal organs, enabling it to process food and reproduce. Powerful muscles are attached to the skeleton to give motion. The cat mates with the opposite sex and the female bears live young that are suckled and reared by her until they are able to survive alone. All cats, whatever their breed, share the same physiology. They differ only in minor ways to produce a more compact or more elongated conformation, with one or two breeds with anomalies of fur balance or bone structure caused by particular mutations.

The skeleton

Cats are much smaller than humans but their skeleton contains more bones; a total of 230 against a human's 206. The cat's skeleton is a semi-rigid framework that supports other, softer structures. A system of efficient levers is provided by the bones of the spine, limbs, shoulders, and pelvis. These are connected to and geared by powerful attached muscles. Other bones, such as the skull and arched rib cage and pelvis, give the body protection. Four distinct types of bone make up the skeleton of the cat: they are known as long bones, short bones, irregular bones, and flat bones.

Long bones are cylindrical and have hollow shafts containing the vital bone marrow in which the manufacture of all blood cells takes place. These bones form the cat's limbs. In the forelimb the long bones are the humerus, running from the shoulderblade to the elbow, and the thick radius, connected by strong ligaments to the thinner ulna. In the hind limb, the femur, or thighbone, is very long and rather fragile. It fits into the pelvis with a ball-and-socket joint, and at the lower end is joined to the tibia, a strong bone, reinforced down its entire length by the thinner fibula.

Short bones consist of a spongy core surrounded by compact bone. They are found in the cat's feet and kneecaps or patellae. The patella is found where the femur joins the tibia. It glides freely over the smooth end of the femur and adds to the graceful movement of the cat in action. The forepaws of the cat are made up of sets of three small bones, each of which forms a digit corresponding to the finger of the human hand. The tiny bones at the end of each digit are highly specialized, however, and articulate so that the claws may be extended or contracted at will. The cat has no thumb as such, and the corresponding digit consists of two bones only that form the dew claw. In the hind feet the bones are longer and the first toe is absent altogether. A diagram of the cat's skeleton shows clearly that the animal walks up on its toes, adding to its speed and accuracy of movement.

Irregular bones are so called because of their varying, irregular shapes. They are similar in structure to the short bones. A long string of these bones make up the vertebral column, or spine, of the cat. Attached to the skull at one end with the atlas and axis bones of the neck, the spine continues with the hollow cervical, thoracic, and lumbar vertebrae which contain the spinal cord. Then, gradually, smaller and smaller bones extend to the tip of the cat's tail. The irregular projections of the bones of the vertebral column serve as attachment points for the various muscles of the back.

Flat bones are made of two layers of compact bone with a spongy layer sandwiched in between them. Such bones make up the skull, the pelvis, and the shoulderblades or scapulae. The skull consists of many pieces of flat bone connected together. At birth, however, the flat plates are separated in some places, and it is important to avoid injury to the kitten's head. The flat pieces of bone are pierced by numerous holes for the passage of blood vessels and nerves. The scapula is a flat bone, roughly triangular in shape, that is jointed to the upper end of the humerus. Unlike us, the cat does not have a fully developed collarbone, and there is a great deal of free movement in the animal's shoulder. The hip bone, too, is connected to the spine in such a way that it allows fluid and flexible movement, making the cat one of the most agile of animals.

Flattened and elongated bones make up the cat's 13 pairs of ribs. These bones are not hollow, but their spongy interiors contain a substantial amount of marrow and produce a proportion of the animal's blood cells. The volume of the chest cavity is controlled by the strong muscles attached to the ribs that cause the lungs to empty and refill.

The muscular system

Overlying the skeletal framework of the cat is a complex network of muscles that give the animal its powerful and typically graceful movement. They are also responsible for its sinuous shape. There are three types of muscles in the body of the cat. The first are the striped or striated fibers attached to the limbs and other parts of the anatomy that are under the voluntary control of the cat, and are known as voluntary muscles. The second group consists of smooth or unstriated tissue that carries out muscular functions

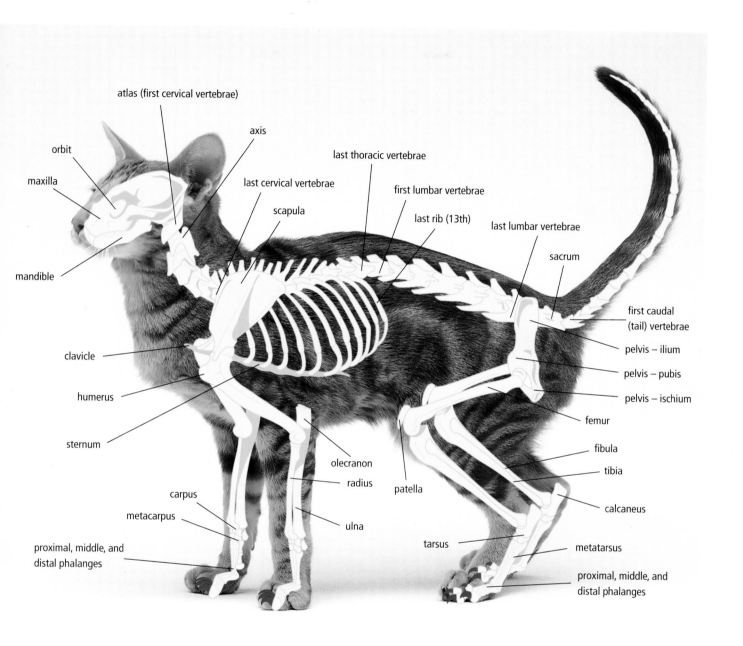

atlas (first cervical vertebrae)

axis

orbit

last thoracic vertebrae

maxilla

last cervical vertebrae

first lumbar vertebrae

scapula

last rib (13th)

last lumbar vertebrae

sacrum

mandible

first caudal
(tail) vertebrae

clavicle

pelvis – ilium

pelvis – pubis

humerus

pelvis – ischium

femur

sternum

fibula

tibia

olecranon

calcaneus

radius

patella

carpus

metacarpus

ulna

tarsus

metatarsus

proximal, middle, and
distal phalanges

proximal, middle, and
distal phalanges

not under voluntary control, such as the muscles of the intestines and the walls of blood vessels. These are known as involuntary muscles. Finally, there is the specialized cardiac muscle that has adapted to carry out the functions of the heart and possesses unique powers of rhythmic contraction.

The voluntary muscles are usually attached to the bones that form a joint. The extensors are those that extend and straighten a limb, while the flexors flex and bend the joint. The muscles that move a limb away from the body are called abductors, and adductors draw the limb back again.

Muscles are attached directly to bone by fibrous attachments at points known as origins, that usually occur at the point nearest the cat's spine. At the other end of the muscles the attachments are called insertions, and the muscles are secured by

above: A cat's skeleton is made up of 230 different bones, fewer in the tailless Manx and Japanese Bobtail.

top: The cat's flexible backbone and well-articulated joints give it a lithe and sinuous body. **middle and bottom:** When walking the cat follows a four-stage sequence: right hind leg, right foreleg, left hind leg, left foreleg, placing them in an almost straight line. As it gets faster, diagonally opposite legs begin to move together, and in a gallop it makes a series of bounds, pushing off with both hind legs and landing on one front paw, then quickly transferring weight to the other, a stride ahead before the hind feet land forward of them ready to push off again.

strong cords of fibers that form the tendons. A muscle may have more than one origin and insertion, and the variety of the voluntary muscles—there are more than five hundred in the cat—enables it to be almost fluid in its movements.

Muscles of head, torso, and tail

The cat can turn its head from side to side, as the cervical vertebrae are supported by exceptionally strong muscles in the neck, enabling the animal to position its head accurately for searching out prey by sight, sound, and smell. The strength of these muscles can be seen clearly as a mother cat carries her young, or when the hunting cat carries prey as large as himself.

The rib cage is lifted by powerful involuntary muscles of the chest. The diaphragm contracts, causing air to be drawn into the lungs through the cat's nasal passages and windpipe.

Arching of the back and strong springing movements are made possible in the cat by the arrangement of the large groups of muscles that run down and along the back, and that are attached to the thoracic, lumbar, and sacral vertebrae. The only powerful muscles in the tail are near the root, and the rest of the appendage is controlled by small muscles and tendons down to the tip. Though small and delicate, these muscles enable the cat to use the tail expressively, as well as balancing the weight of its body when running and jumping.

Leg muscles

In the limbs, the muscles of the foreleg enable the forepaw to be rotated as the radius moves around the ulna as the wrist bones are fixed. This enables the cat to

above: *Powerfully muscled hind legs enable the cat to leap up to five times its own height. Bringing up its hind legs to land, it uses the front feet to stabilize its balance. If a wall proves too high it may use the upward impetus to "run" vertically up the final stretch.*

below: *Cats have extraordinarily good balance and can negotiate the narrowest fence, aided by mechanisms in the ear and the tail that help maintain equilibrium.*

grasp small objects and to use its paw as a scoop.

The head of the humerus, which is held only in a shallow groove in the scapula, can also move freely and is held by muscles to the chest wall. Therefore, the whole forelimb is extremely flexible and can move forward and backward for running, as well as across the chest or up above the head for climbing, washing, or grasping different prey. The hind limb is less flexible and can basically only move forward and backward. The muscles are immensely strong, and form the spring mechanism that enables the cat to pounce from its waiting position with such strength, speed, and accuracy. They enable a cat to jump up to five times its own height.

Perhaps the most interesting and specialized muscles of the cat are those found in the paws. The voluntary muscles attached to the claws enable the cat to extend or retract these at will. The cat uses its claws for climbing and in hunting to grip prey. It also uses them as weapons of defense when cornered and for attack when fighting. The claws are often extended and retracted rhythmically in time with purring, when the cat is very happy and contented, as, for example, when a mother cat is suckling her kittens. Kittens also perform the same action when they are suckling or kneading with their paws at either side of the breast.

The digestive system

The cat is a very successful carnivore, with its teeth and digestive tract specialized for a meat-eating hunter who may not always be successful in catching prey, so may gorge occasionally at a large kill. The cat cannot chew but tears or bites a piece from the carcass, then swallows it so quickly that the salivary juices in the mouth have virtually no time to start breaking down the food. The salivary glands of the cat produce little or no ptyalin, which is the powerful enzyme present in human saliva necessary for the preliminary breakdown of starches into blood sugars. Any starches present in the cat's diet are, therefore, of little food value to the animal. The gastric juices of the cat are much more powerful than those found in the human stomach; in fact, they are strong enough to soften bone. The cat is able to swallow large chunks of rodents and birds, and any parts such as feathers, hair, and bones that are not quickly broken down in the stomach may be regurgitated.

The cat's teeth

The cat's dentition is highly adapted for stabbing, slicing, tearing, and biting, but not for chewing its prey. In the adult cat there are 12 incisors, four canines, ten premolars, and four molars, giving a total set of 30 teeth. When kittens are born, the teeth are just visible inside the gums. They soon erupt, and by the time the kittens have reached six weeks of age the teeth are strong and needle-sharp. It is at this stage that the queen will naturally become increasingly reluctant to feed the babies, who ideally should be given thin strips of raw meat to chew on. Kittens eventually shed their baby teeth as the permanent ones come through. This usually happens without any problems at five to six months. Occasionally double dentition is seen when the early teeth are not shed, and the kitten develops a sore mouth. The veterinarian can

right: Like all carnivores, cats evolved to live by hunting; as a result, a cat's digestive system has adapted to cope with periods of gorging and periods of starvation.

quickly ease out the temporary teeth and the condition soon rights itself.

The digestive tract

In the stomach, protein material is broken down in the first stage of its reduction to simple amino acids, before being combined again to form the building blocks necessary for replacement of cells throughout the cat's body.

From the stomach, the partly digested food passes through a valve called the pylorus, to the small intestine. Here further digestive changes take place, aided by secretions from accessory glands such as the pancreas and liver. Fats are broken down and extracted, sugars are changed structurally, ready for storage, and minerals are absorbed. From the small intestine the now-fluid contents pass into the large intestine, where they are acted upon by the specialized bacteria that are present there. Water is drawn off, and finally the remaining waste material passes into the colon to be voided as feces.

The respiratory system

The respiratory system of the cat is fairly complex. The lungs are situated within the chest or thoracic cavity and separated from the abdomen by a strong muscle known as the diaphragm. Each lung is divided into three lobes and consists of the bronchi, smaller branching bronchioles, and a mass of tiny air sacs.

During respiration, the cat draws in air through its paired nasal cavities. This then passes through the pharynx or

above: The tongue scoops up water and flicks it to the back of the throat. Its rough surface also scrapes the flesh off bones.

throat, down the trachea or windpipe, and on through the bronchi into the lungs. When the air fills the air sacs, gaseous exchange takes place. Carbon dioxide from the blood filters into the air sacs as oxygen passes from the air to replenish the blood. The used air is then exhaled.

The process of breathing is quite automatic, as the chest muscles contract and relax, acting rather like a pump on the ribs and diaphragm, driving the air in and out of the lungs. The breathing rate varies from cat to cat, and is affected by exercise, emotion, or environmental temperature. The normal respiration rate of a resting cat is, however, put at 20–30 breaths per minute.

The circulatory system

Every cell in the body of the cat needs a supply of nourishment, and it is the function of the blood to deliver the nutrients and to take away the cells' waste products. The blood consists of red blood cells and white blood corpuscles contained in a fluid known as blood plasma. Red blood cells contain hemoglobin, a compound that transports oxygen. White blood corpuscles pick up and transport impurities and bacteria that have invaded the cells. Plasma contains specialized platelets that cause cuts and wounds to clot.

The blood is pushed around the body by the heart, a muscular pumping organ that consists of four chambers. The blood's journey starts in the left auricle, or upper chamber, of the heart. Enriched with oxygen from the lungs, the bright rich blood passes into the left ventricle, or lower chamber. It is then forced out into a great artery, the aorta, to run its course through all the arteries and arterioles and into the fine network of capillaries that infiltrate the cat's body, distributing its store of oxygen as it goes. As the blood gives up its oxygen, it collects a great deal of waste matter. Leaving the capillaries, it enters into tiny veins or venules, before passing into the great veins that transport the stream back to the heart.

Muscular movements of the cat and the expansion and contraction of its chest muscles during normal breathing help the transport of the blood back toward the heart. The blood moves quickly in the main arteries, but the rate is reduced by one half on its return journey through the main veins. Extra blood with its nutrients is required by different parts of the body

above: *The dagger-like canine teeth are used for holding and killing prey and tearing flesh. The other teeth also rip and tear, but cats swallow without really chewing.*

right: *Young kittens have a pulse rate of 150–200 and breathe up to 40 times per minute, much faster than adult cats.*

at different times. After a heavy meal, for example, the cat's abdomen draws in extra blood to aid digestion, at the expense of the supply to the brain and other parts of the body. When the deoxygenated blood, with its wastes and impurities, returns to the heart, it passes through large veins, the venae cavae, into the right auricle. The blood enters the right ventricle, and then is driven through the pulmonary artery to the lungs for ventilation and purification. Carbon dioxide is given off, oxygen collected, and the

clean, enriched blood passes into the heart's left auricle to run its course again.

Blood passing through the aorta causes its walls to expand, and a pressure wave (the pulse) passes down the arteries. It is usual to take the pulse rate by placing a finger on the femoral artery on the inside of the animal's thigh. In a healthy, adult cat at rest the pulse rate is 100–140 beats per minute. Kittens have a much higher rate than adult cats, and in both, excitement or fear will make the heart beat faster.

SKIN AND FUR

THE SKIN OF THE CAT is made up of two layers of tissue. The inner layer is known as the dermis and the outer layer as the epidermis. The epidermis is constantly being replaced as the outer surface dies and sloughs away into tiny flakes of dandruff. The skin can be used to monitor the health of the cat in many cases. In a healthy, fit animal the skin is soft and pliable. It is possible to take a fold of skin on the neck, scruff, or back, then release it and watch it immediately regain its normal position. In a sick cat, or one that is in the process of dehydrating, the skin is stiff and unyielding. It may be impossible to lift even the smallest fold, and skin that is pinched up appears to have lost its elasticity, remaining in the pinched fold for some moments. A sudden change in the color of the skin points to severe illness in the cat, as some diseases can induce deficiencies of pigment. A pallid appearance can point to infestation by parasites, a lack of some vital dietary requirement, or even an acute case of shock. Reddening of the skin can indicate an inflammatory disease of the skin or its underlying tissues, while a blue tone can suggest heart trouble, poisoning, or the onset of respiratory disease. Jaundice, one symptom of several serious illnesses, produces a yellowish effect in the skin of the cat. Any change in the color of the cat's skin is usually noticed first on the ear flaps and nose, lips, and gums.

Glands

The skin of the cat contains some sweat glands, but these seem to exist mainly for excreting impurities from the body, rather than playing a major role in controlling the animal's temperature. The true sweat glands of the cat are in the pads of its feet, and this is why most cats leave a slightly damp trail of paw marks on surfaces such as laminated work tops. The cat has sebaceous glands in the skin that open into the hair follicles and produce a semi-liquid, oily substance known as sebum, the purpose of which is to coat each new hair as it grows.

Of great importance to the cat are the various scent glands that the cat uses for marking and identification. There are the temporal glands on the forehead, just above the eyes, the perioral glands by the lips, and other glands near the root of the tail. By rubbing these glands against a surface such as furniture, trees, a post, another animal, or a human friend, it deposits minute scent secretions that mark it with the cat's own distinctive odor.

Nose and paw leather

The hairless skin of the cat's nose leather and paw pads is extremely sensitive to touch, even more than the rest of its skin. The epidermis of the pads is very thick and rough, providing a surface with perfect friction for running, jumping, and climbing.

Claws

The claws are formed of layers of keratin, the same material that forms hair, and grow continuously from the base, like human finger-nails. There are five claws on each forepaw but only four on the

above: Scratching on a tree trunk not only exercises a cat's claws, it removes blunt claw tips, exposing sharp new points beneath. Cats' claws retract into the paw, giving it a very soft tread, but can instantly be extended to grip with or to use as weapons.

hind legs. The fifth claw acts rather like our thumb, helping the cat to grip when climbing a tree or holding prey. The fore claws are usually kept retracted when not in use, but can be rapidly extended when needed to gain balance on a surface or as weapons. In Foreign cats they are sometimes slightly less retractile and can be heard making contact as they walk across a smooth floor surface. Wild or feral cats will wear claws down by friction on hard surface and remove old tips from paw claws by scratching and biting. Domestic pets, especially those who live entirely indoors, will need regular cutting of their claws and provision of appropriate scratching surfaces.

Fur and whiskers

Hair is derived from the outer layer of the skin and acts as an insulatory cover, keeping the cat warm in cold weather and cool in hot weather. Hair forms a dense pelt over the entire body of the cat, and is modified in certain areas, forming eyelashes and whiskers. Each individual hair is a long thin cylindrical structure, pointed at one end and ending in a tiny bulb at the root end, which is embedded

left: An adult cat may have 200 hairs per square millimeter on its belly, about half that number on the back. In luxuriously coated longhairs like this Persian some hairs may be 5 in. (13 cm) long.

below: The cat's whiskers and other vibrissae are much thicker and tougher than ordinary hairs and set deeper in the skin. There are usually 24 arranged in four rows on either side of the nose. The upper rows move independently of the lower ones. The skin on the nose and paw pads is 75 times thicker than elsewhere, and on the nose ridged in a pattern individual to each cat.

in the dermis. Each one is formed quite separately in its follicle, and pigment cells called melanocytes inject tiny granules of color into the hair as it grows, giving the coat its genetically determined coloring.

There are three main types of hair. Shortest, thinnest, and softest are the down hairs that lie close to the body and conserve body heat. Awn hairs that form the middle coat are slightly more bristly, with a swelling toward the tip before it tapers off. They are part insulation, part protection. Guard hairs, which are the thickest, are long and straight. They form a top coat that protects the fur below from the elements. In the wild cat there are about 1000 down hairs to 300 awn hairs and 20 guard hairs, but in domestic cats the ratio varies greatly between breeds.

Special muscles attached to the large follicles enable the hairs to become erect and stand out at right angles to the skin whenever the cat is startled or angry. The coat may also stand out when the animal is ill and has a subnormal temperature.

All hairs, especially the guard hairs, are sensitive to touch without the skin having to make contact, but there is also a fourth kind of hair, the vibrissae, that is even more touch sensitive. These make up the whiskers, eyebrows, and similar hairs on the cheeks and chin and behind the forelegs. They are greatly enlarged and thickened. The whiskers are embedded in the upper lip to a depth three times greater than other hairs and are surrounded by a mass of nerve endings that transmit information about any contact they make and any changes in air pressure around them.

Responding to currents of air and changes of pressure as well as actual contact, vibrissae provide the cat with special information when it is too dark to see. The whiskers can be brought forward to investigate the shape of objects and can also be wrapped around caught prey. They also help the cat to detect changes in the environment.

Molting or shedding is the term given to the regular or irregular loss of dead hair. Some cats shed such hair very lightly throughout the year; others have a considerable change of coat during the spring and autumn months, and even the appearance of the summer and winter coats can vary in some varieties.

THE CAT'S SENSES

THE CENTRAL NERVOUS SYSTEM of the domestic cat consists of the brain and spinal cord, and controls and coordinates all the animal's everyday activities. Information received by the cat's sensory organs is constantly monitored by the system and dealt with according to its degree of importance. Vitally urgent information is acted upon immediately, relatively unimportant signals may be discarded, and other information is passed to the memory region to be stored for future use.

Characteristics of very primitive brains can be found in the structure of the cat's brain, which has three clearly defined regions. The forebrain is concerned with the sense of smell, but also contains the thalamus, which responds to impulses traveling from the spinal cord, and the hypothalamus, which controls internal regulatory processes. The midbrain contains the optic lobes and is the area that deals with signals stimulated by light. In the hind-brain the cerebellum controls balance, and the enlarged end of the spinal cord forms the medulla, controlling the animal's respiratory and circulatory systems.

The core performs the same functions that it did in the earliest vertebrates, regulating endocrine gland production, controlling respiration and metabolism, and maintaining homeostasis (a constant internal environment). Heart rate, blood pressure, and temperature are kept steady by the regulation of mechanisms within the hypothalamus that receive and process feedback from the animal's body.

Digestion is controlled by the limbic system, which is also responsible for all activities requiring a set pattern of sequential response. This part of the brain is vital for the survival of the cat. Hunting, eating, mating, and escaping all require patterns of behavior that must be carried out in the correct sequence in order to be totally effective.

The cerebral cortex is the most recently evolved structure in the brain of the cat. It is deeply wrinkled, or convoluted, giving a great surface area, without the necessity of increasing skull size. The two large and symmetrical hemispheres at the top are made up of many neurons,

left: A cat's eyes have a wide field of view and good stereoscopic vision. This helps them judge distances and enables them to see in dim light.

above: A cat is always alert, both as a hunter and for its own protection. Even asleep its senses are not dormant, for its ears are still listening.

or nerve cells, and are separated by a deep groove that runs from the front to the back of the brain. The left hemisphere controls most of the functions of the right side of the body, while the right hemisphere controls those of the left side, and a network of nerves connects both hemispheres for the correlation of information. The animal's legs are controlled by an area at the front of the cerebral cortex, the body is controlled by an area in the central region, and a section at the back of the cortex deals with the processing of visual stimuli. Auditory processing areas are situated at the sides of the cortex, and there are complex zones specifically concerned with activity, learning, memory, and all other conscious sensations.

Sight

The cat has excellent vision, even in subdued light. It only needs one-sixth of the light humans need to distinguish the same details of shape and movement. Their pupils can open very wide to admit more light, which passes through the transparent, curved cornea and lens to the retina at the back of the eye. Any light not absorbed by the retina meets a special layer of cells called the tapetum lucidum that reflects it back to the retinal cells, reinforcing the information transmitted by the nerves there to the brain. Any reflected light that is still not absorbed creates the familiar effect of the cat's eyes shining yellow, green, or red at night. The delicate mechanisms in the back of the eye are shielded from strong light by the contraction of the iris, which closes down to form a slit-like pupil, thereby also enhancing the sharpness of the vision.

The eyes of the cat face forward, allowing the fields of vision to overlap, and giving stereoscopic vision that is

slightly wider than our own. This makes the cat extremely accurate in judging distances for jumping or springing and pouncing while hunting. The eyes are also more rounded and have a considerably wider overall field of vision. However, being comparatively large and set in deep sockets in the skull, the cat's eyes do not move freely, so the animal will turn its head to bring objects into sharp focus. Cats are very sensitive to subtle differences in the grayness of colors and, although their color vision is not as good as ours, they are not colorblind as was once thought.

As well as the upper and lower lids, the cat has a third eyelid, known as the nictitating membrane, or haw. This is a sheet of pale tissue situated in the inner corner of each eye and normally tucked away out of sight. Any inward movement of the eye within its socket causes the membrane to move diagonally upward and across the front of the eyeball. The function of the haw is to remove dust and dirt from the cornea and to keep the eye moist and lubricated. When a cat is out of condition or incubating an illness, a

above: The large "pinna" of a cat's ear helps it to focus sound and judge direction. Cats can hear through a huge range, allowing them to pinpoint the position of prey.

tiny pad of fat beneath the eyeball contracts and causes the eye to retract slightly into its socket; then the nictitating membrane is extended part of the way across the eye. The appearance of the haw is often taken to be an early warning of disease.

Hearing

The hearing of the cat is exceptionally well developed. It can pick up the high-pitched sounds of its prey, as well as many other noises that are quite inaudible to the human ear. While mature humans can hear as high as 20,000 cycles, and dogs nearly 40,000, cats reach an amazing 100,000 cycles per second. They can hear ultrasonic sounds that precede an activity, which is why they often react before we are even aware that anything is happening. Cats ears may, however, be less sensitive in the lower range.

The ear of the cat consists of three sections. Outside, the pinna, or ear flap, is naturally erect and points forward. It is flexible enough to move forward, sideways, or back, in order to pinpoint the direction of the slightest sound, and forms a funnel to lead sound waves down to the eardrum, which is tautly stretched across the ear canal. In the middle ear three small bones transmit sound to the cochlea of the inner ear. Here sounds are converted into nerve impulses that are passed along the acoustic nerve to the auditory cortex of the brain to be decoded and recognized by comparison with sounds stored in the memory bank.

Smell

In the cat the sense of smell is well developed, possibly 30 times better than that of humans. When the minute particles of odorous substances in the atmosphere are drawn in during normal breathing, or are deliberately sniffed in by the cat, they stimulate highly sensitive nerve endings of fine hairs within the nasal cavities.

A thick, spongy membrane, the olfactory mucosa, with over twice the surface area of that of humans, contains 200 million scent-sensitive cells, an indication of how important this sense is to cats, used in relation to their sex life and essential in their hunt for food.

In the roof of the cat's mouth is a special organ we lack, also lined with receptor cells. Known as the veromonasal or Jacobsen's organ, it is a ½ in. (1.2 cm)-long tube opening just behind the front teeth. When a cat receives a new, subtle, or interesting smell it opens its mouth and raises its head. It may look like a human reaction to a bad smell but the cat is savoring the scent. Its strange grimace, with wrinkled twitching nose and drawn-back lips, is called the flehmen reaction and directs the odor to the Jacobsen's organ.

Cats rarely eat carrion, and most of them find the smell of tainted food highly offensive. Some cats appear to be very

below: *Scent is an important sense for cats. Their urine carries an individual odor that is sprayed to lay claim to their territory and to indicate their presence to other cats.*

fond of perfume, and like to nuzzle into the shoulder or chin of a human wearing after-shave lotion or cologne. The catnip plant emits an odor that most cats find irresistible. How it affects cats is a matter for conjecture, but it appears to excite them sexually while having a simultaneous and contradictory soothing effect on the nervous system. Given the opportunity, even neutered cats and young kittens will roll in the plant, purring ecstatically.

Taste

It is difficult to distinguish between the senses of smell and taste in the domestic cat, but it seems that the cat's tongue can differentiate between things that are salty, sour, bitter, or sweet. Most seem to like salty tastes, but can vary considerably in their reaction to sweet foods. The very positive response that the cat shows toward fresh meat is more likely to be evoked by smell than by taste. Taste alone does not seem important to most cats, but this is how tiny kittens, on first leaving the nest, test most new surfaces

below: *By opening the mouth and drawing in the air laden with scent particles the cat can direct them up to the channel behind its front teeth that leads to an extra scent organ so that it can savor important or pleasurable smells.*

left: Kittens are always investigating new things in their world, and this one may think these flowers smell interesting, but it is just as likely that another cat has left its scent on them.

below: The front paws are particularly sensitive and are used to investigate objects, but whiskers are also used, especially in the dark, to find out about shapes as well as registering changes in air pressure.

and objects, licking carefully and methodically, and with great concentration. Just how the information they receive in this way is analyzed and stored is not known, and it occurs only during the most sensitive period of learning in the young cat.

Touch

Cats use their noses, paws, and whiskers for examining objects by touch, generally after having first checked out the items by smell. Cats rarely burn themselves with hot food or liquids, as they use their noses as thermometers, approaching the dish closely and appearing to sniff. They are, in fact, testing for temperature, and will step back if the food is too hot.

Affectionate cats will often pat at their owners' faces to attract their attention. Hunting cats will touch prey with a paw to see if it is dead or alive. Mother cats often touch their kittens with their paws and faces. And cats use their faces, whiskers, and paws to touch each other.

MATING AND REPRODUCTION

THE AGE AT WHICH DOMESTIC CATS sexually mature can vary widely depending on the breed, but is usually earliest in Siamese and Burmese. In males it will generally be at between 7 and 14 months, in females 4 to 9 months old. In feral or free-ranging cats it may not be until 15 months or longer. Unneutered adult males are prepared to mate at any time and if free-ranging, spend much of their time seeking out the opportunity. Females have limited periods where they are ready to mate. Most females have their first such period of heat at 4–6 months but onset of estrus in the maiden queen (as a breeding female is called) is often determined by the season of the year. In the northern hemisphere, many start their distinctive "calling" in the first February following their birth. Indoor cats, warm all year round and with artificial light extending "daylight" hours, seem to breed at any season of the year, but feral cats tend to have one litter in spring and another in the early summer. Cats can breed throughout their lives.

The male cat

The male's paired testes, enclosed within a bag, the scrotum, are situated outside the abdominal cavity just below the anus. They produce the male hormone, testosterone, and sperm cells, the production of which requires a temperature slightly cooler than that of the cat's body.

The testes descend from the abdominal cavity into the tiny sacs of the scrotum either when the kitten is still within the uterus of its mother or shortly after birth. Very occasionally, however, one or both testes fail to descend in the normal way, resulting in a sterile, or partially sterile, cat. If fertile, they may pass on the condition to their offspring, so should be neutered.

The female cat

In the female cat paired ovaries lie on either side of the spine, just behind the kidneys. The ovaries produce the female hormone, estrogen, and ova (eggs). Ovulation is not cyclic, as in humans, but is a response to the stimulus of mating. When ova are expelled they pass down into the coiled fallopian tubes, where they may be fertilized by the sperm from the male cat, a process of fertilization that can take place up to three days after mating. The tiny, fertilized egg cells spend five or six days in the fallopian tubes; during this time they divide, forming blastocysts. This is a critical time in the development of the embryos, for it is during this stage that the ovaries of the mother cat begin to secrete another hormone, progesterone, required for their successful implantation in the uterine wall. Having become implanted in the lining of the uterus, the kittens gradually develop to their full birth size.

Recognizing e~~~~s

A queen in estrus is often said to be "in heat," "in season," or "calling," from the calls that she makes. The signs of estrus are easy to recognize. In the preparatory stage, pro-estrus, when the reproductive organs undergo changes in readiness for mating, fertilization, and pregnancy, the queen becomes extra-affectionate and restless. If confined, she will pace the floor and spend some time looking out of the window. She begins to produce a particular smell, more noticeable to cats than to humans, and will rub her scent-glands against things, and may roll from time to time. At this stage she may be interested in the male cat but is not ready for mating. Pro-estrus lasts from one to five days and is followed by estrus. This is the period when mating will take place readily, and has a duration of about seven days. The queen becomes increasingly agitated. She rolls vigorously on the floor and cries, often quite fiercely, with a distinct cry—"the call." If confined, she will try to escape; her cries will become deeper and more urgent, and she may reject food. If stroked along the back while in this condition, she immediately takes up the mating position and may be touchy if handled. A frustrated queen may neglect her cat box and spray furniture and walls instead.

Courtship and mating

The male is attracted to the female by her calling and by her smell, which carries a considerable distance. Under natural conditions several male cats may pay court to the calling female. The queen rolls and postures but may be unwilling to mate at first. The males square up to each other and a characteristic cater-wauling begins as they decide the order of supremacy. The actual battles may be bitter, bloody, and fought in comparative silence. The queen may be mated by a subordinate male while two dominant males fight, but it is more usual for the strongest male of the group to mount her first. The queen decides who to accept first and may be mated many times during estrus and by more than one male. When she is ready to accept a mate she crouches down, head extended, with the chin near the ground and hindquarters raised with the tail to one side.

The male cat may circle her and attempt to sniff her; if he is not rebuffed he quickly approaches and takes the loose skin at the scruff of her neck in his jaws. After a moment to check her reaction he places his forefeet astride her shoulders and treads alternately with his hind paws on her haunches, encouraging her to raise her tail. If she is receptive, she too will tread with her hind legs. Crouched over her body, the male tries to effect penetration, which may take some time as the queen wiggles and moves around. Eventually penetration occurs and the queen growls fiercely, moving forward. The male cat holds her scruff firmly in his teeth until he has ejaculated, then releases the queen and leaps away. The reason for this is apparent as the queen, usually growling fiercely, turns to attack him with teeth and claws. Then she rolls on her back on the ground before licking her genital area thoroughly. As soon as the queen begins her toilet, the tom attends to his own, and washes his penis. He constantly glances toward the queen, and as soon as she relaxes and shows signs of regaining the mating posture, he is ready to mount and mate her again.

The pregnant queen

The gestation period in cats averages 65 days. However, it is not always certain exactly when conception occurred and many queens carry litters a little longer. The first sign that a cat is pregnant is a pinkness and slight enlargement of the nipples about three weeks after mating. It is more easy to notice in a first conception, and is by no means an infallible test. A week later a veterinarian should be able to feel tiny embryos within the uterus, but this is not something for untrained hands to try.

Treat the mother normally during pregnancy. About halfway through, the increase in weight and differences in its distribution will make her take more care in jumping and in passing through narrow openings. She will spend more time on grooming and her appetite may increase; a mid-day meal in addition to her usual breakfast and supper is better than giving bigger meals. The enlargement of the uterine horns may press on the stomach, limiting the food that she can cope with at one time.

At six weeks' gestation, the cat is obviously pregnant. Do not allow her to gain too much surplus weight, and encourage her to exercise. The kittens are growing rapidly, and it may be necessary to add calcium to her diet of high-protein foods. Some cats like milk and get their calcium requirements from this. Others, especially the Oriental varieties, find milk products intolerable, but the veterinarian can advise in such instances.

right: Kittens are born about nine weeks after conception. Movement of the fetuses can be felt from the seventh week. This cat has about ten days to go before giving birth.

From six weeks the abdomen increases in size and the pregnant cat's coat blooms with health. She spends her time quietly grooming herself, resting, and prowling in the yard, if allowed to do so. If she appears to be slightly constipated, oily foods such as tuna in oil or sardines can be given. As the kittens move inside her, the queen rolls and stretches her body sinuously along the floor, then washes her enlarging nipples vigorously. In the seventh week the nesting instinct becomes apparent as she looks into cupboards and dark corners for a suitable place to give birth. It is now time to prepare a kittening box.

Use a sturdy cardboard box, with sides about 20 in. (50 cm) long. In one side cut a round hole about 8 in. (20 cm) in diameter and 6 in. (9 cm) from the floor. It lets the queen in and out without letting in drafts. Place it in a convenient corner, using newspaper to insulate the bottom. She may shred this until it forms a soft bed. Sheets of torn kitchen paper towels make a soft, absorbent, and disposable mattress for the birth. A sheet of cardboard makes a removable lid. If the room is chilly, an infrared heating unit can be suspended over the open top instead. When the kittens start to leave the nest at around four to five weeks, a new box can be provided and the old one discarded.

In the last ten days of the pregnancy, the queen should be gently groomed to remove all dead hair and to tone up her muscles, and fine-combed to ensure she is free of parasites. If carrying a large litter, she may be unable to clean her anal area; sponge this twice daily with warm water. If her nipples are dry or scaly, gently rub on a little vegetable oil. Clip overlong claws. With longhaired queens, clip hair surrounding the birth canal and near the nipples to facilitate suckling.

Giving birth

When the queen first feels the pangs of labor, she may go to her litter box and strain, looking behind herself in an agitated and puzzled manner. She may pace around growling or crying softly. She will usually refuse food for several hours before the birth; refusal of a favorite meal is a sign that the birth is fairly imminent. The first signs of labor may last for several hours in the maiden queen, but be barely perceptible in an older cat.

Most queens go into their nesting box as second-stage labor begins, but some may need encouragement to do so, as they may want to stay with their owners. In both cases the removable lid enables you to reassure her and check that all is well. Fierce contractions soon ripple down the queen's flanks as the first kitten moves into the birth canal. The queen may lie on her side and push her hind legs against the side of the box. When the head or tail of the first kitten is presented, she may sit up, pushing downward until it is expelled. The kitten may be presented either head first or tail first. Only when a tail-first kitten is presented with its legs turned forward instead of extended does the cat seem to have any problems in delivery. Prior to the expulsion of the first kitten, a sac of fluid may be passed. This prepares the birth canal for the passage of the first kitten.

After the delivery of the first kitten, the mother usually licks the membranes of the amniotic sac away from its head and body. Her rough tongue stimulates the kitten into taking its first breath. As the queen licks the kitten, she lifts it forward and the placenta passes from the vagina. Most queens then eat the placenta and then chew along the cord to a short way from the kitten's body.

The whole litter may be born in a matter of an hour or so, or they may be spread over a period of 24 hours, with long rests between kittens. When all are safely delivered, clean, and dry, the queen cleans herself before settling down to nurse the kittens. She will appreciate a bowl of beaten egg, hot milk, and glucose at this time. Then, gathering all the babies to her, she will curl around them and rest for about twelve hours.

Birth problems

Occasionally, things go wrong and intervention will be necessary. A kittening kit can be prepared before the birth, ready for any emergency. It consists of an old terrycloth towel, cut into small squares that have been washed and boiled to sterilize them, then stored in a plastic bag; a pair of sterilized blunt-tipped scissors; a bottle of astringent antiseptic lotion from the veterinarian; a roll of cotton; a rubber hot-water bottle, and the vet's emergency telephone number.

The birth of a maiden queen's first litter can be a long and frustrating business. There is no need to call the veterinarian unless the cat has strained without results for two hours or shows signs of exhaustion or anxiety. Sometimes a kitten is half presented and, despite strenuous pushing by the queen, appears to be stuck. Place a small square of towel over the protruding part to help you grip it firmly and gently. As the queen strains again, ease the kitten slowly and steadily downward and between the queen's legs, until it is free. Do not pull the kitten, just ease it forward; if it is a breech presentation, the body may need to be very slightly rotated in order to free the head.

Sometimes the queen is so busy producing the next in line that she does not have time to attend to the last-born kitten, and prompt human assistance is necessary. The kitten's head must be freed from the sac without delay, and the mucus cleared from the face and nostrils. After the membranes have been wiped away, place the kitten on the palm of your hand, head downward, and rub it firmly but gently from tail to head with a square of towel. This clears any fluid from the lungs and nostrils and encourages the kitten to breathe. The placenta may still be inside the queen, attached to the kitten by the cord. If this is so, pull the cord gently as the queen strains until the placenta is delivered.

Place the cleaned kitten near its mother's head where she may eat the placenta, and sever the cord. If she does not, cut it about 1 in. (2.5 cm) from the kitten's body with the sterilized scissors. Their blunt blades crush the cord as it is cut, preventing bleeding. The astringent antiseptic should then be applied to the cut end of the cord with some cotton.

Experienced breeders prefer to sever the cord by pulling it gently apart with well-scrubbed fingers and thumbs, having been instructed in the art by the veterinarian. This method breaks the cord at its natural place of severance, and no bleeding takes place, but it should not be tried by the novice.

If the mother ignores a kitten, it should be rubbed with a towel square until dry, then placed on a hot water bottle until the queen is ready to nurse it. Bouts of labor pains might make her temporarily unwilling to care for one or all of the kittens, and they must be cleaned and kept warm until she completes her kittening and accepts them.

Most feline births go according to plan, and cats make excellent natural mothers. There are times, however, when things do go wrong When a queen has labored hard, with strong contractions, for two hours without any signs of the kitten's head or tail appearing, a vet should be called. If wrongly presented, kittens need gentle manipulation by the vet before they can be born.

Genetic inheritance

When the kittens are born, unless the mating has been carefully planned, there may be some surprises. The kittens may look just like their mother, but they could also look very different from their parents. The appearance and characteristics of each kitten are determined by the

left: The mother must bite or lick away the amniotic sac that surrounds the newborn kitten and lick it dry. In doing so she stimulates independent breathing.

below: The number of kittens in one litter can be as many as 15, although four is the average.

parents' genes. Each cell in the body has 19 pairs of chromosomes, rod-like structures that carry the genes, each parent contributing one of each pair. Where genes from both parents carry identical information these are described as homozygous for that feature; when not, they are heterozygous. When they are homozygous the kitten will have that feature, but where they do not match its development depends upon which feature is dominant, as some genes override the influence of a recessive partner. The recessive gene remains in the new genetic code and can be passed on to offspring; hence, a kitten inheriting identical recessive genes may show a feature that is not visible in either parent.

If the ancestors of each parent and their other relatives are documented it enables breeders to assess their potential genetic makeup and plan for mating for a particular result. This is why a pedigree is important to breeders, together with a knowledge of which factors are dominant and which are recessive. White, for instance, is dominant to all other colors. Black is dominant to blue. Tabby (agouti) is dominant to non-tabby. Short hair is dominant to longhair. Full coat is dominant to rex coat. Manx is dominant to normal tail.

KITTENHOOD

AT BIRTH THE KITTEN IS CLEANED by its mother's rough tongue as she removes the amniotic fluid and traces of the sac from its fur. The licking also helps to stimulate circulation and respiration in the tiny creature. As soon as it is breathing properly, guided only by a strongly developed sense of smell, the kitten crawls toward its mother's nipple. This is the stage at which it is easiest to sex kittens. The soft fur in the genital area is still damp and the organs clearly defined. Once they have dried off it becomes more difficult, but they can be checked again at about four weeks, when the differences between the sexes become more obvious (see page 124).

Newborn kittens, although blind and deaf, stake claim on a particular nipple, and fight off the other kittens with strong scrabbling movements of their forepaws. For the first few days of life, they merely sleep and suckle, often treading on either side of the nipple with their forepaws to stimulate the milk flow. The smells of the birth process give them a sense of security for the first few days of life. Excessively soiled paper in the nest box can be replaced, but the birth secretions are sterile and most should be left until the kittens' eyes are open, when they will be less stressed by the change in their environment. In their first days kittens seem to prefer certain places in the nest box. Their legs are too weak to support them so they push themselves forward on their bellies, leaving scent trails that they can recognize. If the kittens are cold, they cluster together, forming a little heap; if they are warm, they spread out.

The birth weight of kittens is very variable: long-haired and short-haired breeds weigh in at about 4 oz. (114 g), Siamese often as little as 2 oz. (57 g).

Much depends on the size of the parents and how many kittens are in the litter, although there can be some variability within a litter. Kittens gain weight steadily from birth onward if they are receiving adequate nourishment. Weigh each kitten once a week and chart their progress. If individuals fall below the general rate of growth, check for signs of illness or deformity. If all the kittens show poor rates, check their mother's diet and milk glands.

Caring for the mother

The queen should always have some fresh drinking water available. She may be fussy about her food but, if she has eaten the placentas, that will sustain her for some time. She may be very reluctant to leave the kittens at first, but encourage her to stretch her legs and to pass water. Sometimes, placing the queen in a fresh litter box has the desired result. Ensure that her milk is flowing properly; gently examine her nipples the day after the kittens are born. If any are blocked, bathe them with warm water, then massage them gently with olive oil until the milk flows freely.

The lactating queen should be given four good meals daily, and plenty to drink. Meals should be small, well-balanced, and fed to her fresh. Do not give her cold food straight from the refrigerator, or she may get diarrhea. Serve the food at room temperature. Meat, which takes several hours to digest, should be fed at midday and last thing at night. Other meals can consist of fish, cheese, eggs, or milk products.

Awakening senses

Kittens generally open their eyes when they are two to ten days old, and are sensitive to strong light at this time. Siamese often begin to open their eyes on the second day, but some kittens can take as long as twelve. There is no need to worry unless there is any discharge or swelling of the lids. Any stickiness can be bathed away with a saline solution. Hearing gradually develops, too, and with the increased sensitivity the kittens begin to explore their limited environment and to show signs of playful behavior. At first the young kittens pat at each other in a clumsy manner, but as their eyes focus better and their sight gets stronger, they can be seen to watch their mother entering and leaving the box. Even at birth, the blind and helpless kittens may hiss if picked up, and can continue to do this for two or three weeks. Once they recognize the smell, voice, and possibly the sight of their handlers, this behavior stops.

At the age of three weeks kittens can stand quite well and toddle around on their short, unsteady legs. They keep their heads close to the floor at this stage and can be seen to rely greatly on the sense of smell, often retracing their steps to the safety of their special corner of the nest box. At this stage they can roll over and right themselves, and play with their siblings with paw pats and bites.

By the end of their fourth week the kittens may decide to explore outside the

left: Mother and kitten.

below: Some teats give a better milk flow than others. Kittens may compete for the best place to suckle, but usually establish claim to a particular nipple from birth.

left: *left: If mother decides to move her kittens she carries them by the scruff of the neck. The kitten curls its feet up to help it clear the ground.*

nest box. Their legs are now much stronger and their sight and hearing are used as much as smell in testing out the environment. During their first excursions, kittens rush back to the safety of the box when frightened by loud noise or sudden movement. It is now that they test new surfaces by licking and chewing, so it is vitally important that in the area where they play and explore no toxic disinfectants, detergents, or polishes are used—many of those sold for domestic use are harmful to cats. Kittens will now begin to show an interest in their mother's food. As they eat more and more solids, their excreta change, and the mother cat stops cleaning up after them.

right: Play with mother, siblings, and on its own enables a kitten to try out and perfect the skills it needs in adult life.

below and bottom: Mother cats must feed, protect, and train their kittens. They are very tolerant of kitten antics but will begin to leave them alone at times or to refuse to let them suckle as part of the weaning process.

It is time to provide them with their own litter box. If they do not learn to use it from their mother, place them in it after every meal. They will eat a little more solid food each day but continue to take milk from the queen for several more weeks if they are allowed to do so.

Stimulation and handling

The brain of the young kitten is functional at birth, but its intelligence depends to a large extent on the number of synaptic junctions that form during the first few weeks of life. Proper stimuli and slight amounts of stress during the first critical weeks help to develop the brain and so produce a smarter cat. Kittens should be handled frequently between the ages of four and eight weeks. This period is roughly equivalent to the nest-changing age in the wild, and is the time for young kittens to recognize the difference between safety and danger. It is also important to start gentle grooming at this age, especially in the long-haired breeds, with particular emphasis given to inspection of ears and mouths. Training carried out at this stage is invaluable and lasts for life.

At five weeks of age a kitten's brain is almost mature, with the synaptic junctions formed and fully operational. Motor development, however, including the coordination of the limbs and muscles, takes longer, so the small animals should be protected from any possible injury at this stage.

Weaning kittens

Kittens will now be adventurous and need space to play with each other and their toys. Golf balls, feathers, and balls of paper make excellent toys. They enjoy diving into and out of large paper bags and cardboard boxes. A wide variety of food at this stage prevents a kitten from developing into a finicky cat.

right: Kittens use shrill alarm calls to demand food or rescue before their hearing is operative, and mother cats use a range of croons and calls to reassure the kittens. In adulthood it is largely cat-human communication that a cat vocalizes.

At six weeks kittens, though still suckling, take a lot of solid food. If they seem reluctant to eat, rub some food on their lips until, in licking it off, they get to enjoy the taste. Some breeders wean kittens by giving them milk mixed with baby cereal, but many kittens naturally prefer their mother's milk to this. Others provide meat to simulate prey: raw meat cut in long narrow strips for the kittens to growl over and chew. At first kittens must be watched while they eat solids. Their lack of technique may result in lumps of food becoming wedged across the palate. If this happens, a match stick or plastic spoon handle can be used to pry the food gently away from the roof of the mouth.

Kittens should always be fed fresh food at every meal. Any that is not cleared up in ten minutes should be taken away. In this way the kittens will become used to feeding at regularly spaced intervals. Their stomachs are still only about the size of a walnut, so giving small meals at frequent intervals helps to avoid any gastric upsets. Some kittens seem reluctant to drink, and can become slightly constipated. If this happens, stir a little water into meat meals. A touch of table salt added to the food will also increase thirst and encourage them to drink more. Serve warm water or milk; do not take it straight from the refrigerator. Many adult cats are now fed dried complete foods so it is important that kittens learn to drink plenty of liquids. They will now be regularly using their litter box, so remember to change it frequently.

Acclimatization

Kittens must be taught acceptance of strangers, children, and dogs, and should be accustomed to household noises such as washing machines, vacuum cleaners, and doorbells. The ones that are destined for a show career should be picked up and stroked by visitors to the house so that they enjoy being handled by everyone they meet. This socializing period should not be underestimated. Kittens that do not receive the proper stimuli and treatment during this early period may be difficult to handle later in life, every time they are removed from their own environment, or when they are with strangers. Most veterinarians and boarding cattery proprietors have to bear the brunt of "difficult" cats, who may be perfectly tractable in their own homes but elsewhere are nervous, irritable, and bite and scratch if handled. Their owners will often confirm that such cats were once stray or farm kittens that were taken in and tamed after the critical period. Kittens should be handled, petted, and groomed as often as possible during the weaning period. They must learn to come when called by being given a reward, either food or a petting. They should get used to have their mouths opened and inspected and their ears cleaned without fuss, and should learn that being brushed is a most pleasurable experience. Gentle handling produces happy, gentle cats.

Learning from play

Play is very important in the development of the kittens, and the role of the mother cat should never be underestimated. Even when the litter is very young she will be seen to entice them to play with the end of her tail. The queen also teaches the youngsters when to run for cover by growling when danger threatens. Through play kittens practice social, hunting, and fighting skills to equip them for adult life. From the age of eight weeks their play patterns become more sophisticated, and hunting and killing actions are apparent in their games. They practice using their forepaws to grasp while they administer neck bites to their litter mates. Hind legs are used for raking at the body of another kitten while the forepaws grasp it firmly around the neck. Kittens jump on their mother's tail, simultaneously biting at the part just in front of their grasping paws. Small toys are dribbled across the floor before being passed through to the hind legs, which perform kicking and treading movements. Kittens learn to carry small toys in their jaws, and may growl when another kitten approaches. When offered strips of raw meat, each takes a piece and growls ferociously if a litter mate approaches. If touched at this time, the kitten will strike out, accurately and fast, toward the teasing hand.

Independence

The mother cat forces her kittens to be independent by refusing to allow them to suckle at around the eighth week. With a large litter she may show reluctance to allow them to nurse from about the sixth week, while the queen with one or two kittens may be prepared to feed them until they are really well grown. As the kittens get older, their needle-sharp teeth start to hurt the queen as they suckle, and if she is allowed to roam freely, she may bring in some prey for the litter. Confined cats often carry pieces of food to their kittens, uttering a distinctive cry. After the kittens have examined the meat, the queen eats it in front of them.

If kittens persist in suckling and need to be forcibly weaned, the kindest way to do this is to remove the kittens from the mother's nipple for long periods at the seventh week, then take half the litter, usually the largest of the kittens, completely away during the eighth or ninth week. The following week the remaining kittens are also removed. If the mother still has milk, her water bowl should be taken away for a few hours, and her food cut down, so that any milk that she produces can be reabsorbed by her body.

If the kittens are fed six small and well-spaced meals a day, they will quickly forget their mother's milk. They are quite capable of eating enough food at this time to satisfy their body's needs. They may need a calcium supplement, especially if they are of Oriental or Siamese blood lines, and a course of gentle worming tablets may be started. Plans should now be made with the veterinarian for their first vaccinations against feline diseases, and they should always be immunized before they go to new homes.

About twelve weeks after birth, a kitten should be independent enough to go to a new home. Although still developing physically and mentally, it should have learned that it is a cat, and how to behave itself as a pet animal. If it is to be kept without other pets, a kitten should be given lots of toys, fuss and attention during its first few months so that it grows into a well-balanced and happy cat.

below: In sibling play-fights an instinctive restraint mechanism prevents them from doing serious damage to each other.

right: A kitten must not only practice physical actions and coordination but must learn to understand and interpret the world around it.

CAT BEHAVIOR

LTHOUGH CATS HAVE NOW been domesticated for well over three millennia, they have a much longer history as a wild animal and still retain the instincts of the wild cat. Many, both feral and pets, have lives essentially unchanged except for the support they get from their owners. Even with house cats the main effect of domestication is the retention of juvenile, kitten-like characteristics into adult life; the root of their behavior lies in their original life as wild animals. Neutering, if carried out before behavior patterns are firmly established, will further modify some behavior, but do not blame the cat because it is a natural hunter and wants to defend its territory, and to get out to mate. Knowing something of cat behavior and the way cats communicate will not only help you to make its life happier but will enable you to get more from having a cat as a companion.

Cat conversation

Many people talk to their cats and their cats talk back—and sometimes they seem to understand each other. Cats have a considerable vocabulary; one researcher claimed to have identified at least one hundred different sounds, and some people have tried to translate them precisely. Certainly some sounds seem to be fairly universal and easy to interpret, and owners will learn to recognize some of what their cat is communicating. Cats appear to retain their kitten signals to communicate with their owners, who still hold a mother-like relationship with them, while using an adult repertoire of speech with other cats.

All cats purr, although some so softly that vibrations can only be felt when stroking their throats. Cats usually purr with contentment or affection, but some-times a deep purr means pain. Purring can begin when a kitten is about one week old, and it is usually heard as it contentedly suckles. Young cats purr in a monotone, while older ones purr with two or three resonant notes. Many other calls and cries express different needs and emotions.

A queen and her consort have a whole language of love calls, and mother cats communicate with their kittens in a range of different cries, mews, and chirrups. Growls are also variable, and range from the scream of fear to the guttural choke of anger. Cats can also hiss and spit. Whatever method the cat chooses to communicate, it leaves one in no doubt as to its feelings and intentions at that particular moment.

Body language

Cats also communicate with a wide range of facial expressions and body postures. The alert cat has a very direct gaze, with forward-pointing ears and whiskers. If it is also slightly nervous, the nostrils may twitch slightly as the cat tries to identify and recognize using smell as well as sight and sound. When the scent has been identified and recognized as friendly, the cat raises its tail and approaches, slightly stiff-legged, in greeting. If the visitor is another cat, then some mutual rubbing or grooming may follow preliminary nose-touching. Adult cats may greet each

above: A cat approaching looking ahead with its tail held high, the tip often curled forward, is an alert and confident cat offering a friendly greeting.

left: In a play fight one kitten begins to adopt a submissive posture, but its ears remain alert.

other, then indulge in some play, either a mock battle or a game of tag.

A normal and nonaggressive cat in its own territory may receive a threat, perhaps from another cat or a strange dog. At first the cat will freeze and look at the intruder, then its tail will start to flick slowly from side to side. Its whiskers and ears point forward and its nose will start to quiver as it attempts to identify the threat object. As the intruder approaches more closely, the cat changes its stance. The point of the lifted tail turns downward, the chin is drawn in, and the ears flatten as the cat begins to turn slowly to one side. Gradually, the hairs on the cat's back and tail will rise up until the animal has assumed its aggressive posture.

This typical display continues if the intruder comes forward, and is very menacing. The cat faces the enemy but turns its body sideways to present as large and formidable an area as possible. The hind legs become tensed and ready to spring

above: The arched back and bristling fur demonstrated by this kitten look aggressive; the tail is confidently upright and the rear stands firm while the front of the body retreats and the fur is erect to make the cat look bigger.

below: Crouched low, this cat is not ready to submit; with chin tucked in, ears turned to show their backs and whiskers forward ready to face the threat.

left: A cat rubbing up against an owner is both greeting him or her and leaving its scent mark. By exchanging scents with each other in this way, cats find it easier to identify friends.

below: Territory will also be marked by rubbing with the scent glands on trees and roots, as well as by spraying urine.

forward in attack or away in flight. The weight of the front of the body is poised on one foreleg while the other, claws unsheathed, is prepared to strike out. The cat's chin is drawn tightly in to protect its throat, the ears are laid flat to its head, and the lips are drawn back, showing the teeth as the cat snarls fiercely.

If the unwelcome visitor backs away from the threatening cat, the latter may move forward a little, smacking its lips and salivating, while continuing to growl. When the threat has disappeared entirely, the cat will sniff at the invaded ground and may spray, defecate, or strop its claws before regaining its normal appearance and composure.

The signs of extreme agitation when a cat is threatened are easy to recognize. The eyes will be wide open, glancing rapidly from side to side, while the body is crouched, chin held down and the ears held out at the side of the head. A cat showing these signs should be coaxed gently. If you touch it before eyes and ears regain their normal appearance it may bite and scratch you in defense.

Cats can also communicate affection to a human by posture. The tail, in particular, is most expressive. Carried erect, it indicates a feeling of contentment, and if it is carried straight up, it can also be a gesture of welcome. Even when the tip of the erect tail waves slightly to and fro, the cat is contented; but when it lashes from side to side, it expresses extreme annoyance and may presage an attack. A cat that stands perfectly still with the tail held out in a straight line is almost certain to attack. With all the tail hairs erect, it looks like a bottle brush, and when this is also accompanied by the erection of all the body hairs, the cat appears to grow to twice its normal size.

Contented cats will often purr and start to knead their owners with their forepaws, replicating the action of tiny kittens, kneading while suckling.

Scent messages

Scent is personal to the individual cat and scent signals in the air or left on objects tell other cats about sex and readiness to mate, who has been in a place before, and how long ago. Scents are left on each other's bodies when friends meet, helping to avoid confrontation. People leave their own scent on cats when they stroke them and when someone comes into the house the cat can gain information about where they have been from the scents on them.

As mentioned before, cats deposit scent by rubbing their scent glands against things. Both head and tail glands are used for marking. Marking with the forehead and lips seems to give a cat pleasure, for it may knead with its forepaws and purr while carrying out the rubbing. If another friendly cat has marked the same spot, it may drool and salivate while carrying out its own lip-marking, rubbing its jaw and chin firmly on the object, sometimes even rearing up on its hind legs in order to rub even harder. Having used the temporal glands for the initial marking, a cat may then turn around to complete the mark with its tail gland. This type of marking is most easily observed when a cat winds itself around its owner's legs, leaning inward, and allowing its forehead and the side of its jaw to rub the area first. The body moves forward to rub over the same area, followed by the tail, which winds around the leg to wipe it with its entire length.

One of the most important uses of marking is to indicate a claim on territory. Male cats generally spray droplets of strong-smelling urine onto every convenient object along the perimeters of their ranges. The tom examines a post or bush, turns his back on it, raises his tail, then, with two or three pedaling movements of his hind legs, urinates high and accurately. Sometimes he will turn again to examine his signature, or back up and rub his tail and hindquarters against the damp patch. Occasionally, the tom turns and smells the mark, then strops his claws vigorously.

Female cats sometimes develop the habit of spraying, either when their hormonal balance has been upset by doses of contraceptive pills or when they have become frustrated by frequent periods of heat. Such queens adopt the typical male position and direct their urine backward in a fine jet.

An emotional disturbance may trigger the spraying habit in the neutered cat, generally when its position in the household seems threatened by the arrival of a new baby, a new kitten or puppy, or in some cases by the arrival of a new piece of furniture or carpet. It is particularly annoying if a cat persists in spraying indoors. Neither females nor neutered cats produce spray that smells anything like the pungent urine of the male cat—which is also sticky and difficult to clean from household furnishings.

When a cat feels particularly upset, it may defecate as well as spray, and may choose to do this where it will have the most devastating effect; in the middle of the carpet or on the best cushions. The spot chosen is always very conspicuous,

and totally unlike the procedure normally carried out when emptying the bladder and bowels, when the meticulous cat tries to and hide its excretions.

In investigating the scents left by other cats a cat may show the characteristic flehmen reaction (see page 100), drawing back its lips and raising its head so that every vestige of the smell can reach the Jacobsen's organ in the roof of the mouth, so that it can savor, test, and identify the odor.

Territories

Wild cats occupy a territory of a size matched to their hunting needs. Where prey is abundant the territory can be smaller. Females will usually defend a central area against outsiders, and males will usually have a larger territory which may overlap that of several females. Domestic cats, whether living feral and scavenging as well as hunting or fed by owners, do not need large areas to hunt but still have a strong sense of territory. House pets usually treat the home as territory shared with their human household, although with some core areas that

are specific to themselves or others. They will accept that they are not allowed in certain places, at least if that territory owner is around, and may claim a particular chair or cushion as their own unless forced off it by a more dominant member of the household.

Outdoors, cats lay claim to an area that they defend against those from other households. This does not necessarily match human house and yard divisions and may include places not on the boundary with their home. A new arrival who finds its own back yard already claimed, and who is unable to drive off the occupant, may occupy somewhere several doors away. In highly built up areas where there are no gardens a cat may be reduced to an outdoor territory of little more than a rooftop or window ledge. Some areas and much-used routes connecting areas, often walls, may be shared among several cats.

Hunting

Kittens usually begin to show the first signs of predatory behavior at about six weeks, when the mother offers them prey

right: Having got as close as possible without alerting its prey, a cat may wait patiently in ambush.

below: When domestic cats "play" with prey they have caught it may be because they are too well-fed to want to eat, but their strong instinct to hunt makes them prone to this activity.

below right: A cat seeking out prey must have all its senses alert.

left: Some cats become excellent at fishing. They dip a paw beneath the water and flip fish onto the bank.

or pieces of meat. She calls to the kittens and pats the offering around before eating it in front of them. This is when they start to practice hunting techniques, using their siblings and toys as mock prey, crouching, pouncing, and making mock attacks and head- and neck-biting movements.

Even the most docile of pet cats will occasionally go hunting, given the opportunity, unless it is very overweight. Well-fed but fit cats hunt whenever they can, rarely eating their prey but obviously regarding it as enjoyable sport. Farm cats kept for killing rats and mice prove more efficient in their job if fed properly, and are less likely to be injured by vermin bites. Most cats hunt alone, but cases of cooperative hunting by cats from the same family have been known.

Cats usually hunt at twilight or dawn, when their ability to make the best use of poor light conditions stands them in good stead. Acute hearing also helps in pinpointing prey, before making the final, death-dealing pounce. Cats generally prefer to hunt in their own carefully defined territory, and country cats usually have set beats through favorite copses, woods, and hedgerows. Their safe passage through dense undergrowth and pathways is ensured by the use of sensitive whiskers, eyebrows, and ear-tufts. Their soft pads with retracted claws enable silent, swift movement, and the powerful muscles of the hindquarters produce the final attacking spring. Victims are grasped between the forepaws, with claws fully extended to give extra grip, and the killing bite is delivered to the neck region.

Hunting birds in the open requires great skill, and birds are less often a victim than is generally thought. First a cat will flatten its body to the ground and glide forward in long, fluid movements. The hips and shoulderblades are kept level and low, and the head extended forward with flattened ears. When it is within springing distance, it will pause, swinging its hips and tail rapidly from side to side, gathering impetus for the forward leap. Suddenly it catapults forward, often pinning the prey to the

strings, feathers, and catnip-stuffed mice all help to exercise a cat and stimulate it into a close simulation of a serious hunt, thus maintaining the link with its natural past.

Sleep

Cats have two distinct sorts of sleep. A very light sleeping state occurs during the many catnaps of the day, during which the blood pressure remains normal and the temperature drops slightly, while the muscles are slightly tensed. In deep or paradoxical sleep, however, the temperature rises, the blood pressure falls, and the muscles relax. Electroencephalograph recordings taken during light sleep show a typically slow wave pattern, while recordings made during paradoxical sleep show short, sharp patterns. During paradoxical sleep cats can be seen to dream, sometimes purring, twitching, fluttering their paws, or making running and jumping movements of the limbs. Sucking movements of the lips may occur, or the tail may switch and the ears twitch. Why cats dream or what they dream about there is no way of knowing, but it is possible that, during dreaming, the events recently learned during the waking hours are being sorted and important information is being stored away in the memory banks.

One third of the cat's sleeping time is spent in this deep paradoxical sleep, and cats deprived of enough of it can become quite ill. In experiments cats were kept without deep sleep for several weeks, and were found to have accelerated heart rates. After the experiment the cats spent

ground with its claws. Unless taught by their mother, cats do not automatically learn a good killing bite and sometimes they seem to defer death for awhile to practice hunting techniques. The hapless victim may try to escape, but will often be tossed, patted, caught, bitten, and played with for some time before it dies. The cat may become highly aroused during such play and continue to toss the small body around long after it is dead. Some cats like to hide their victim's body under a rug or piece of furniture, then walk away as if they have forgotten about it. Then they turn, run, and pounce, hooking it out of hiding with a sweeping forepaw in mock-serious play. When a cat decides to eat its prey it often

devours the entrails, and then it may or may not finish off the rest of the body. Larger animals, such as rabbits, are usually eaten over a period of time, the cat returning to the carcass until it is finished. After that, it may not eat again for two or three days. Smaller prey, such as mice and small birds, are often eaten entirely within a few minutes, starting with the head. The less digestible portions such as the fur or feathers may be regurgitated later.

Hunting and killing are built-in features of the domestic cat. Confined cats need compensation for the lack of facilities for these natural pursuits. Caring owners provide toys and games for their pets as substitute prey. Paper balls on

a great deal of time sleeping, as if trying to catch up on the lost sleep, but it took several weeks before the heart rates returned to normal.

Newborn kittens spend the first week of their lives in paradoxical sleep, broken only by short periods of wakefulness in which they suckle their mother. From the age of one to four weeks they spend longer periods awake, but slip straight back into paradoxical sleep without any transitory light sleep phase. From the age of four weeks onward kittens start experiencing light sleep phases, too, which coincide with the completion of the development of the synaptic junctions in their brains.

Cats can sleep at any time, day or night, and seemingly in any position. While asleep their hearing becomes even more acute than when awake, providing warning of any danger. Although they prefer warm cosy beds, cats can relax on any surface no matter how uncomfortable it seems to humans. When waking up, a cat usually goes through a routine of stretching and flexing, particularly of the spine and limbs, but if it has been a long sleep, it may be reluctant to exercise much for awhile and decide instead to have a drink and a wash before going about its business.

Washing and grooming

The action of light and warmth on the coat usually stimulates the washing reflex in cats. To wash, a cat employs both tongue and paws, and in this way is able to clean most of its head and body. The tongue of a cat is covered with tiny projections called papillae that scrape meat off bone and carry food backward in the mouth. They are also used to wash and comb the coat. The cat sits up and licks its mouth and lips; then, licking a paw until it is damp, passes this over its head, into and around the ears, over the eyes, and down the side of the nose. The paw is licked again and again, and the washing motion is continued until the cat feels clean; then the other paw washes the other side of the head and face. Each shoulder and foreleg is licked in turn,

then the sides and flanks, the hind legs and genital area, and the tail.

Tangles and burrs in the coat or between the toes are bitten out, and mud on the pads is removed with great care. Cats often mutually groom each other as a sign of great affection, usually after a meal and before settling down together to sleep. Young kittens begin to wash themselves in a rather ineffectual way at about three weeks of age. When they are eating solids, however, at about six weeks of age, they are able to wash their paws and faces quite well, and clean up their tail ends every time they use the litter box.

Cats that refuse to wash may have trouble in the mouth, and the first thing to check is for the presence of tartar. Queens that stop washing their genital areas could have a distasteful discharge, and, again, this needs checking out. Full males that appear to have a greasy patch on the tail probably have "stud tail." This must be treated with soap and water to remove the grease and the tail then needs to be kept scrupulously clean.

As well as using their tongue to keep their coats clean, cats will lick themselves dry when they get wet and, if feeling too hot, will apply saliva over their fur; this helps reduce their temperature as it evaporates.

Behavioral problems

In view of the constraints and relatively abnormal conditions under which domestic cats live, it is surprising how few revolt against domestication or exhibit strange behavior patterns, but shock and trauma can produce disorders. Rough, unkind handling can result in a totally unbalanced and unpredictable cat, and any form of severe shock may result in reactions that induce collapse of the cranial nerve and death. This can also happen to over-humanized cats on which care and love have been lavished; the attack is a direct result of the overstimulation of the nervous system.

Pet cats rarely become aggressive unless they are being teased or ill-treated. Sometimes a cat reacts violently to being touched because it is reacting to another

left: Cats are resourceful at getting things they want. Scooping dry food out of a box uses the same skills used by some cats in the wild to remove small prey from holes.

left: A cat can use a curtain as a hiding place and as something to attack, but if you want to preserve your furnishings, direct a cat's play to safer substitutes.

threat; it may be watching a menacing dog or a noisy vacuum cleaner when its owner tries to pick it up and it thinks that it is being attacked by the cause of its fear. This behavior is an understandable response by the cat's complex defense mechanism.

Drugs and food additives can cause unusual behavior in cats. For instance, benzoic acid, a food preservative quite safely used in the preparation of dog food, causes a nervous condition in cats. They become wild, hysterical, very sensitive to light, and finally develop severe muscular spasms.

Introducing a new kitten, puppy, or human baby to the household can cause fear in some cats and antisocial behavior in others. As well as deliberately urinating or defecating, some have been known to refuse all food for several days until they become quite ill. Others methodically break every small ornament that can be tipped off mantels and shelves. Some cats start to shred every soft furnishing in the house. Occasionally the disturbed cat will indulge in self-mutilation, licking at paws, flanks, or tail until the area chosen is raw and bleeding. Others sit and pluck out the fur on their chest or flanks. One Siamese, jealous and unhappy, was placed in a boarding kennel while his fate was decided, and, in five days, chewed half his tail away.

Cats that are extremely bored, or badly reared, may indulge in excessive self-grooming. This may happen during long confinement in a cattery where there is a total lack of stimuli. Cats in this situation will lick and groom their bodies until some areas are raw. They may suck at their paws, tail, or rear nipple, purring and kneading, regressing mentally into kittenhood.

Wool-eating or sucking seems to be related to self-sucking and sometimes occurs in otherwise well-balanced cats, especially some strains of Siamese. It is probably easiest to accept this habit and let the cat have its own piece of cloth to suck at. But if the attraction is for man-made fibers and the cat swallows large amounts of the material it could become impacted in the stomach and intestines and need surgical removal.

Sexual disorders sometimes manifest themselves in pet cats when they are not neutered and become frustrated. Neutering usually brings about a marked improvement in behavior and general health.

Cats can also take great pleasure in idiosyncratic behavior. Some like to play with water, particularly with dripping taps, or even to swim. Some are clever enough to use the toilet. There are cats that like snow and ice, others that will not go outside in the rain. Some like to roll on cold concrete or paw at window panes. They can also demonstrate that food they don't like needs covering up like mess in their litter box—and they can sulk, backs to their owners, when they have been teased.

Part Four:
Care of the Cat

CHOOSING A CAT

THE FIRST QUESTIONS TO ASK in choosing a cat are ones to ask yourself. Why do you want a cat? Are you really prepared for the demands in time, effort, and money that caring for it will make on you? A cat can live for upward of 14, even 20, years and you will be responsible for it all that time. You must provide food and regular grooming, change litter boxes, meet veterinary bills, be available for play and company, and find others to do all these things if you have to be away from home. If you take a lot of vacations or your work involves frequent trips away from home, what happens to your cat? If you are prepared to take on all this, the pleasure a cat will give you will make it all worthwhile. Think then whether you might take on not just one cat but two, if there are not already other pets for company. Cats will be much happier with a companion, especially if you are going to have to leave them alone for many hours. Two cats brought up together usually become inseparable friends. Never think of giving a cat or kitten as a present unless you are absolutely certain, not only that this is what the recipients want, but that they are prepared and can afford to provide all that the cat requires throughout its life. Such considerations may seem obvious, but animal welfare organizations still have to cope with thousands of abandoned animals that their owners felt unable to care for.

Where to find a pet

Unless you know a friend or neighbor with a cat who needs a home, the first place to look for a cat is your nearest animal shelter. A number of animal charities take in stray or unwanted animals and others confiscated from cruel owners, and are always in need of new homes for them. There will be kittens and mature cats and, especially if you prefer a more placid pet, you might consider giving a final home to one of those elderly cats who are sometimes more difficult to place. While shelter cats are mainly animals of unknown pedigree, you may find cats of many different breeds and mixture to choose from. With a shelter cat, as well as finding yourself a pet, you have the added pleasure of knowing that you have probably saved a life, for many unwanted animals still have to be put down. The shelter may want to check you out to ensure that you can provide a proper home, and will usually charge a small fee as a contribution toward their costs.

If you have set your heart on a pedigree cat of a particular breed you should seek out a breeder to obtain one. Breeders will usually only have kittens for sale, but they keep in touch with enthusiasts for the breed and may know of someone with a mature cat that needs a new home. The best place to see lots of pedigree cats and kittens is at a large Championship Cat Show. Most major cities have at least one such show each

left: All kittens are adorable but you have to choose, or let the kitten choose you. If you select a kitten this young, you must wait until it is fully weaned before you can take it home. If you have no other pets to keep it company, and especially if you are out all day, consider taking two.

below: When visiting a breeder to see kittens, check out the whole cattery. What sort of conditions are the cats kept in? Do all the other cats look fit and well?

Please Do Not Touch The Cats

Always try to see a cat in its home environment before deciding on a purchase. This will not only give you the best opportunity of assessing its character but enable you to judge the hygiene of the establishment and the quality of its rearing. With kittens you will be able to see them interacting with siblings and their mother, and perhaps other close relations. This will give a further indication of their potential character, and perhaps also allow you to chose a favorite kitten from a litter. Some cats are quiet and staid in their habits, while others are extroverted clowns. It is even possible to recognize kittens of both types in the same litter. A noisy, busy household with young children and other pets is not the place for a timid and sensitive kitten, and an outgoing, mischievous kitten might prove a little too lively for a quiet and peaceful home.

Pedigree or pet?

An elegant cat at a cat show or a cuddly kitten in an animal shelter will probably produce the same response in the cat lover. The one that you finally choose is up to you.

Pedigree cats are not more loving, more clever, or more naughty than other cats, and their beauty is a matter of individual taste. Some breeds tend toward having a particular character; Siamese and Orientals, for example, tend to be more demanding and involved with their owners, while Persians are on the whole more placid, but an animal's character is also determined by family and rearing. Some breeding lines seem to show particular kinds of personality, which you can assess by seeing them in their homes. Often the attraction will simply be a cat's appearance—but it is important to

year, and they are widely advertised. They give the opportunity for people to see many different breeds and to make contact with breeders. Exhibitors are usually delighted to explain the virtues of their specialized breeds, but remember that they may be slightly biased toward their own breed. Veterinary practices may be able to put you in touch with local breeders if you have difficulty in finding them.

Many cats are still sold through pet stores. The best will not usually have animals on the premises but arrange for you to purchase from reputable breeders. A cage in a store is not a good environment

for a cat. It is easy to lose your heart to a plaintive kitten in a shop window or to want to rescue an unhappy-looking cat, but buying it means that it will be replaced by another unhappy animal and you may be getting a frail and sickly cat or one with potential behavioral problems. A badly reared kitten, particularly one starved of essential proteins, vitamins, and minerals in the first few weeks of life, may never develop properly. Lavish care and mounting veterinary fees have not prevented kittens from dying of gastritis or nonspecific enteritis soon after settling in their new homes, much to the distress of their new owners.

remember that longhairs will require much more grooming and will also cause more problems for anyone allergic to cat fur. Orientals tend to shed less heavily, while Rex and Sphinx breeds produce even less fur in the air. Rigorous grooming will minimize random shedding.

What is certain with a pedigree cat is that you know what it will look like when mature. Some pedigree cats can be expensive to obtain, especially if they are rare and in demand. If you do not want to breed, you may find kittens that are not quite of show quality available as pets. These are not so expensive to buy. Or you could choose a crossbred kitten from an accidental mating, or one not suited to a breeding program could become available. In such cases the breeder may insist that the cat be neutered so that you cannot breed from it.

Kitten or cat?

Many people only think of acquiring a kitten, but that may not be the best choice. A young kitten needs someone to give it meals at intervals through the day and may find it frightening to be introduced into a busy family. The character of an older cat is easier to see and any difficult traits will already be apparent. For an elderly person or one with limited time available, a cat with a more mature lifestyle may be easier to accommodate.

Male or Female?

If you are going to breed from your cat you will have a clear idea of whether you want to raise kittens or set up a stud. If not, and your cat is to be a pet, then it should be neutered and the question of the sex of the kitten becomes much less important. Males may grow a little larger and be slightly more aggressive, but in the neutered cat there will be very little difference—no more than the difference that occurs between individual cats.

Choosing a cat or kitten

A cat or kitten should look clean and healthy, with a firm, lithe body. The backbone and hips should be well covered, but there should not be any sign of a pot belly, which could denote the presence of worms. The eyes should be clear and bright, with no sign of any discharge, and the third eyelid or haw should not protrude at the inner corner. The ears should be spotlessly clean inside, without any black grits, which could indicate canker or mites. The coat should be soft, with clean separated hairs, and when parted behind the ears and at the root of the tail, must be free from the tiny round black grains that are excreted by fleas. With a young kitten, also check that there is no discharge from the nostrils and that teeth and gums are fresh and healthy. Finally, look under the cat's tail

for any yellow staining that could mean that the kitten is suffering from diarrhea.

If the kitten passes all these tests, it should be safe to take home. If not, it should be left in the environment it knows until it is treated.

Reliable breeders will always agree to a sale subject to a veterinary check. They may also want you to prove that you are a suitable new owner. Always make sure that the kitten is fully weaned, and with an older kitten or cat ask whether it has been fully immunized.

Strays

If think you have found an abandoned cat or a cat tries to move into your home, you must make every possible attempt to trace its possibly grieving owners. If it has no identity tag or embedded microchip, you should still inform the authorities in case it has been reported missing. The problem with such a stray is that you know nothing about it, so it is worth having it checked by a vet for any problems and for neutering if necessary.

below left: In a female kitten, the vulva is a vertical slit almost joined to the anus like a letter "i."

below right: In a male kitten, the tip of the penis is hidden in an opening ½ in. (1 cm) below the anus, with the scrotal sacs in between.

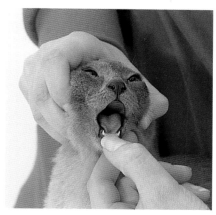

top left: *Look inside the mouth. Gums should be a healthy pale pink, teeth clean and white, and the breath fresh, without odor.*

middle left: *Eyes should be bright and clean with no discharge. The third eyelid (haw) should not be raised and there should be no discharge or blockage around the nostrils.*

bottom left: *Check ears for any wax deposit or discharge. Dark lumps of wax may indicate ear mites, so watch the cat to see if it scratches its ears.*

below: *If you have decided on a pedigree breed, take a look at the cattery, as well as the cats. This will give you a good guide to the hygiene and care surrounding the cat's breeding.*

Collecting the new cat

No kitten should leave its mother until it is fully weaned. If you purchase a kitten at a show, do not take it straight home. Shows take a lot out of a small kitten, and its lowered resistance might make it liable to develop a minor infection. It is better to pay a deposit and collect the kitten a few weeks later. This will also give you time to make things ready to receive it. With any cat the transition from one home to another must be made as quietly and as comfortably as possible to avoid any unnecessary stress.

When collecting any cat you will need a safe carrier to take it home in. Cats should not be carried unconfined in cars or on public transport. Carriers are available in wicker, plastic, wire mesh, nylon, or cardboard. A good one will last for years and be worth the investment, so buy one big enough to contain the grown cat. Inexpensive cardboard carriers have the advantage that they can be disposed of. Plastic or plastic-covered metal will be easier to wash and keep hygienic.

The carrier should be lined with layers of newspaper topped with an old sweater or piece of warm blanket. If it is made of wire mesh, line the sides with paper too, especially on a cold day. With a small kitten you might like to add a rubber hot-water bottle beneath the blanket. A cat may protest at being shut inside the carrier during the journey home, but the lid should not be opened under any circumstances. If you are a passenger, and not busy driving, then talk to it and reassure it all the way.

Make sure that you get a proper briefing from the breeder or previous owner of the cat, preferably in writing. Also check that you have information on the diet the cat is currently used to, its immunization certificates (if it has been immunized), which will carry vaccination dates and the types used, and its full pedigree and registration certificate if it has one (see page 139). If you wish to breed or show the cat yourself, make arrangements with the breeder for official transfer of the ownership of the cat to you and for registration, if this has not already been done.

MAKING A NEW CAT AT HOME

below: *This is a traditional cat bed, but a cardboard box will serve just as well. Place it in a quiet place where people are not constantly walking past.*

right: *A scratching post will give a cat somewhere to exercise its claws without doing any damage to your furniture. Make sure it will be stable when in use.*

SOME PREPARATION IS NECESSARY to make ready for a new cat's arrival. The first essential is to provide a warm bed in which the cat can rest and sleep. If you are taking on an adult cat that already has a bed, ask to take it with you. It will be a familiar base and you can replace it if necessary when the cat has settled in. For a kitten, a solid cardboard box is better than a wicker basket at this stage. Its firm sides keep out drafts and, if soiled, it can be replaced. Line it thickly with newspaper, putting a blanket on top that can be pulled up around the sides to form a nest-like depression in which the kitten can curl and sleep. It is a refuge from which to explore or to retire to if the the cat feels threatened.

A shallow litter box must be provided. Discover what filling the cat is already used to and begin by using that. You can gradually convert it to the proprietary cat litter or other filler you prefer after the cat is used to its new toilet.

Food and water bowls are needed, of course, and a starter supply of the food the cat is used to. Again, you can try new foods to change its diet later.

Cats need to exercise to stretch their claws and remove blunt tips, so supply a piece of wood on which they can do this. Ideally, it should be set vertically, not just laid on the floor. Special posts are commercially available, but some have carpet covering, which could encourage the cat to use any piece of carpet for the purpose. A rope covering is better. Outdoors, a cat will claw on a tree trunk, stretching up and scratching with delight.

Finally, kittens need toys, and many adults will enjoy them too. Another cardboard box makes a good fun cave; kittens love to climb into boxes to play. Cut some kitten-sized holes in every side and toss some toys in. Kittens will enjoy diving in and out. There are many pet toys for sale, but avoid any with long pieces of cord or elastic attached, glass eyes, tiny bells, or any other object that can be chewed off and swallowed by a kitten. Synthetic rubber and plastic can also be chewed and swallowed by a teething kitten. Simple toys, crumpled balls of paper, table tennis balls, spools, feathers, and a simple cloth mouse filled with catnip with a short string tail, all give great pleasure and encourage play. This helps to build up muscles and sharpen the reflexes. If a cat already has small toys it likes, ask to have them; they will already have its smell upon them.

As a long-term provision, if a cat is able to have access outdoors, a cat door can be installed to allow it in and out without having to open a door. However, no cat should be allowed out until it has become accustomed to its new home, and it is best to wait until a kitten is three or four months old before teaching it to use its own way in and out. A good cat door will be weighted to prevent it from swinging in the breeze, and have a catch so that it can be secured if you want to keep a cat in. Some have a magnetic

catch, operated by a small magnet worn on the cat's collar. This also prevents strange cats from making their way in.

On first arrival

The new cat, especially a kitten that will be missing its mother and litter mates, should be given plenty of attention on its arrival in its new home, but if it wants to return to its carrier or box do not fuss over it. At first it should be confined to one room where you have set up its bed and litter box so that it can get its bearings. Show it the litter box and scratch around in it to make it obvious what it is for. Offer the cat a meal and after feeding the cat, indicate the box again. With a kitten, place it on the litter to teach it this lesson. Let the cat explore further afield at its own pace, always leaving the way open for it to retreat to its secure bed area. Make sure there are no open windows or chimneys, unguarded fires, electric wires from lamps, uncovered fish tanks, or poison-impregnated fly strips that could be hazardous to an exploring kitten.

If there are already established pets in the house, make sure that they too get plenty of attention so that they do not feel their security and status threatened by the new arrival. It may help to take some of their bedding, or even a little soiled litter from their tray, and rub it on the kitten to transfer their own smell on

above right: For a cat allowed outdoors a cat door saves continual door opening. Prop it open while the cat learns this is the way in and out.

right: A litter box is essential, even if you propose to let your cat go outside. Covered types stop the litter from being scattered outside the tray.

to it before they have the chance to meet it. Feed them separately at first and do not leave them alone until the spitting and hissing has stopped between cats. It may take a week or more for an older cat to accept a new kitten, even though the kitten is obviously willing to be friendly. It is very rare for a cat to fail to accept a kitten in the end, no matter how strong its initial reactions are.

Most animals are tolerant of the young, even of other species, but if you have a jealous dog it may attack the newcomer, even when it is a tiny kitten. Introduce the two in stages, and do not

leave them alone together until they have become obvious friends. Always serve the cat's food separately from the dog, who will probably quickly finish its own meal, then demolish that of the cat. Serve them either shut in different rooms or at different levels, the dog on the floor and the cat on a high shelf.

Once the new cat is feeling at home you can move the bed and litter box to their permanent positions, or if you have other pets you may find they prefer to sleep together. However, it is always good for a cat to have an area established as a core territory that it can call its own.

FEEDING YOUR CAT

WHEN THE CAT EVOLVED and adapted to a strictly carnivorous diet, it virtually lost the capacity to digest and utilize plant foods. The cat just cannot exist on a low-protein diet. It requires large amounts of meat daily, in relation to its size. The only way in which the cat can digest carbohydrates is in the cooked state, such as in baked biscuits, bread products, and boiled root vegetables. It needs a relatively high level of vitamin A to keep its body cells working properly, but far less vitamin D in relation to A than is needed by dogs or humans. Vitamins of the B group are important for the maintenance of the central nervous system.

Natural food yields a high level of calcium and phosphorus, which the cat requires for the growth of its bones. These elements may be lacking in the meals fed to the domestic cat. The signs of deficiency show as fractured or deformed bones, especially in a kitten of four to six months. Cats are often seen to chew grass; this supplies folic acid, necessary for their well-being but lacking in cooked meat diets.

Following digestion, the food undergoes the process of oxidation within the body, and energy is released. The energy is measured in units of heat called calories. In a healthy cat the number of calories it requires balances the number of calories that its body uses each day. If this balance is well maintained, then the cat stays fit and healthy and its weight remains constant. A cat that is underfed gradually loses weight and condition as the body draws on the reserves of fat or protein to make up the deficiencies.

Depending on its pattern of activity, the normal female cat requires 200–250 calories per day, while the male needs 250–300 calories. Kittens need more calories in relation to their body weight; because they are growing rapidly, their smaller bodies are subject to more heat loss, and their energy requirements are always higher.

It is always best to feed your cat a varied diet and discourage finicky eating. A particular food may go off the market, and cats addicted to one type risk problems. Carcass meat is low in calcium, vitamin A, and iodine; eating that alone may lead to osteoporosis ("brittle bones"). Too much liver can cause excess vitamin A, resulting in bony outgrowths around the joints and spine that make movements painful. Too much cod liver oil can have the same effect.

Meat can be fed cooked, canned, or raw. Raw meat must be fit for human consumption. Always wash your hands after handling it and before touching anything else. Cooking destroys many vitamins, although these can be replaced by adding supplements.

Milk is rich in protein and an acceptable food for some cats, but some cannot digest the lactosein, which can produce persistent and severe diarrhea. Others show an allergic reaction to the protein in cow's milk; they may be able to drink goat's milk instead, but otherwise must not be given milk. Many breeders use canned evaporated milk for rearing their kittens and to provide extra calcium for pregnant and lactating queens. Diluted with an equal quantity of hot water it is acceptable to most cats, but if diarrhea results, it should be withdrawn. Calcium can easily be added to the diet by means of specially formulated tablets, or by feeding sterilized bone meal as a supplement.

Water, in a clean bowl, should be put down every day so that it is always available to the cat.

Commercial pet foods

Pet food is now a vast industry that spends millions on research and testing (as well as advertising). Canned food varies in quality and many more expensive kinds seemed aimed at the buyer's taste rather than the cat's, but food sold

right: Make sure a feeding bowl cannot be easily toppled over, and that it is easy to keep clean.

by the leading makers is carefully balanced. Vitamins lost in the cooking process are replaced, and the ingredients are carefully selected before being prepared under conditions of hygiene and efficiency.

Complete dried foods are also available and are carefully formulated to contain everything a cat needs to stay healthy. Cats fed on dried diets should be fed only one third of canned food, by weight, and must be given plenty of water. Watch to ensure that they drink well. A pinch of table salt added to the food will encourage a cat to drink. Kittens weaned onto dried foods usually drink adequate amounts of water and do well; older cats, given a dried diet later in life, may be too lazy to drink enough, and health problems may occur. Dried food helps keep teeth healthy but some cats become easily addicted to a favorite brand. It may be best to use dry food as just one part of the diet.

left: Cats eat grass as a source of folic acid. It may also act as roughage and help them to regurgitate fur balls.

A varied diet

A mixed diet for an average cat with a weekly calorie requirement of 1,400 to 1,800 units can be made up in many ways. These are some suggestions using a variety of foods over seven days.

1 7 small cans of cat food and 1 pint / 600 ml of milk
2 1 lb. /450 g dried diet and ½ pint / 300 ml of milk
3 2 lb. /900 g rabbit; 8 oz. /225 g liver and ¾ pint /450 ml milk
4 1 lb. /450 g beef, 1 lb. /450 g melts (spleen), 8 oz. /225 g oily fish, and ½ pint /300 ml milk
5 4 cans of food; 4 oz. /112 g dried diet, 8 oz. /25 g white fish and ¾ pint / 350 ml milk

When to feed

In the wild state the cat hunts, kills, feeds, then rests. It may gorge itself on a whole rabbit one day, then go without food for the next two or three days. Adult pets do quite well if fed only one meal daily, but two meals a day may add interaction and interest and especially helps to alleviate the routine in catteries. Whichever you

choose, gradually reduce the number from the kitten's multi-meal day. For pregnant and lactating queens give three or even four meals. There are no hard and fast rules, but for a young adult a morning meal might be 2–3 oz. (57–85 g) milk with a few drops of cod liver oil added twice a week and an evening meal of 6–9 oz. (170–255 g) varied canned or fresh food, depending on the size and

activity of the cat. If a cat becomes overweight or underweight, loses its coat, has foul breath, flaking skin, or shredded claws, the diet could be at fault. Infertility, uncertain movements, neurotic behavior, and sensitivity to light can all be the result of inadequate or incorrect feeding. A thorough checkup and an accurate list of the cat's diet will help the veterinarian to pinpoint the problem area.

Feeding guide

Age	Body weight (lb./kg)	Daily food requirements (oz./g)	No. of meals per day
Newborn	¼ / 0.12	28 / 1	10
5 weeks	1 / 0.45	3 / 85	6
10 weeks	2 / 0.9	5 / 141	5
20 weeks	4½ / 2	6 / 170	4
30 weeks	6½ / 3	7 / 198	3
Adult male	10 / 4.5	8 / 241	1
Pregnant female	7½ / 3.4	8½ / 241	2–3
Lactating female	5½ / 2.5	14 / 396	4
Neuter	9 / 4	6½ / 184	1

GENERAL CARE AND TRAINING

THE DOMESTIC CAT MUST LEARN to accept the limitations of domestic life and obey the rules of sharing a human home. Owners must, on the other hand, undertake responsibility for the well-being and protection of the cat. As well as providing food and shelter in a safe environment, they must undertake regular grooming (see pages 136–7), during which they should also monitor the animal's physical condition and watch for changes in behavior that could be symptomatic of problems. Immunization against disease is periodic, and neutering a one-time procedure, but most cat care should become a regular routine. Inevitably, some veterinary bills will be incurred. Various companies now offer insurance plans to cover pet health care costs. These are worth consideration, but check and compare what coverage they give before choosing one. If a cat or kitten is not already equipped with a collar, then get it one.

Identification tags and chips

All cats should carry identification whenever allowed outdoors. The conventional way is an identity tag carried on a collar, but the collar must have an elastic section or be designed to break easily if caught on a nail or twig, as it could choke the cat. Cats have sustained injuries from loose collars, often because they have lost weight after becoming trapped somewhere without food. A paw pushed through the collar leaves it

cutting into the skin at the top of the leg. Instead, or better in addition, a tiny microchip can be inserted under the skin. This carries a personal identification number registering the cat, and can be read by a device held by veterinary surgeries and police stations. It does not hurt to insert, has no effect on the cat, and ensures that, even with no collar or if deliberately stolen, your cat can be identified as yours.

Immunization

All cats should be vaccinated against Feline Infectious Enteritis (FIE), Feline Leukemia Virus (FeLV) and two respiratory viruses: Feline Viral Rhinotracheitis (FVR), and Feline Calcivirus (FCV). Shots are usually given at the same time; the first at about nine to twelve weeks, with a second injection three weeks later and then an annual booster injection. It is wise to get a certificate of vaccination. Veterinary practice and types of vaccine vary; some may require a booster only

every two years, but follow your vet's advice. These are dreadful diseases and every cat needs protection. Cats at shows and those placed in boarding kennels are at particular risk, and admission to either is usually dependent upon a current certificate of vaccination being produced. Do not use a kennel if they do not ask for one.

Neutering

Unless a cat is to be used for breeding, have it neutered to avoid unwanted kittens. If you have a female, would like to raise a litter, and are confident that you can place any ensuing kittens in good homes, a female can be spayed after having her first litter. Entire females not allowed to breed will make every effort to escape. Their frustration leads to behavioral and sometimes health problems. Stud males are confined to their cattery, but full males allowed their freedom soon develop unsociable habits: spraying their territories, fighting other males, and wailing through the night.

Neutered male cats are castrated; a simple operation during which the testes are removed through a small incision in the scrotum that does not even require stitches. Usually performed at six months, it can be done at any age over four months and even on older, battle-scarred toms has no ill-effects.

Females have the ovaries and uterus

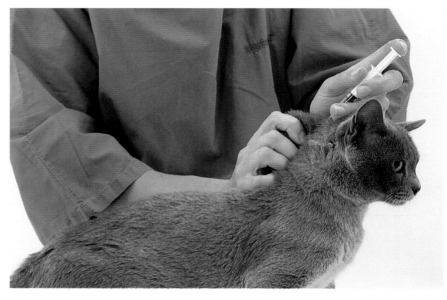

right: All cats should be vaccinated against the main infectious feline diseases and given regular annual booster shots. It is a simple procedure that does not hurt the cat.

left: *The general health and well-being of your kitten can be assessed through physical examination.*

above: *A covered litter box will help to prevent spilling out when the cat scratches to hide its leavings. The top is easily removed for replacing the litter.*

right: *In administering ear drops, hold the cat's head gently and massage the drops from the base of the ear. Eye drops should be given equally carefully, not holding the bottle too close to the eye.*

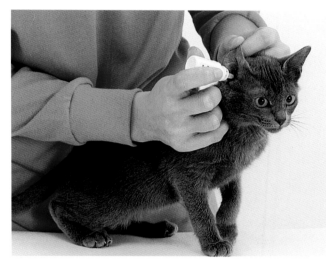

right: *Teeth and mouth should be part of your regular inspection. Kittens lose their first teeth from about five months old.*

removed, commonly known as spaying. Under a general anesthetic, the operation site is shaved and cleaned to prevent infection. In the U.S.A., an incision is usually made mid-line (along the middle of the abdomen from the navel toward the hind legs); in Europe and Australasia it is more common to make a small incision in the flank. Once the organs are removed, two or three stitches close the incision and can be removed about a week later.

The female may be neutered at any age from about four months. Unless vital for other reasons, females should never be spayed when in season, when reproductive organs are enlarged and there are more risks involved.

For 12 hours before the operation cats must go without food or fluids, but both males and females are usually playing, eating, and drinking within a few hours of their operations. Females with mid-line incisions may take slightly longer, normally about 48 hours, to recover. The neutering of pedigree or show cats is often delayed to allow their full physical development.

Litter boxes

A variety of litter boxes is sold. Some have covers to prevent litter from being spread around, others have filters to drain out liquid, and a variety of proprietary litter materials is available, several of which reduce odor. Wood shavings or torn paper are sometimes laid beneath the litter to reduce the amount needed. The litter must be changed frequently, and the box washed with a mild solution of household bleach, or a cat-safe disinfectant; never use one containing phenol (for example, Lysol or Jeyes Fluid). Scalding water can be used to sterilize the box. A kitten should already be toilet trained when it leaves its mother. If it does not use the litter box properly, check first that it is not a protest against overused litter.

Physical checks

Get to know a cat well and it will be easy to spot any limping or awkwardness of movement, difficulty in urinating or defecating, or unusual behavior; these should prompt an investigation of the cause. Make a habit of looking for signs of injury or infestation while grooming, with a special check at least once a week.

Make sure that the inside of the ears is spotlessly clean with a very slightly moist appearance. Wipe away any grayish wax with a dry cotton swab. If a cat has a lot of hair inside the ear, wax may clog around it. Use cotton lightly moistened with warm water and baby soap to wipe it away, but do not allow water to trickle down inside the ears, and never poke inside the ear canal itself.

Black or dark brown gritty material in the ears usually indicates the presence of ear mites (see page 153). Kittens' ears can get dusty, and need wiping out constantly. It is important to teach the kitten to enjoy having its ears cleaned by making it a part of petting, before feeding.

Accustom the cat to having its mouth examined. Kittens need regular checking to ensure that their teeth are erupting properly, and that the milk teeth are

right: Brushing with special feline toothpaste will help prevent the buildup of tartar on the teeth. Let the cat get used to the brush before trying to use it in the mouth.

left: Claws will need regular clipping, especially if a cat does not go outdoors. Use strong nail clippers, not scissors.

being shed. When kittens refuse all food it is usually because new teeth are coming through; the milk teeth are still present, and the kitten has a very sore mouth. A small strip of raw meat each day helps to avoid early teething problems, helping to remove the first teeth quite naturally as new teeth come through. Soft foods can cause a buildup of layers of tartar along the gum margins. Regular checks ensure that this can be controlled by using a special toothbrush or soft wooden dental sticks impregnated with an oral antiseptic. Cats seem to enjoy the procedure. A

few hard pellets of crunchy cat food also help to keep teeth and gums healthy.

If a cat salivates excessively but is otherwise well, it may be due to an extreme buildup of tartar. This must be removed by a vet without delay. If it is neglected, the teeth may need to be extracted.

On the feet, examine paw pads for thorns, cuts, or abrasions, and at the same time gently squeeze each foot to extend the claws. A broken claw can become infected, and a swelling may be found up in the claw bed. Bathe the whole foot to give relief. Sometimes the area around each claw bed becomes neglected and dirty. If this happens, wash each foot carefully and thoroughly with warm water and baby soap, then rinse and dry. Examine each claw to make sure that there is no sign of infection, for this is the site most commonly attacked by a fungal disease such as ringworm. Check the length of claws and trim them if necessary. With some cats this is easy to do on your own, but some people find it easier to have a helper hold the cat or ask the veterinarian to do it. Some people have cats declawed. If you would seriously consider doing so, then you should not keep a cat.

While grooming, also check for any skin wounds and lesions. Puncture wounds, usually made by teeth or claws in fights but sometimes made by prey,

can often be infected and turn into abscesses. Look out for any sign of infestation or skin problem. No cat with any scratch, scab, or patch of bare skin is allowed to enter a cat show. Look out for small spots like blackheads around the chin, whisker-pads, and on the top of the tail. These are blocked sebum glands and can be washed away.

Necessary training

Cats can be trained to behave in an acceptable manner so that they fit into a normal family routine. Cats do very much as they please most of the time, and the training really consists of observing their behavior, ignoring them when this is totally acceptable, and scolding them when it is not.

First a cat should learn its name. Choose one that is distinctive and

different from that of any other household pet or family member. Use it when you are doing things the cat likes, offering food or stroking it, greeting it when it is coming toward you. Never use its name in censure: say "bad cat" or something similar. If you have several cats it may not mean that the right cat will answer your call, but it makes sense to try. Some breeders with several house cats perform this party trick: when all the cats are asleep together, they quietly call one name; when that cat looks up, they then call the next name, and so on, until each cat has individually responded.

Short sharp words of command should be taught. "Get down" seems to be effective, used most often when cats jump up where they should not, or steal from kitchen counters. Teach it by using a firm, sharp voice and clapping the

left: Part the fur so that you can see down to the roots and to check skin condition for any sign of fleas or their droppings, or other parasites.

below: *Indoor cats need play to give them exercise, but there are times when they just want to retire to a basket to rest or wash.*

hands together at the same time. They soon learn to understand a disapproving "No." Use it if a cat starts to scratch the carpet, then firmly place it by its scratching post. Do the same if your cat makes a mess or wets in the wrong place—reprimand it sharply, and then put it on its litter box. Establish one place for the litter box; do not move it around or the cat may go to the place where it used to be.

If the cat is to be taught that toilet facilities are outdoors, it must be a gradual process. Move the litter box near the door; then, over a period of a few days, put it outside for a few hours, eventually in the area in the yard you want the cat to use. Then place some soiled litter on the spot and take the box away. If possible, however, the cat should be allowed to use a clean litter box whenever it needs to do so. In this way a careful check can be kept on its motions for any signs of constipation, diarrhea, or worms. Any kidney or bladder trouble will also be noticed. The cat is also less likely to pick up infection if it has indoor toilet facilities.

Many cats spend their entire lives indoors due to heavy traffic and other hazards. They are quite contented and healthy, if they have not been used to an outdoor life. If a cat is to be kept permanently indoors, it should be started off as a young kitten, so that it knows of no other form of life. The indoor cat must be given plenty to occupy its time and another pet as a companion. Pots of grass and scratching posts help to compensate for the facilities of the yard, and some form of climbing frame is appreciated.

Scold a cat immediately when it does something wrong, not when it comes running to you. Some people use a water pistol to squirt water at a cat to signal

disapproval, but this should always be combined with a verbal reprimand.

The elderly cat

The company of an aging cat in good health is delightful and soothing and as rewarding as playing with a tiny kitten. The old cat's reactions are sharp, his movements are subtle, and he may deign to chase string and pat feathers, as long as he is not made to look foolish. Old age in the cat can be anything from nine to nineteen years, but the cat can be considered old when it starts to take things easy and spends even more time than usual sleeping. Elderly cats need a great deal of love and affection, and should not be ignored just because they sit around the house and are rather undemanding and quiet. Everything should be done to keep them feeling as good as possible.

This is the time to begin to feed a good light diet and to groom the cat every day, for the cat may not spend enough time in caring for its own coat and toilet, often neglecting the tail area in the process of self-grooming, so extra attention may be necessary. Grooming powder can be used in the coat, if necessary, to keep it clean and soft.

An old cat needs especially careful attention to ears, teeth, and claws. Do not allow it to get overweight, as this would put undue strain on the heart. Have its mouth, teeth, and general condition checked by the veterinarian at regular intervals for any sign of kidney disease.

If an elderly cat's teeth deteriorate, a soft diet can be given, and if the kidneys begin to fail, a low-protein diet extended with rice and pasta can be started. Fresh clean drinking water is even more important to the cat in old age. Extracting bad teeth often dramatically improves an old cat's health. Its strength should be kept

left: Most cats live between 9 and 15 years, although the better feeding and care now available makes longer lives not unusual. Several cats have been recorded over 30 years.

below: Old age has little effect on appetite but movement becomes less flexible, grooming less thorough, and daily routine more fixed.

up while the mouth heals by feeding a light liquid diet for a few days.

If an old cat has trouble walking, its pads may be cracked, and it should be confined to the house for a few days while vegetable oil is rubbed into the skin. A little oil added to the diet might also help the condition of the skin.

It is common to obtain a new kitten when one cat is getting old. This can be a good or a bad decision, depending on the temperament and nature of the old cat. If the established cat likes the new kitten, its presence could bring a new lease on life. The kitten's keen appetite may stimulate the old cat to eat better and take a renewed interest in life generally. On the other hand, a cantankerous older cat, perhaps with general discomfort from its kidneys or stiff joints, may resent the playful antics of a kitten. The kitten's attempts to involve an older cat in its games could be met with hostility, and the old cat may be so resentful that it stops eating, becomes depressed, ill, and incontinent. If the old cat is the only one in the household and has always been a loner, it would be better to postpone the acquisition of a new kitten. If, however, the old cat is one of several family pets, he probably would not have any objection to a newcomer.

As a cat ages, so a certain amount of tissue degeneration occurs. This is inevitable and cannot be prevented, although, with care, the effects can be eased. Regular visits to the veterinarian are important; every six months unless treatments are required. Disturbed behavior patterns may be the result of chronic illness in the old cat. For example, a previously clean cat may have accidents, making puddles on chairs and carpets. It is best to confine the old cat to areas of the house where the occasional lapse of manners will not matter. It is cruel and unfair to chastise or ban him from the house for something that is beyond his control.

Eventually, the old cat sleeps more and more, and is increasingly reluctant to exercise. It may drink lots of fluids but take very little food. While it is able to function normally, if only in this modified way, it is probably quite happy and contented. If its bladder and bowels begin to fail and the cat is unable to eat, veterinary advice must be sought, for the only humane thing to do in these circumstances is to have the old cat put down, allowing him to die in dignity.

GROOMING

GROOMING IS ESSENTIAL for a cat's well-being. It keeps the coat in good condition, removing dead hair and flakes of dead skin; it cleans and separates the growing hairs; it stimulates the circulation; and it helps tone up the muscles. Different methods are used for grooming longhaired and shorthaired cats, and for exhibition purposes more sophisticated techniques are employed. Grooming should start as young as possible and become a pleasurable experience for the cat.

Grooming the shorthair

Shorthaired cats should be groomed at least once a week, more frequently if they are shedding a quantity of hair or are entered in a show. Use a moderately stiff brush to brush lightly but thoroughly from head to tail to remove any loose hair. Pay particular attention to the throat, armpits, and inner thighs. Check for any signs of the black grits which show the presence of fleas.

If necessary, a pesticide suitable for cats, or a correctly formulated coat dressing, may be applied and worked into the coat. Next, use a fine-toothed comb all over the cat from head to tail, to remove loose hairs, scurf, and parasites or grit. A pad of soft cloth or a chamois can be used fairly firmly along the muscular areas to raise a sheen on the coat; then the hands are used all over the cat, smoothly and firmly, to promote muscle tone. Finally, the ears, eyes, anal region, and claw beds are examined and cleaned if necessary.

Hand grooming (heavy stroking) will also free loose hair, and some cats even enjoy the sensation of having their hair brushed back from tail to head.

Grooming the longhair

Longhaired cats require daily grooming, with an extra-special session once a week in which the ears, claws, and teeth are checked and cleaned if necessary. Some cats need powdering every day if the coat is especially soft and easily mats; others only once a week or so. Specially formulated grooming powder is best, but baby powder may also be used. Sprinkle it lightly into the coat, work it in with the fingertips, gently separating the hairs. While the powder absorbs grease from the fur, tease out knots or tangles with a wire rake or special mitten. Use it carefully so that the skin is not scratched or damaged. When clear of tangles, brush the powder out of the coat, then comb all over with a coarse, blunt metal comb, finishing off by working up from the tail to the head against the lie of the coat.

If a longhaired coat is neglected, the hairs clump together in thick, matted lumps. They are impossible to tease out and they must be cut off at the roots. A seriously neglected coat may have to be completely clipped or de-matted, often needing to be done under a general anesthetic by a veterinarian. As the new hair grows, it must have daily attention so that it never mats again, but in such soft-coated cats it is a good idea to keep the underneath of the body clipped fairly closely, unless the cat is going to be competing at shows.

below from left to right: Longhaired cats need daily grooming: (1) Brush first from the head to the tail, first back, then tummy and paws. (2) Comb out loose fur without pulling on tangles. (3) Wipe around the eyes with cotton dipped in clean water, using a new piece for each eye. (4) Finish off the facial hair with a toothbrush.

The bran bath

A very soiled or oily coat may be cleaned with a bran bath. Spread 4 oz. (112 g) of bran on a baking sheet and heat it in a warm oven until it feels comfortably hot to the touch. Tip it onto a large sheet of newspaper, place the cat on it, and massage the bran into the roots of the fur. Then wrap the cat in a hot towel and pet it soothingly. After about ten minutes, remove the towel, stand the cat on the newspaper and brush and comb the bran from the coat. It will bring any dust, scurf, dirt, and loose hairs with it. The next day, thoroughly groom the cat again to remove the last traces of bran. The coat will look greatly improved and have a good sheen.

Shampooing

If fur becomes contaminated with chemicals it is best to dunk the cat in water. For petroleum products and turpentine, first use vegetable oil or margarine, then wash with some mild soap or specially formulated cat shampoo. If one is not available, a baby shampoo could be used, but never use shampoo intended for adults—it is too strong for cats. A very greasy coat or the need for a perfect coat for a show may call for a less urgent wet shampoo. If cats are used to bathing from kittenhood they may get to enjoy it, but an assistant will usually be necessary. Do not do this in the bath, which will mean bending over; use a double sink or two bowls, and fill with water that is comfortably hot. Place the cat firmly in a quarter-full bowl or sink. Ladle water over the cat, head first, until the coat is saturated. A little shampoo may help the water to penetrate the hair. When the coat is thoroughly wet, massage in the shampoo. Avoid massaging the shampoo on the face. One person can hold the cat by the scruff while the other rubs in the shampoo.

Use the second basin of hot water to rinse out all the shampoo. Pour gently over the cat until every bit of foam is removed. It may be necessary to change the water in which the cat is sitting. When the coat is rinsed clear, dry the cat thoroughly with a thick towel. Some cats will allow themselves to be finished off with a hair dryer or fan heater; others have to be put in a very warm spot inside a mesh carrier until they are dry. Most cats help by licking the fur vigorously to dry it. As soon as it is dry the hair can be groomed into place.

Trimming claws

To shorten the cat's claws use a pair of nail clippers with a spring handle. Scissors must not be used, as they will splinter the claw and make it sore. Holding the cat comfortably, squeeze gently on the paw and the claws will protrude. Each has a pink area toward the base, the sensitive quick, easily seen under the paler keratin. Keep clear of this quick, place the clippers across the claw, and clip firmly. If the cat gets fractious do not persist. Do the rest on another occasion.

VISITS AND VACATIONS

SOME OWNERS LIKE TO TAKE their cats away with them to weekend cottages, to visit friends, or even to their office. For all cats there will be some excursions to the veterinarian's office, the cat show, or the kennel. It is essential, therefore, that cats get accustomed to traveling in a cat carrier.

If cats have to be left behind when the owner is away, provision must be made for them. A neighbor or friend who looks after them should get to know them well beforehand. Caregivers should spend time playing with and stroking the cat, if it will allow it, not just pay a quick call to give food and change litter. Ideally, try to have someone come to live in while you are away. A cat is very territorially conscious so it is not usually wise for it to stay in someone else's house; it may try to find its way back home, but an apartment that it cannot leave may be safe. If there is no one to look after the cat while you are away, then you will have to put it into a boarding kennel.

Using a cat carrier

The first requirements of a carrier are to contain the cat and to be easy to carry, but it should also be comfortable and protected from drafts and weather while you are in transit. It must be well made with secure fastenings that a clever cat cannot open. A frightened cat could scratch and chew through a cardboard or wicker carrier, and no cat should be sent unaccompanied in one. Line wire mesh and open wicker carriers for protection against the weather. A top-opening carrier is easier to lift a cat in and out of than one that opens at one end.

Get a cat used to its basket before you use it. Make it a component of a kitten's play area, put a blanket that has the cat's scent inside for use as a bed. Lay some paper in the carrier and feed a favorite meal inside. Do this with the door or lid left open, then after a few times with it closed. Make a fuss of the cat afterward. The carrier should become associated with good things and carry familiar smells. Put a blanket carrying the cat's scent inside when it is being used.

In an emergency, if no carrier is available, punch holes in a cardboard box and tie the lid down. As a last resort, a sturdy, zipped-up overnight bag or shoulder bag may be used.

Leads and collars

If a carrier is not available—but never do this if driving a car alone—a cat can be restrained and controlled to some extent with a leash. It should be attached to a harness that fits over the body, rather than a collar. A determined cat may wiggle out of a collar and can be half strangled by pulling on the leash. Harnesses are made to fit comfortably without rubbing. Slip the loop of the leash around your wrist so that a sudden jerk cannot pull it out of your hand.

Some cats learn to walk on a leash, usually if they have got used to the idea in early kittenhood. If your cat likes to walk alongside you there is a chance of success. Begin with holding the leash very slack. With the cat less than the leash distance away, call it to you and stroke it. Then begin to try the same thing, moving away slightly. With luck the cat may follow you.

Training a cat for travel

If a cat is going to have to accompany its owners on journeys quite regularly, it must be trained to accept this from as early an age as possible. Take it out for short journeys—in a car, on public transport, or just walking down the road. To make it feel secure, put its blanket and favorite toys in the carrier. It will get used to outside noise and traffic and the motion of being in vehicles—fortunately, cats rarely suffer from motion sickness.

Some cats like to watch everything going on around them. They like the attention other people give them on a bus or train and to look out of car windows, but never let them out of their carrier unless on a leash and never by the driver where they could dive under the pedals. On a long journey most cats get bored and soon go to sleep and often it is better to put them where there is nothing to see.

Public transport and international travel

Always check with airlines, railways, and bus companies before traveling with a cat, as they may have special regulations. Some, but not all, will allow a box or carrier in the passenger section. If cats are only allowed to travel as cargo, they must be packed in specially constructed, crush-proof wooden crates.

Strict regulations apply to the transportation of cats between various countries of the world, and these should be carefully studied before you attempt to take a cat from one country to another. The animal may need to have specific injections and certificates for entry into some countries. It may also need to be confined in quarantine kennels for several months on entry into others.

Quarantine, mainly as a protection against the spread of rabies, currently applies in Hawaii, Australia, New Zealand, Eire, and the United Kingdom, although there are proposals for changes in the British legislation.

Vacation travel

Some hotels permit visiting pets but, except when on a leash, the cat will have to be securely confined to one room, and hotel staff must be alerted not to let it dash out when the door is opened. Preferably, it should not be left alone. An inquisitive or frightened cat could too easily go missing for this to be a recommended practice. However, where time is regularly spent in a second home, the same procedures should be followed as when introducing a cat to any home. Certainly, do not allow it to go outside until you are confident it has become established in the new area. Let it out after several weekend visits, or the first three or four days of a vacation at least. Confine the cat some time before returning home, or it may be missing when it is time to leave.

Boarding kennels

Seek recommendations for boarding kennels from veterinarians and other cat owners, and always visit first to inspect it before making a booking for your cat. Such establishments vary greatly. Some are built and run exclusively for cats, and others are annexed to dog boarding kennels. The best have a small, warm, and well-ventilated building for each cat, in which there is room for its bed and

belongings, food, and water, plus space for it to exercise itself. Adjoining is a secure outdoor run, giving no chance of escape, floored in easily cleaned concrete, with a covered or indoor litter box and a sunning log or shelf.

Indoor boarding kennels are not very satisfactory as there is a greater risk of infections spreading from cat to cat if there is not adequate airflow.

above: *Cats should always be transported in a secure carrier. The more used they are to travel, the less disturbing they will find it.*

below: *If you need to board your cat, check the kennel and make arrangements as far in advance as possible to make sure they have a vacancy. Take its bed and some favorite toys along so that not everything will be new and strange.*

Part Five:

The **Health** of the **Cat**

GENERAL HEALTH

ALL RESPONSIBLE OWNERS will ensure the best possible health for their cats by providing a balanced diet, good hygiene, and appropriate immunization for kittens, with regular booster shots. By knowing your cat and its behavior you, as the owner, are best placed to recognize the signs of illness when it does occur, enabling early treatment to give the best possible chance of a cure. Grooming sessions provide the opportunity for regular checks, but any change or odd behavior should always be investigated.

Cats suffer from a wide range of diseases and conditions, some paralleling those in humans, from cancers and arthritis to diabetes, but there are few that can be passed from humans to cats and vice versa. The most serious disease they can catch is rabies. Ringworm is a fungal disease that can be transmitted to humans, and certain mites and fleas can pass from cats to humans (although fortunately cat fleas prefer a cat host). Bacteria from a cat may infect open wounds on humans, and scratches and cuts should be carefully cleaned and covered to avoid contact. Bites and scratches that are inflicted by cats should be carefully cleansed and antiseptic should be applied.

A protozoan parasite, Toxoplasma gondii is possibly the most worrying such disease. It is carried by many humans—90% in some countries—and

probably by 50% of cats, and the cats spread infective cysts by voiding them in feces. It produces mild symptoms in the cats and rarely in humans, but it can affect unborn children in the womb, and pregnant women should therefore try to avoid changing cat litter or, if they have to, always wear gloves. Both humans and cats can contract the disease from raw or undercooked meat.

left: A healthy cat is alert and constantly grooms and cleans its fur.
right: You are the best person to recognize when your cat is off-color and lethargic.

Signs of illness

Generally speaking, if a cat loses its appetite, either partially or completely, an owner should check for an obvious cause. Even a finicky cat will have a pattern to its feeding habits and any change should sound a danger warning.

Any changes in appearance and behavior can also indicate the incubation of illness. Look for signs such as the cat's coat being held slightly erect, giving an

right: The raised nictitating membranes (haws) of this cat are a sure sign that all is not well.

instructions to the letter, and call with a progress report and for further instructions the following morning. The veterinarian would far rather help with advice during a false alarm than be presented with a cat in an advanced stage of infectious illness. Always arrange a firm appointment for the examination of a cat you suspect has an infectious disease, as it is very unfair to take such an animal into a crowded waiting room where other cats are at risk. In some countries the veterinarian is prepared to make house calls; in others, cats have to be taken for examination and probable hospitalization. In all cases early diagnosis and the administration of prompt treatment are important for the well being of the cat.

Symptoms to look out for

- Weight loss
- Coughing/sneezing/nasal discharge
- Difficulty in eating
- Loss of appetite
- Vomiting
- Blood in urine/difficulty in passing urine
- Lethargy/fever
- Increased thirst
- Marked change in behavior
- Scratching/licking
- Signs of acute pain
- Diarrhea
- Constipation
- Haws showing
- Difficulty in breathing
- Ulceration of mouth
- Pallor of lips and gums
- Swollen abdomen
- Stiff or unsteady gait
- Lameness
- Fur loss/failure to wash or self groom

open and spooky look, dull eyes, and the nictitating membrane (haw) appearing across the eye from the inner corner. A cat may seem thirsty but be reluctant to drink, crouching with its head over its water bowl, or it may drink copiously with gulping movements. It may go repeatedly to its litter box but seem unable to pass urine or feces despite straining. It may resent handling, spit when touched, or stop cleaning its fur. Bad breath, sneezing, drooling, vomiting, diarrhea, and discharges from the nose or eyes are all danger warnings. In some diseases the cat may cry out when passing water, or its abdomen may look very distended. It may spend a great deal of time licking its genital region and return to its

litter box several times in an agitated manner. All these signs are signals of danger that should be noted carefully and passed on to the veterinarian to aid diagnosis of the specific trouble.

Vomiting, though an important symptom, is not always sign of an emergency. If it occurs once or twice over a couple of days it is probably a minor stomach upset, and the best treatment is to starve the cat for 24 hours and then give a bland diet for a few days. However, if the vomiting persists then a vet should be consulted. But it is not recommended to watch your cat all day and then decide to call the veterinarian at midnight. If you are worried, call for advice during the daytime, follow the

ACCIDENTS AND FIRST AID

ROAD ACCIDENTS CLAIM MANY feline victims. If not killed instantly, cats may be stunned and bruised, or sustain multiple fractures or severe internal injuries. They may lie unconscious at the side of the road, or try to drag themselves back home. Some crawl away to die, leaving their frantic owners devastated and never discovering what happened to them. A vehicle impact is usually easy to identify as a cause of injury because the cat grips the road surface on impact, and the claws become fragmented.

Domestic hazards

Cats' natural curiosity sometimes gets them into trouble. Discourage them from jumping onto tables, shelves, and working surfaces. A cat used to jumping up to investigate tempting smells may end up colliding with a pan handle or landing on a hot stove burner. Blistered pads are difficult to treat and cause great pain. Hot oil may scald skin, cause deep burns and loss of hair. Boiling water is another danger. Household cleaners, disinfectants, air fresheners, and insect sprays may all be toxic to cats. Some cats climb into refrigerators and washing machines and get shut inside, so do not leave them open and unattended.

Kittens seem especially attracted to electric wires and cables and will play with any draped across the floor from appliance to wall socket. They pat at the cable, roll over and kick at it, grasp it in the paws and then bite hard in a mock "kill." If the end of the wire is connected to a live socket and the sharp little teeth pierce the casing, contact is made and the kitten will be electrocuted.

In the garage, antifreeze compounds made for car radiators spell death for the cat. For some inexplicable reason, cats find the substance strangely attractive, and attempt to lick the can. The toxic component is ethylene glycol, which causes rapid death.

Outdoors

Cats allowed to roam freely may be accidentally poisoned by pesticides such as slug bait, which if eaten by the cat can cause convulsions, arrested respiration, and death. Rodent poisons can be ingested directly or by eating a poisoned animal. Garden sprays may contain organophosphorus compounds, which cause acute diarrhea and muscular tremors leading to collapse. They can be fatal in high concentrations.

Insect stings usually occur when a cat attacks the insect and tries to bite it, so most stings are in or around the mouth. A cat frantically clawing at its mouth may have been stung, in which case the area will be seen to swell fairly quickly, but it may be trying to remove a piece of bone, or other foreign body, wedged across its palate or embedded in its tongue or inside the lips, so inspect the mouth.

Cats who fall into water barrels or pools can swim, but if unable to get out they risk drowning when they become exhausted. Play it safe and keep these hazards covered.

First Aid

Burns and Scalds: Cool the burned area with iced water, cover with clean cloth such as a handkerchief or tea towel, place the cat in a warm carrier and take to a veterinarian.

Electrocution: Turn off the power supply, using rubber gloves or some wooden item to prevent getting a shock yourself. Get the cat warm by rubbing its body and wrapping in warm blankets until professional help can be obtained. Artificial respiration may be necessary if the cat stops breathing (see below).

Poisoning—external: Poisonous substances on the coat or feet of the cat should be washed off immediately with

below: A feline first aid kit is much like one for humans, but all antiseptics must be suitable for cats. Add flea spray and worming pills and make some Universal Antidote (see page 171).

plain soap (not detergent) and warm water. Professional advice is essential.

Poisoning—internal: Keep the animal as warm as possible and seek professional advice without delay Take any suspect products along, so that the correct antidote may, if possible, be given.

Stings: Look for the sting and remove it. Bee stings are acid; neutralize them by gently rubbing on household soda. Wasp stings are alkaline; bathe the wound with vinegar or lemon juice. Keep the cat warm and quiet. If the area swells alarmingly, or if the cat becomes feverish or distressed, veterinary advice should be sought.

Drowning: Lie the cat on a table with its head hanging over the edge, and allow the water and mucus to drain from the mouth while rubbing the body fairly vigorously. If breathing stops, artificial respiration is necessary until professional help arrives or can be sought.

Road Accidents: An injured and unconscious cat should be carefully eased onto a towel or jacket so that it can be lifted without disturbing its limbs or internal organs, which may be damaged. It should be taken to a veterinarian without delay, and kept warm and quiet on the journey. If the cat is hemorrhaging from the mouth, attempt to keep the airways open on the journey.

Bleeding: If blood is spurting from a wound, it may be coming from an artery and must be controlled. A folded handkerchief can be pressed firmly over the bleeding point until professional help is available. If the bleeding is from a limb, a tourniquet may be temporarily applied. Tie a handkerchief around the limb above the wound, place a piece of stick or a pencil beneath it, then twist the stick until the material is tight enough to stop the hemorrhage. After ten minutes gently release the tourniquet, to avoid the possibility of tissue damage. A cat hemorrhaging from the mouth, nose, or ears must receive urgent veterinary attention and should be kept warm and still until help is available.

Fractures: A cat with fractures should be moved with the utmost care onto a tray or piece of board before you attempt to transfer it to the veterinary hospital. It should be covered with warm blankets and kept still and calm.

Foreign bodies: Bones stuck across the palate can be removed by prying them off with the handle of a plastic spoon. Sewing needles may be stuck in the tongue, lips, or throat and need expert attention for safe removal. Burrs and thorns may be causing trouble in the cat's pads, and can be removed with tweezers before bathing the affected paw in a solution of Epsom salts to reduce the tenderness and swelling. Grass seeds sometimes get under the eyelids of the cat and must be flushed out with a syringe and warm saline solution.

Artificial Respiration: Necessary only in extreme cases to save life, artificial respiration can be carried out in two ways: (1) Place the cat on its side, head slightly forward, so that the airways are clear. Ensure that mouth and throat are clear and that the tongue is forward (in cases of drowning allow the cat's head to hang over the edge of the table). Gentle pressure is applied to the chest of the cat, then released. This is repeated rhythmically, four seconds being taken to apply pressure and four seconds to release it, until the cat takes a breath. (2) The cat is held head down by its hind legs (grasped firmly, close together) and swung in a wide half circle, gently and smoothly, until the cat breathes.

above: Wounds can be cleaned at home with salt water and cotton.

left: A bandage over the neck or upper body can be made more secure by anchoring it around the foreleg.

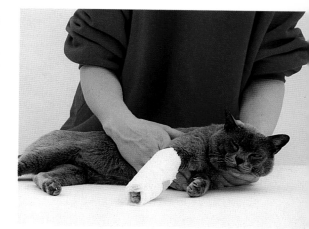

above: Bandaging around a leg can be secured top and bottom with adhesive strips.

CAT DISEASES

Viral diseases

Fortunately, of the several infectious viruses that affect cats, vaccines are now available to give protection against some of the most serious, although not yet against Feline Immunodeficiency Virus (FIV—cat AIDS).

Feline Infectious Enteritis (FIE), also known as **Feline Panleucopenia (FPL)**, is highly contagious, with an incubation period of two to nine days, but usually less than six days. It is characterized by its very sudden onset and the cat can quickly die. It mainly affects young cats, who will appear depressed, refuse food, and may vomit white froth or yellow bile. The temperature can rise as high as 105°F (40.5°C) in the early stages, then quickly falls to subnormal. Dehydration is noticeable and rapid; the cat usually sits hunched up with its coat erect and staring, and its head drooping over its water bowl. It may look as though it intends to drink, but instead may gulp, or lick its lips. If touched or lifted, it may cry out in pain, and its body feels cold and rigid in contrast with its normal warmth and suppleness. The virus attacks sites of white blood cell production, hence the alternative name Panleucopenia. If the cat lives for more than a few days, diarrhea may develop.

Early treatment is essential for survival. Antibiotics to counter secondary infections and warm liquids given intravenously with constant careful nursing may stem the course of the disease. All wastes must be burned and all equipment kept sterile. The nurse should wear disposable or easily sterilized clothing when handling the sick cat and contact with all other felines should be avoided during the course of the illness and the subsequent period of

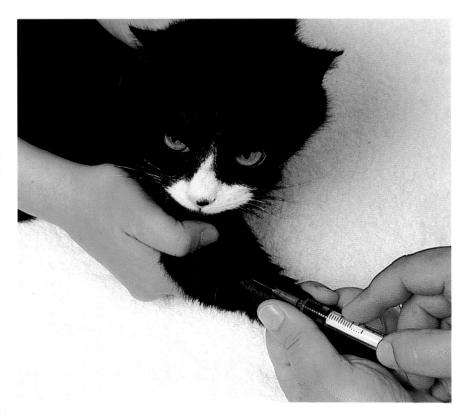

quarantine. The mortality rate is very high and cats that do very slowly recover may shed viruses for some time, and therefore must be isolated from any chance of contact with other felines. The virus, which is impervious to most disinfectants, can be transmitted by airborne particles, on hands, clothes, or through fleas, and can survive away from a host for a considerable time. Vaccination is essential as the only effective way of combating the disease.

Feline Leukemia Virus (FeLV) is a contagious disease that is transmitted mainly when shed in saliva. Fortunately it cannot live long outside the cat. It can cause arthritic diseases, breeding problems, red blood cell abnormalities,

tumors, and immunosuppression in addition to leukemia, so the symptoms are very variable. There may be gradual weight loss or difficulty in breathing, but many cats show no signs of infection and the effects are comparable to those of FIV (see above) and human AIDS. Cats developing recurrent infections or who are slow to recover from a disease are tested for the virus. A vaccine, though not 100% effective, gives protection if given prior to exposure. Many adult cats, if exposed to infection in small doses, develop their own antibodies, but young cats are particularly vulnerable.

Cats in catteries and colonies are particularly susceptible; vaccination and regular testing is the only way to

left: *A young cat suffering from advanced Feline Infectious Peritonitis, when the disease has begun to produce abdominal swellings and inflammatory growths.*

eliminate the disease from them. Those being boarded or attending shows should, therefore, always be vaccinated.

Feline Infectious Peritonitis (FIP), a strain of Coronavirus, is usually associated with intestinal disease. It is most frequently seen in young cats. Carrier cats are thought to be important in spreading the disease, which is probably most commonly passed orally. Initial symptoms are lethargy, loss of appetite, and fever. It may then develop either as a

"wet" form with a buildup of fluid in the abdomen, which becomes distended; alternatively, this disease can develop as "dry" form, with symptoms according to the organs affected. These might include include poor coordination, paralysis, deafness, degenerative blindness, or kidney disease. FIP is generally fatal and only in its terminal stage can a positive diagnosis be reached. A vaccine has been released in the U.S.A. that has had limited success.

Feline Viral Rhinotracheitis (FVR) and **Feline Calicivirus (FCV)** are both diseases of the upper respiratory tract caused by viruses, and vaccines are available to give protection from them. In cat colonies especially, many clinically healthy cats carry the disease and continue to shed the virus, especially at times of stress. The main signs are fever, sneezing, saliva hanging from the mouth, conjunctivitis, discharges from the nose and eyes, and often a cough in addition. FCV is usually milder, and sometimes the only sign is ulceration of the tongue or paws.

Antibiotics are given to counter the secondary effects of these diseases, and vitamins are used to counter depression and stimulate appetite. Suspected cases should be taken to the veterinarian by appointment so that they can avoid contact with other cats. Stricken cats must be isolated and require careful nursing, and may have to be hand fed and helped to the litter box or they may be incontinent. Many cats overcome cat flu, even if they have also had pneumonia, and are completely restored to health. Others are left with permanent after-effects such as sinusitis, permanently damaged eyelids or conjunctiva, "snuffles," noisy breathing, or a persistent cough. Some cats have periods in which they seem perfectly well, only showing signs of these after-effects in cold, damp weather, or when they are subjected to any form of stress. The majority of recovered cats remain carriers of the disease.

Rabies is also a viral disease. It is transmitted in the saliva from the bite of an infected animal. Cat-to-cat transmission is rare, and in the United States bats seem to be the main source of infection. When introduced to the body, the virus invades the nervous tissues, producing the disease and culminating in a particularly

left: *A vet may take a blood sample to help with the diagnosis, or to confirm the indications given by physical and behavioral symptoms.*

right: *A Chinchilla Persian with breathing difficulties, a symptom of cat flu.*

below: This cat's eyes already show that it is sick, and its nasal discharge may indicate a case of one of the respiratory diseases commonly known as cat flu.

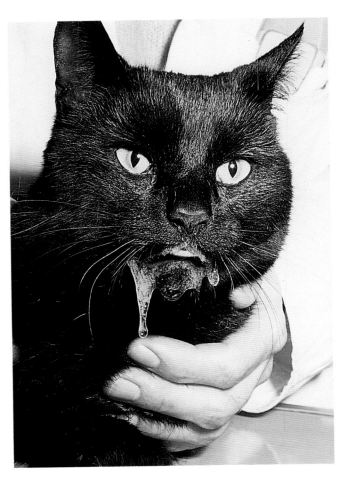

right: Heavy strings of saliva hanging from the mouth are another symptom that may indicate cat flu.

dreadful death. Quarantine regulations have kept some countries free from its menace—notably Britain, Australia, New Zealand, and the U.S. state of Hawaii. The incubation period depends on the distance of the site of a bite from the central nervous system and can be from 9 to 60 days or possibly as long as six months; hence the long periods of confinement in quarantine quarters enforced by various governments. In many countries where rabies occurs (including the other U.S. states), vaccination is compulsory by law.

The first symptoms of rabies are subtle changes in the animal's temperament, with a tendency to hide, a slight temperature rise, and dilation of the pupils. This stage lasts for about three days, after which the excitative stage develops. During the next four days the cat becomes increasingly nervous and irritable, showing exaggerated responses to sounds and lights. It then becomes increasingly aggressive and will attack and bite other cats, dogs, or humans that are foolish enough to approach it. Eventually all muscular control is lost; the jaw droops, and the cat salivates uncontrollably; paralysis spreads throughout the body; and death follows two or three days later. This final stage is known as dumb rabies and in some cases none of the earlier symptoms appear. There is no effective treatment for this disease at present.

Feline Immunodeficiency Virus (FIV), cat AIDS, like the human disease, affects the immune system, preventing it from fighting back against other diseases. It was not discovered until 1987, although it had been present in cat populations since the early 1970s, and is still not fully understood. It is thought to be transmitted mainly in the saliva through bites. It is a relatively unstable virus and cannot survive long in the environment, and transmission through feeding bowls and contact is not thought to be an important mode of transmission. The virus may be passed between mother and fetus, but the significance of this is not yet clear.

Once infected, a cat's immune system cannot eliminate this virus. Infected cats initially show a mildly raised temperature that lasts a few weeks, with enlarged lymph nodes that may persist for several months. After this initial infection there is a latent phase with no clinical signs, but after a time signs of immunosuppression become apparent as the virus destroys the white blood cells called lymphocytes that are involved in the immune response. Symptoms are varied, dependent on the secondary disease present. Typical manifestations include gingivitis, stomatitis, ocular signs, weight loss, chronic diarrhea, fever, pneumonia, and tumors. FIV is suspected when an animal suffers repeatedly from infections or fails to recover from an infection. There are a

right: A cat with an ulcerated tongue; this can be a symptom of several diseases.

below: Gingivitis produces a red line of inflammation running along the gums next to the teeth. It is a symptom of a number of conditions.

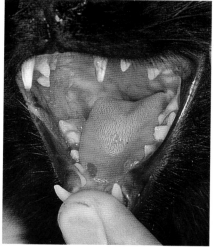

number of diagnostic tests available, but no known treatment and as yet no vaccine. Expensive drugs, such as AZT, can slow the progress of the disease but not cure it. Castration to reduce aggressive behavior and restriction to supervised outdoor access are measures for stemming the spread of the disease. Transmission risks are low in a peaceful multi-cat household.

Diseases of the digestive system

Mouth infections Injuries, bacteria, viruses, and fungal infection can all cause inflammation and infection in the mouth. Bad breath, dribbling, and loss of appetite all suggest mouth infection, and bleeding gums or gingivitis, a reddening along the gum next to the teeth, may be present. Gingivitis is most often seen in cats when plaque builds up on the teeth, undermining the gums and exposing the roots of the teeth. If untreated, teeth can become loose and fall out, or abscesses develop at their roots. Affected cats often grind their teeth, salivate, and go off their food. Most cats need dental scaling and polishing at some point in their lives, after which dry food is often recommended to provide abrasion and reduce buildup of plaque.

Gastritis is inflammation of the stomach, commonly caused by an unbalanced diet, swallowed irritants licked off coat or paws, bacteria, parasites, or hairballs. The main symptom is vomiting, which is often clear and frothy, sometimes bright yellow, occasionally bloodstained. However, vomiting is a symptom of many things, usually not one of those which cause gastritis, including obstructions and organ failure, and diseases such as FIE and hepatitis. If a cat vomits once or twice over a period of a couple of days the best advice is to starve the cat for 24

hours, then give it a bland diet for a few days. Naturally, if the vomiting persists, a veterinarian should be consulted. Hairballs can be avoided by regular grooming, and giving mildly laxative food to such cats during the seasons they are shedding their hair.

Enteritis is inflammation of the intestine; when both stomach and intestine are affected it becomes gastroenteritis. The first sign is diarrhea. Some cats are constipated and may vomit in the early stages, then develop diarrhea. The diarrhea may be very pale and milky, it may be bright yellow, or it may be very much darker than a normal stool, possibly with signs of blood. Boiled water should be given to prevent dehydration while waiting for veterinary assistance.

There are many causes of enteritis in the cat, but the symptoms must not be ignored. If the animal passes a loose stool but otherwise appears well, it should be observed for twenty-four hours, and given plenty of fluids but no solid food. If the cat also vomits, then small drinks only should be given. The chances are that the cat will be back to normal the following day and was merely reacting to having eaten something disagreeable, such as a poisoned flying insect. Some common cleaners, polishes, disinfectants, and air sprays produce these enteric

symptoms in cats. Any cat that regularly has mild attacks of diarrhea or vomiting should be examined by a veterinarian.

Feline infectious enteritis (FIE, see page 146) and other viral diseases, bacteria such as Salmonella and Escherichia coli (both transmissible to humans), and various other causes, including worm infestations in kittens, can also produce enteritis.

Fortunately, acute diarrhea is more often a reaction to a sudden change of diet, but persistent diarrhea may have a number of causes that need treatment. There is serious danger of dehydration; careful nursing will be needed.

Diseases of the uro-genital system

Kidney failure can occur in an acute form due to toxins such as ethyl glycol, heavy metals, some drugs, and bacterial infections, but can also be caused when a reduced blood supply to the kidneys is the result of severe dehydration, hemorrhage, heart failure, or obstructions to the urine outflow. Symptoms are depression, increased thirst, loss of appetite, occasional vomiting, and the production of small amounts of highly concentrated urine. The cat usually sits in a typical, hunched-up position, crying when touched or lifted. Ulceration of the mouth may prevent the cat from drinking, and immediate treatment is required. If recognized in time it is reversible. Recovery is slow and is maintained by a special low-protein diet.

Chronic kidney failure is common in elderly cats. The cat drinks excessively, and is particularly partial to water from puddles, fish ponds, and flower vases. Large quantities of pale urine are passed, the cat may have offensive breath, and the mouth becomes ulcerated. The condition known as uremia sets in when the kidneys fail to filter the waste products from the blood, and the cat begins to vomit, and appears anemic.

Affected cats can be fed on a special diet that provides good quality protein reducing metabolic waste, and is low in phosphates to reduce the release of calcium from the bones, which aggravates the condition.

Feline Lower Urinary Tract Disease (FLUTD) is common in cats, particularly lazy overweight ones, that are fed on a dry diet with little water intake. They visit the litter box frequently but after squatting and straining pass only a

above: Excessive straining in the litter box or attempting to urinate or defecate without result can be as important a symptom to report as diarrhea or vomiting.

right: The swollen abdomen of this cat is due to fluid and one cause could be pyometra, though swelling is not always noticeable in this condition.

small amount of urine that may be streaked with blood. The straining is often accompanied by a moan or cry of pain. Crystals are usually present in the urine. If urinary retention is severe, the bladder can be felt like a hard, round ball. At this stage they need gentle handling on the way to the veterinarian because the bladder may rupture.

In males and very occasionally in females the urethra becomes blocked with crystals. If they are not removed the bladder will rupture. The obstruction is removed by catheterization and a diet prescribed to prevent reoccurrence. In cases where the crystals cannot be dissolved they may require surgical removal.

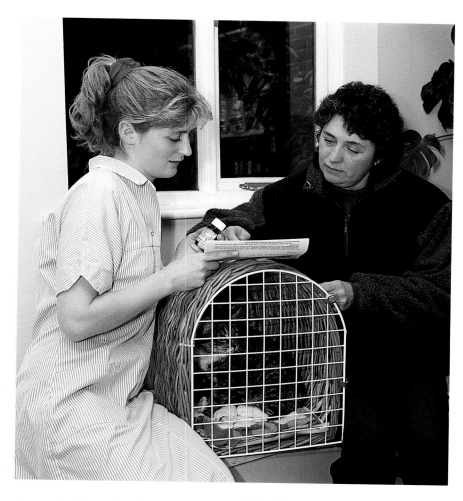

Uterine disorders After kittening, puperial metritis can occur due to retention of a placenta or a dead kitten. The cat attempts to wash her genitals and then stops, turns away and gives a plaintive cry, and there is an offensive discharge. Urgent treatment is then required to save the queen and her kittens.

In older, nonbreeding queens a condition known as pyometra can occur. Pus forms in the uterus and the abdomen distends. The cat is depressed, is thirsty, but refuses to eat, has a high temperature, and may vomit.

Endometritis, an inflammation of the uterine lining, may occur for no apparent reason in females of all ages and is the most important cause of reproductive failure. Repeated abortions, stillbirths, and vaginal discharge all suggest it. If untreated it often develops into pyometra. If treatment is not successful, spaying may become necessary.

Skin diseases

The majority of skin problems in cats is due to parasites or allergies. Sometimes hair follicles become blocked. This usually occurs on the chin, producing blackheads that can be treated by washing with soap and water (see page 137). If it is complicated by bacterial infection, which can also produce pus in the follicles, veterinary help will be needed. Excessive licking, usually in areas easily reached by the tongue such as groin, inner leg, or belly, can produce a raised, wet, swollen area known as a lick granuloma, which is usually treated with corticosteroids. In linear granuloma, cause unknown, raised, pinkish-yellow nodules appear on the skin. It is treated in the same way.

In a few cases, mainly neutered shorthairs, some temporary hair loss occurs, possibly due to hormonal imbalance. A more common condition is a

swelling, or hematoma, caused by bleeding from a broken blood vessel, usually on the ear.

Skin allergies can have several causes, including a reaction to foods, inhalation of particles, contact with foreign substances (that frequently turn out to be dyes in fabrics or domestic cleaners and polishes), parasites, and other causes. The most common types of reaction are known as Miliary dermatitis and Symmetrical Alopecia, both resulting from an allergy causing itchiness. Cats suffering from allergic reactions tend to overgroom rather than to scratch, so the condition is often unnoticed because it is interpreted as a healthy cat being very clean.

In Miliary dermatitis, crusty lesions usually appear around the base of the tail, neck, and spine. These are associated with broken shafts of hair and hair loss. With Symmetrical Alopecia, broken shafts are located around the inner thigh and the rear of the abdomen. They can be distinguished from hormonal hair loss because the shafts are still actively growing.

External parasites can be diagnosed by taking coat brushings or skin scrapings. Evidence of fleas is very easy to find, even if the fleas themselves are not evident, in the black specks of flea feces. If you have any doubt as to what these are, drop them into water or onto damp paper, and a brown or bloody discoloration will be seen. Flea bites are a considerable component in the production of Miliary dermatitis, and treatments for other allergies should also ensure that the cat is rid of fleas.

PARASITES OF THE CAT

THERE ARE A NUMBER of parasites that live on the skin of the cat. Fleas, lice, and flies are all insects; mites and ticks are arachnids, related to the spider. Fungal infections can also feed off the cat's skin. Internal parasites include thread-worms, whipworms, and flukes, which rarely cause problems (though liver flukes are considered an important cause of disease in Florida and the Bahamas), and a variety of other worms detailed below. Some single-celled protozoans can also affect a cat. Isopora, which burrows into the intestine wall, usually has no ill effects, but in kittens can sometimes cause enteritis. Toxoplasma, although again often having no ill effects on the animal, can be a dangerous infection for pregnant women to catch.

right: Flea larvae are not easy to see, except under the microscope as here. Droppings are more noticeable, but the almost certain presence of eggs and larvae means that treatment must be repeated to kill them when they become adult.

External parasites

Fleas bite and suck blood. They are not limited to one host, although they prefer a particular species, and can transfer themselves with enormous leaps. They actually spend most of their time off the host and can lay eggs either on the skin or in the environment, such as on bedding. Typical signs are a cat scratching its neck, twitching muscles along its spine, or when it often turns to bite at the base of its tail. Small black grits can be found on the skin at the base of the ears and along the spine near the tail root.

Remove fleas with the fingers or a fine-toothed comb. Crush immediately. Coat and bedding need to be treated with insecticidal products. Check regularly for any signs of reinfestation.

Lice are host specific and spend all their life on the cat and spread only by direct contact. One kind sucks tissue fluid and blood, another eats hair and dead skin.

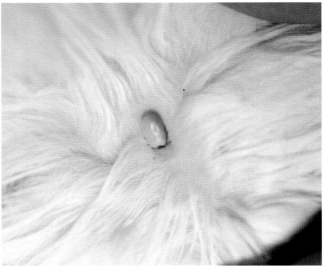

left: Ticks are easily visible when inspecting a cat's fur. Never try to just pull them off. Their tenacious jaws may stay in the skin and cause an infected wound. A dab of rubbing alcohol will make them release their grip.

They are rare except on cats who are failing to groom themselves properly, with young cats being more severely affected. Signs of infestation are when the cat scratches its head and neck. Slow-moving, pear-shaped yellowish-white lice may be seen in the coat, looking like scurf. Tiny, clear, bead-like eggs (nits) are cemented to individual hairs.

The coat should be sprayed, dusted, or bathed with prescribed insecticide. Hairs with nits should be combed out and burned. Then check the animal regularly for any reinfestation.

Ticks are rare on cats but can be picked up from vegetation outdoors. They seem to cause no irritation or distress, although since they suck blood may be

right: Excessive scratching is a symptom to look out for. It is a sign of fleas and other parasites and, directed to the ear, of otodectic mange.

debilitating. They are seen during grooming as a blue-gray wart-like growth attached to the skin.

Most flea treatments kill them, or a dab of rubbing alcohol will make them relax their jaws and they can be picked off with tweezers—do not just pull them off or the jaws may remain in the skin.

Harvest mites (red bugs, chiggers) inject their saliva and then suck back the resulting "soup." They are parasitic only in their young stages. Infested cats may hold down their ears, scratch their heads, or bite their toes. On examination the tiny mites can be seen as orange-red specks clustered closely together, usually on the ear flaps or between the toes. Most flea treatments will kill them.

Mange mites—there are several types of mite whose infestation is commonly called mange, some dealt with separately below. One kind, Noteoedric mange, is highly contagious to other animals and people. Fortunately rare, it is caused by a burrowing mite whose entire two- to three-week life cycle is spent on the host. Hairs break off and lesions usually appear on the head and neck, with reddening of the skin and visible scales and crust formation.

The cat must be isolated and the affected skin softened with soap and water before applying skin preparations. Treatment is repeated at intervals until new growth of hair indicates the final destruction of the mites.

Also uncommon, Demodetic mange produces lesions around the cat's eyes and occasionally on the forelegs. More generally, scaling of the skin is common, with itching that makes the cat constantly scratch. Treatment is with skin applications.

Cheyletiella mites live on the skin of many different animals and are not strictly species specific. Dandruff, especially along the upper part of the back, is the most common sign, and may then lead to miliary dermatitis, but sometimes a cat scratches continuously with no other symptoms. Owners may develop a rash on their wrists, chest, and stomach. The mite is identified from skin scrapings and coat brushings. Insecticide kills the mites but must be reapplied after an interval.

Ear canker is produced by Otodectes—ear mites, which can sometimes also spread to the head and body, but they usually live and breed deep inside the ear, causing intense irritation. The cat will shake its head and vigorously scratch at the back of its ears, which accumulate dark brown exudate in the ear canal. When this is removed the tiny white parasites may be visible. Secondary infections quickly invade the inflamed ear, so rapid treatment is necessary.

The exudate is removed and ascaricidal drops applied, then antibiotic cream is applied to treat any secondary infection, in severe cases even before the mites

left: Dirty wax buildup inside the ear is an indication of ear mite infestation.

have been eradicated. Repeat applications are necessary, but veterinary instructions must be followed carefully. The drops can dry out the ear canal and interfere with natural wax secretion. These mites are contagious; irrespective of which one appears infected, always treat both ears, and those of any other cats and dogs in the household.

Ringworm is not a worm but a fungal infection that appears, mainly around the nose, lips, forehead, front legs, and claw beds, as small circular or oval lesions, sometimes like pimples with small scabs, with broken hair shafts within each "ring." Alternatively, there may be clumps of apparent dandruff spreading like cigarette ash on the skin, or as small white scales clustered around small clumps of hair. Some cats are symptomless carriers, and lesions are discovered on human members of the family before the disease is suspected in the cat. Ringworm will often produce fluorescence under ultraviolet light, but diagnosis is confirmed by microscopic examination of infected hair or if necessary by growing cultures.

Treatment is a fungicidal antibiotic that is given orally for up to six weeks with a variety of lotions and creams. Strict isolation and quarantine procedures must be carried out when cats are affected with this serious disease. Shed hair and bedding should be burned and other equipment disinfected with formalin as instructed by the veterinarian.

below: To treat ear mites, ascaricidal drops are squeezed into the ear and then spread around it by gently massaging around the base of the ear.

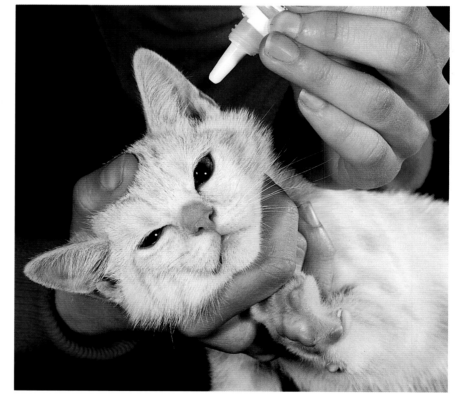

Internal parasites

Roundworms are common in the domestic cat. Only major infestations will do much harm to adults unless they are suffering from some other debility. They can, however, be serious in kittens, who can pick them up from their mother. They can also make it more difficult to deal with any other infection. Roundworms in the stomach are often vomited by the cat and curl up like thin corkscrews of spaghetti, usually about 3 in. (75 mm) long, although they can be twice that length. Eggs are passed in the feces. Roundworms are to be suspected if a cat or kitten has diarrhea, a potbelly, loses good coat condition, and seems fussy with its food. Kittens especially

left: A louse egg attached to a cat's fur, greatly enlarged. To the naked eye they look like scurf, but may be seen to slowly move.

left: Cheyletiella mites produce a layer of dandruff that can be seen on the skin when the fur is parted.

may sometimes cough and there may also be bad breath.

Queens should always receive a course of worming pills well before mating takes place. Young kittens should be wormed under veterinary care, while still nursing if necessary. The treatment usually works at four weeks, then every two weeks until five months, then every eight weeks until a year. Outdoor cats should routinely be wormed three or four times a year, and indoor cats at least once. Your veterinarian will recommend what is best for your area and your cat. Prescribed treatments will usually deal with a range of worm infections; some pet shop pills do not.

Tapeworms live in the intestines of cats. Their eggs are ingested by eating intermediate hosts such as fleas and ticks, or in some species rodents, and develop to adulthood in the cat. Egg-bearing segments of worm break off, are excreted, and can often be found looking like grains of rice in fur around the anus. This may be the only sign of infection, but sometimes the nictitating membrane will be raised, the cat may seem restless and eat a great deal though still seeming in poor condition. The chances of infection are minimized by keeping a cat flea-free and preventing it from eating carcasses of wild animals, and by routine worming; outdoor cats three to four times a year, indoor ones annually.

Coccidia are a range of protozoan parasites that burrow into the lining of the cat's intestines and cause coccidiosis, a condition fairly common in kittens that are kept in overcrowded, unhygienic conditions. Affected kittens may show no symptoms, but with major infestations they will often vomit, especially on waking in the morning. They will also produce offensive, often blood-stained diarrhea, become anemic, and look pale around the lips. If they are not treated, they become increasingly emaciated. Fortunately, good hygiene will reduce the infestation and prevent any reinfection.

Toxoplasma is another protozoan parasite that may be carried with no ill effects but is dangerous to pregnant women. In an acute form in young cats it can produce loss of appetite, fever, jaundice, breathing difficulties, diarrhea, and vomiting, lasting for about two weeks before the cat succumbs. In older cats it may take a chronic form with some of these symptoms developing gradually. Eventually the disease attacks the nervous system, causing fits, blindness, and heart failure. Some treatment is possible but not usually recommended because of the public health risk.

Heartworms are roundworms transmitted by mosquito bites whose normal host is the dog. Cats show no ill effects until, after six months, the parasite matures. They then affect heart action and circulation to the lungs, with symptoms ranging from none to severe breathing difficulties. Treatment at that stage is difficult because dead worms can block blood vessels.

Hookworms attach themselves to the bowel wall where they suck the blood of the animal. They then release an anticoagulant and when they move to a new site the old one continues to bleed. Their larvae may be eaten or burrow through the skin when picked up from damp infected ground. Some of the regular worming treatments will normally deal with them.

HOME NURSING

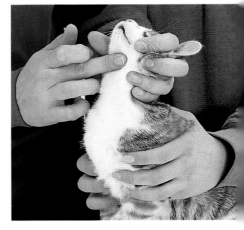

A SERIOUSLY INJURED or dangerously ill cat is better nursed in an animal hospital than at home where full facilities and skills are not available. However, many less serious cases can be cared for at home following the veterinarian's instructions, and efficient home nursing plays an important part in any cat's recovery from illness. Being close to friends and familiar smells and surroundings can reduce stress and give the cat valuable support. As well as providing adequate liquids and nourishing food, the cat must be kept clean and warm and its interest kept alive. Each illness has its own characteristics and special nursing that the veterinarian will explain. Strict quarantine is necessary with infectious diseases, and those handling the cat must change their outer clothing and wash their hands before making any contact with other cats. Sick cats should not be allowed outdoor access in case they hide themselves away, and doors and windows should be securely shut. The cat's bed should be in a quiet area that can be shielded from light. An infrared heat emitter suspended over the cat's bed may make it easier to maintain a suitable and even temperature.

General nursing

Most home nursing is an extension of general cat care. The cat will probably need help with grooming, or even rely on the owner entirely for its cleanliness which is important in maintaining its will to live as well as its comfort and hygiene. Sick cats are seldom very cooperative. They feel vulnerable and defensive, so always be wary of their claws and teeth if you have to handle them or do something for them they do not feel happy with. Some cats can be very trusting of people they know, but restraining their legs and claws in a towel until they feel confident about procedures can sometimes be necessary. If you need to restrain a cat use as little force as possible. Stroke it first to calm it. If you have it standing on a con-

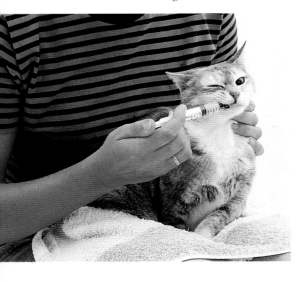

venient surface you may find it necessary only to hold its head with one hand while your forearm holds its body against your side. For more rigid control hold it by the scruff of the neck in one hand while restraining its legs with the other.

To groom a sick cat follow the same procedures as you would for a healthy cat but paying particular attention to the eyes, ears, nose, mouth, and the hair around the urinary and anal passages, which should be washed with warm water and a diluted cat-safe antiseptic. Dry surfaces carefully afterward. If there is any inflammation of the eyes, nostrils, or lips, the veterinarian may suggest applying an antibiotic ointment or clear petroleum jelly.

A sick cat that will not eat or has difficulty in eating may have to be fed by syringe. Going for a day or two without food is not life threatening, and in many cases it may be preferable to force feeding a reluctant animal, but dehydration is dangerous, so liquids should be administered. In both cases, soft food or liquid is drawn into a syringe and given in the same way as described below for medi-

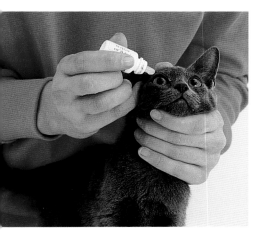

cines. Give only a little at a time and then a little more when that has been swallowed. Small pellets of food can also be administered like pills.

Giving medication orally

Liquid medicines are most easily given with a syringe, as anyone who has tried to spoon liquid into a cat's mouth will know. A syringe is not a hypodermic needle but a tube with a plunger that can be filled with liquid by inserting the nozzle and pulling up the plunger. Syringes come in various sizes and are often marked with scales that make it possible to measure an exact dose. Hold the cat with one hand behind the neck and the fingers gently tilting the head upward, then insert the nozzle of the syringe between the side teeth with the mouth shut. Slowly push down the plunger to discharge the liquid. Make sure you see the cat swallow it.

The cat's mouth must be open to give it a pill. Hold the head from behind with fingers and thumbs stretching around to either side of the mouth, then apply a gentle pressure with the tips of the fingers and thumb. This will make the cat open

its mouth. Hold the pill between finger and thumb of the other hand and press on the lower jaw with the ring finger while popping in the pill as far back on the tongue as possible. Close the mouth and hold it closed while stroking downward on the throat. Make sure that the pill has been swallowed before releasing the cat. Some cats give the appearance of swallowing and as soon as you are not looking spit it out, so keep watching for a few moments afterward. If you find even this simple action difficult to handle there are pill "guns" commercially available that consist of a short tube that you insert into the cat's mouth and push the plunger to release the pill.

Ear and eye medications

These usually come as ointment or liquid that can be squeezed out of tubes or plastic containers. If necessary, clean the eyes first with moistened cotton. From behind the cat, grip it firmly around the muzzle with one thumb above the eye. Lift the eyelid with a finger and squeeze the medication onto the cornea. Make sure only the medication, not the container, makes contact with the eye.

To give ear drops, restrain the cat and turn the head to one side, folding back the ear a little if necessary to ensure that the drops enter it properly. Gently massage behind the ear to spread the drops.

Administering food by a syringe

If a cat finds difficulty in eating, it may be necessary to administer food directly into the mouth with a syringe. Owners should learn to do this as well as how to give pills, medicines, and ear drops.

Bandages

When applying or changing bandages, do not make them so loose that they fall or can be pulled off, nor so tight that they restrict circulation. Tube bandages can be very useful on limbs. Do not secure bandages with pins, but tie them or secure them with a piece of adhesive tape. If bandaging the end of a paw, start with a vertical piece down the paw, around it and up again before circling the paw again. To cover the abdomen, a cloth that is cut into points at either side can be wrapped beneath and the points tied over the back. If a convalescent cat needs dressings and bandages changed, get the veterinarian or nurse to show you how.

"Elizabethan" collars

A collar will prevent a cat from licking off medication or a dressing. These are available in plastic but can be improvised in cardboard. Cut a circle 12 in. (30 cm) across, then cut out a 4 in. (10 cm) circle at its center. Remove a one-quarter to one-third segment from the ring. Fit it around the cat's neck, lacing or taping the straight edges together.

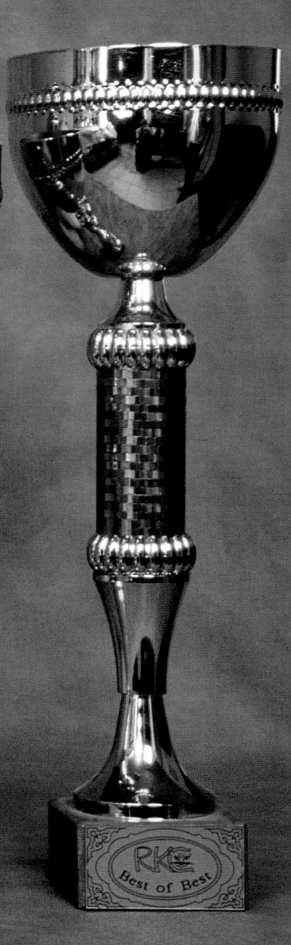

Part Six:
Shows and Showing

THE CAT FANCY

As LONG AGO AS 1598, at the annual St. Giles Fair in Winchester, England, prizes were given to cats competing for best ratter and best mouser, but the first cat show in the modern sense was held at London's Crystal Palace in 1871. It was organized by artist and animal lover Harrison Weir to show different colors, markings, and breeds of cat. An entry of 170 cats and kittens included Siamese, a French-African cat with soft brown fur, and an enormous English tabby weighing 21 lbs. (9.5 kg). Cats were entered according to color, and prizes included one for the fattest cat. This show's success soon led to many others being staged, including the first bench show in America, at Madison Square Garden, New York, in 1895.

It was about the time of these first shows that planned breeding began. The owners of unusual cats started to keep careful records, and so the first written pedigrees were established for cats. Groups interested in the same type of cat formed clubs, and societies of the Cat Fancy came into being.

Governing Bodies

The National Cat Club was formed in Britain in 1887 and published the first stud book in 1895. Most clubs in Britain ran shows under its rules. A rival club appeared in 1896, but in 1910 they joined forces with the Governing Council of the Cat Fancy (GCCF) which controlled all cat affairs in Britain for the next 73 years, until a parallel organization, the Cat Association of Britain (CA) was set up in 1983.

The American Cat Association (ACA) was the first American registry, active since 1899, but there are now a number of North American bodies, often with reciprocal arrangements so that the Canadian cats can be shown in the U.S.A. and vice versa. The largest is the Cat Fanciers' Association (CFA); others include the Canadian Cat Association (CCA), Cat Fanciers' Federation (CFF), The International Cat Association (TICA), United Cat Federation (UCA), American Cat Council (ACC, which holds "British-style" shows), and the American Association of Cat Enthusiasts (AACE, which organizes shows for breeds that are not accepted by larger organizations).

Australia, New Zealand, and South Africa all have their own bodies, many of which follow GCCF rules.

In Europe, many countries have at least two cat bodies, one of them usually affiliated to the Federation International Feline (FIFe). The CA, FIFe and many

left: A show winner
proudly displays his
championship trophies.

left and below: A handsome
Persian bicolor, winner of the
Cat of the Year at the National
Show in London.

U.S. associations have programs for training judges, with tough examination. GCCF judges do not have to qualify in an academic way, but breeders of long standing, experienced in stewarding for existing judges and approved by their breed clubs, are nominated as potential judges. If approved by a Council meeting they become probationers judging kittens, and later progress to full judges.

Recognized Breeds

Each Cat Fancy, or governing body, has its own list of recognized breeds and varieties and sets rules for the way in which they must be bred. They also draw up standards of perfection for each variety, with a points score allocated for each of a cat's features. These sometimes vary between countries and between bodies in the same country. The overall picture of breeds standards is given in Part Two: Cat Breeds of the World, but anyone seeking to register or show a cat under the auspices of a particular body should obtain that body's official standards for, as well as variations between, bodies; amendments are sometimes made as a breed becomes more established or new colors judged acceptable.

Different organizations have different requirements for recognizing a new breed of cat. In general, they require evidence that a new breed is distinctly different from any variety already recognized. They also usually ask that it has bred true over a minimum number of generations (enough to produce at least 100 viable examples in the case of the CFA), and that it has no harmful defects or handicaps.

Breeding Programs

Occasional mutations occur, such as the folded ears of the Scottish Fold or the curled hair of the Rex cats, that can form the basis of a new breed, but most new breeds are based on existing breeds or breed types. Despite the many established varieties to choose from there are still more not yet created.

Registration of a cat's pedigree, its family tree for the preceding generations, enables breeders to trace blood lines and identify the potential generic makeup of each cat.

With careful planning, a color, type of coat, or other physical characteristic can be introduced from one breed to another and, by careful pairing, become firmly established to breed true through genetic inheritance. Nevertheless, such breeding programs must follow rules laid down by registration bodies. Even in the breeding of established varieties only certain cross-matings are allowed, while others are taboo.

CAT SHOWS

IN BRITAIN SHOWS ARE normally one-day events, but in Europe and the United States of America, two-day shows are common. American shows and those of the CA in Britain consist of several "rings," each of which is a small show within a show. This allows exhibitors to get the very best value for their money by enabling cats to be judged on open-breed competition for championships, without the need to go to several shows on different days and at different venues.

Shows may be all-breed affairs, or specialized shows for Longhairs, Shorthairs, or specific breeds. Some smaller shows are really only social affairs, with no meaningful awards, such as championship certificates, ribbons, or points being awarded. A few shows are designed for the assessment and authentications of new breeds or color varieties of existing breeds. Many shows also allow non-pedigree cats to take part.

The largest cat show in the world is run under GCCF rules and takes place in London each year. It is organized by the National Cat Club, the same club that started it all in 1887. Over 2,000 cats take part, and each is judged in one open or breed class, plus a range of miscellaneous classes, and some offered by specialized breed clubs. Despite its size, this show has no climax, such as the Best in Show or Supreme award. The GCCF hold a Supreme Show each year that is unlike any other cat show in the world. Entrants must qualify by winning open breed classes at previous shows. They are judged in rings, in a fashion similar to that used in some American shows, and special awards are offered to winners. The cats are exhibited in decorated pens in the main body of the hall while awaiting judgment in the ring, and the climax of the day comes with the awarding of the supreme rosettes to the Best Cat, Best Kitten, and Best Neuter of the pedigree exhibits, and to the Best Non-Pedigree Kitten and Neuter.

The CFA also has a National Invitational Show that is the culmination of the Regional Qualifying shows held in October each year. Winners at the

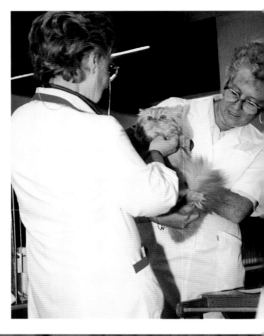

below: *Judges tour the benched cages to judge the cats at shows run under the GCCF rules. Owners are not allowed to be present when judging is taking place.*

below right: *At British and American ring-judged shows cats are taken to the judges, and the public, including owners, can watch the judging in progress.*

right: *Judges make a very thorough appraisal of every cat to assess it according to the points system established for that breed.*

National Invitational Show can win substantial prizes as well as great prestige.

Ring-Judged Shows

In the United States, most cat shows are conducted on the open-ring system and this method has been adopted by the Cat Association of Britain. Open-ring judging is exciting for all participants. Exhibitors are able to dress their show cages, making them comfortable for the cats and colorful and interesting for the general public. They can include prizes won at previous shows and all sorts of information about their breed. Judges do not enter the body of the show hall, so there is no danger of them being influenced by a cat's previous triumphs or its ownership.

In American open-ring shows, the owners bring the cats to correspondingly numbered cages in the judging ring. The judge takes each cat in turn, assessing it before an enthralled audience and then awarding the placings. In British and Scandinavian open-ring shows, stewards carry the cats to the judging rings, while the anonymous and excited owners sit in the audience. Depending upon the rules of the association, judges write a points-score form, give only verbal critique, or they write a full critique for each cat. All but the very top awards are usually presented at the time of judging, and the owner or a steward can take the award back to the cat's own cage for display.

In most open-ring shows, cats may accrue points or certificates to earn titles on one day, reducing the stress and risk of infection from that of closed-ring shows where cats are usually only judged once and need to win at least three different shows to gain a major title.

In most European countries, ring judging is common, but the rings are isolated from the show hall and the judges work in private. The cats are brought to them by skilled stewards who carry the cats displayed along one forearm and gently restrain them with the opposite hand. In closed-ring judging the judges usually write a critique and allocate places that are marked on the critique forms. An official collects these and the show team distributes the certificates, ribbons, and rosettes.

On-Floor Judging

In On-floor judging, as practiced by the GCCF, the judging is carried out in the body of the show hall, with each cat sitting anonymously in the numbered pen and allowed only a white blanket, white litter box, and a water bowl. The judges go from cage to cage, each accompanied by a steward, taking out each cat to assess it. They then decide on the placing of exhibits and send official prize slips to an administration table for processing. Prize slips are then posted on an awards board, and the administrative team allocates prize cards and, at some shows, corresponding ribbons or rosettes, which are then placed on the show cages.

ENTERING A CAT SHOW

YOU CAN FIND OUT ABOUT cat registration bodies, cat clubs, breed societies, and forthcoming shows from the press, especially the specialized cat magazines and on the Internet. At a cat show you will not only see lots of cats but will be able to talk to breeders and other enthusiasts who will be a fount of information about the cat fancy in your region. The experience may make you want to exhibit your own cats.

It is usually necessary to have your cat registered with the appropriate body before entering a show run under its rules. However, most associations allow non-pedigree cats to be shown in household pet classes without being registered, although they may not be eligible to win any very special awards. A few associations, notably the TICA in the United States and CA in Britain, have special fac-

ilities for non-pedigrees to be registered and to compete for such titles as Master and Grand Master, CA Champion Pet, CA Grand Pet and CA Supreme Pet.

Membership of a club or association not only ensures that you can enter its shows and be eligible for its prizes but often brings other benefits: reduced entry fees, free vouchers for catalogs and show admission, and the opportunity to attend meetings and social events. Membership can be passive, or if you enjoy such things, you can participate in show administration and organization, introducing you to an absorbing and often very stimulating hobby.

Applying to enter

By contacting the relevant cat associations you can obtain an official show list, rules, and registration information. Then,

having decided on a show that interests you, you can write to the show manager or director for a schedule and information about the show in which you are interested. You will need to plan ahead as show entries may close well before the show date. In some smaller organizations this may only be three weeks or so before, but with larger shows it may be two months prior to the show date.

Study rules carefully, for they vary considerably. If you have any uncertainties ask the advice of an experienced exhibitor, or contact the show manager for help in filling out the forms. You need accurate details about your cat, so use its registration form for reference. Send the form with payment for appropriate fees to the show office, enclosing a stamped, self-addressed envelope if you need acknowledgment of entry or a reply to queries. You will usually be mailed a set of show documents prior to show day that you will need to take to the show. Sometimes this documentation is collected on arrival at the show hall.

Preparations for the show

Your first requirement will be to get your cat in peak condition. The cat should be wormed if necessary, and it is a good idea

above: *Lining up to be vetted-in before a popular show. Shows make considerable demands on both cats and their owners.*

right: *Some cats enjoy the experience of appearing in a show and remain unfazed by the process of judging.*

left: *A cat must be in top condition for a show, with preparations continuing up to the last minute.*

below: *For British shows under GCCF rules, cages must be undecorated; just a white blanket, bowls, and litter box. Each cat wears a tag with an identification number around its neck.*

to have the veterinarian check over its teeth, ears, and claws. (In the U.S.A. it is also necessary to clip the cat's claws before it is benched.) It is a gentle process to build up to peak condition for the show day. The cat's coat should be lightly but carefully groomed every day in the way recommended for its breed. Use a pad of cloth or a buffer to lightly bang the muscles of the shoulders, back, and thighs. This promotes good circulation and a bloom on the coat. All dead hair should be taken out, and the ears and claws should be kept very clean.

The cat should be friendly with all humans and ideally, should have been accustomed to being picked up by strangers. If a small pen can be obtained, the cat will benefit from being shut in this, perhaps at mealtimes, over a few days to get used to show conditions. Show cats need to travel well, so the cat should be accustomed to going in its carrier and being transported without any fuss. Some breeders even play noisy tapes of crowds at home to accustom their cats to the hustle and bustle of a show.

About five days before the show it is a good idea to give a shorthaired cat a bran bath and sometimes a shampoo. Shampoos are certainly advised for very pale shorthairs and all longhairs. Do not do it later than five days or the fur may still be too soft at show time. As a final stage, groom with grooming powder or talcum powder, which can be left on overnight, but ensure that it is completely brushed out before the show, as if any remains it could ruin your cat's chances.

As show day approaches, the show equipment as laid down in the rules must be prepared. In GCCF shows, in which show pens must be plain and anonymous, strict rules are laid down for what may be put in them. For other shows you will need to make provision for dressing the cage. The cat will need food, drinking water, and litter for its box, and if it has to wear a numbered tag or tally, you will need to attach a ribbon around its neck. This is something else that you must get your cat accustomed to. Take some favorite toys along too, although in the GCCF-type shows these may not be put in the pen until all the judging is completed.

On the eve of the show day the cat should be thoroughly groomed and inspected all over. All the equipment and any necessary documentation should be checked and packed, along with the cat's favorite food in a sealed container. Do not, however, feed fishy or strong-smelling food just before the show. It is a good idea to take along a small bottle or flask of water for filling the water bowl. Strange water can upset the digestion of some cats. Then make sure your cat gets a good night's sleep for an early start!

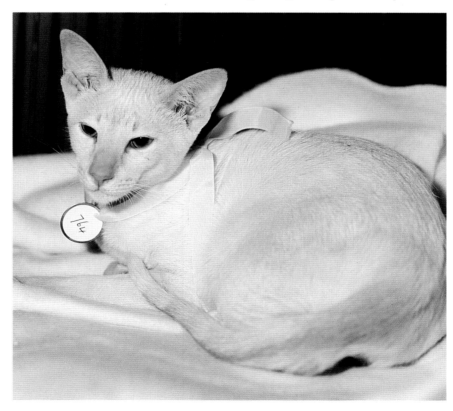

AT THE SHOW

AT MANY SHOWS and all British ones, all cats exhibited must pass a veterinary check on arrival. Cats that are dirty, show any symptoms of illness or parasites, signs of pregnancy or recent kittening, fail to have proof of necessary up-to-date immunization, or meet other conditions of the show will be refused entry. Since some cats can show signs of stress from their journey, these may be consigned to a quarantine area for a time to see if, for example, a high temperature falls once the cat has settled down. Any cat rejected on health grounds must produce a veterinary certificate of good health before it can enter another show.

Plan to arrive at the show hall for checking-in or vetting procedures as early as possible. If you can avoid the long wait in line you reduce the risk of infection through contact with other cats who do not pass the health check.

Inside the hall the array of numbered pens can be confusing, but if the numbers do not run consecutively, there is usually a floor plan on display. Stewards and officials wearing distinctive badges are generally on hand to help if asked, and most shows will also have an information table.

Having found the right pen, clean it or wipe it with disinfectant if you wish, although it will have been steam-sterilized before the show. If you have had a long journey your cat will almost certainly want to use its litter box, so put a little litter in first and after it has been used you can replace it with fresh litter for the rest of the day. Arrange the cat's equipment in the pen, then lightly groom the cat, settling it into place with much petting and coaxing. Stow its carrier and any spare bags neatly out of sight under the pen. In shows where the cats are taken to the judges it is now time to settle down to wait for the action.

In shows where the judges assess the cats at their pens, an announcement will be made to clear the show hall. When this comes it is important to go swiftly, making sure that nothing that can identify you or the cat is left on the pen. Rules may also require you to remove food from the pen while judging takes place. It is only a short time before the breed class results are posted on the awards boards, and the suspense ends as the cat's placing in the class can be seen.

After judging, or at the appointed time for the admission of the general public, it is permissible to go to the cat's pen to feed and reassure it and give it any toys you have brought along. Whether you win or lose, make sure your cat knows how much you appreciate it putting up with show conditions.

In some countries the judging of miscellaneous and other classes continues in the afternoon, but the hall is not cleared again. It is forbidden to speak to the judge or stewards while judging is in progress. However, most judges will be pleased to give a verbal opinion of your cat, if approached courteously when it is obvious that they have completely finished for the day.

In ring-judged shows, check for what times are estimated for when your classes will be judged, then keep your ears open for your cat's pen number to be called over the public address system. At this time, you (or when appropriate a steward) must take the cat to the ring and place it in an appropriately numbered pen behind the judging table. If your cat is entered in several classes, then it will be called separately for each class.

Whether they win or lose, most exhibitors thoroughly enjoy cat shows, and pack up their belongings, cat, rosettes, and ribbons at the close of the

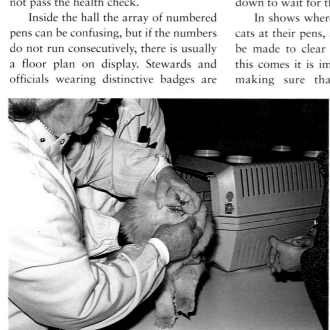

left: Vetting-in, when all cats are given a medical examination before being accepted as entrants.

left: *Cat shows not only give an opportunity to see the many different types of cats, but exhibitors include cat welfare organizations, specialized cat clubs, and accessory manufacturers.*

right: *National Cat of the Year at the National Cat Club 1998 show was this Tipped British Shorthair, seen with owner and judge Mrs. R. Gowdy.*
below: *With prizes.*

show, happy in the knowledge that they have taken an active part in an entertainment for hundreds of cat lovers. After the journey home you should allow your cat to rest for two or three days and watch carefully for any signs of infection picked up at the show or induced by the stress of the unaccustomed activity and exposure. If your cat does show any symptoms, you should seek veterinary advice and also inform the show organizer without delay. Luckily, due to veterinary inspection beforehand, very few cats contract any illnesses at shows.

Most cats enjoy the experience of a cat show and normally show no after effects. If, however, your cat is one of the few who hate every moment of the proceedings, do not subject it to any more such traumatic days. Instead, if you want to go on participating, buy a kitten to train for the show bench, or go to the shows in another capacity. Perhaps learn to steward, to act as an administrator or, if you are a good organizer, work toward becoming part of the all-important show team. Cat shows can add another dimension to the life of all who truly enjoy everything to do with cats.

GLOSSARY

Abscess *a localized collection of pus or matter, forming a lump under the skin. This usually results from a bite or other injury. If not treated it can burst and discharge.*

AACE *American Association of Cat Enthusiasts.*

ACA *American Cat Association.*

ACC *American Cat Council.*

ACF *Australian Cat Federation.*

ACFA *American Cat Fanciers Association.*

Affiliation *term applied to clubs and associations when attached to a larger governing body or other organizations.*

Affix *a cattery name used at the end of a cat's registered name. In the U.S. this is known as a suffix.*

Afterbirth *see placenta.*

Agouti *the wild type of coat pattern found in cats in which the hairs are banded, giving a ticked effect.*

AIF *Association International Féline.*

Albino *a cat with a lack of coloring due to a recessive gene, causing the coat to appear white (not to be confused with Dominant White).*

Allergy *a state of hypersensitivity that may be due to drugs, parasites, food, or cleaning materials.*

Alter *to neuter (see castration and spaying).*

Amnion *the fetal envelope enclosing the fetus.*

Amniotic fluid *surrounds the fetus, cushioning it and protecting it within the amnion. This fluid is seen when the amnion ruptures during the birth process; the term "waters have broken" is commonly used.*

Anestrus *the resting period of the estrus cycle.*

Anorexia *loss of appetite often associated with the onset of several feline diseases.*

Antibiotic *a chemical compound derived from or produced by living organisms and used in the treatment of infection.*

Antibody *a substance formed in the body to exert a specific destructive, restrictive, or protective action on invading bacteria, foreign proteins, or toxins.*

AOC *Any Other Color (term used in registrations and show literature by some bodies).*

AOV *Any Other Variety (term used as above).*

Ataxia *a loss of control of movement resulting in an unsteady or staggering gait. Found in some feline diseases or poisoning or following street accidents or concussion.*

Bacteria *types of microscopic organisms, some of which cause disease.*

Balanced *a term given to a cat with good proportions in relation to the standard of points for its particular breed or variety.*

Banding *areas of dark pigmentation in individual hairs of the cat's coat giving rise to the agouti effect.*

Barring *a form of tabby marking required on some tabby cats but considered a serious fault in self-colored (solid-colored) varieties.*

Benching *placing a cat or kitten, with all its show equipment, in its pen at the cat show, ready for judging.*

Bicolor *(bi-colour) a cat with patches of white and any other solid color*

Bite *the term given to the way in which the cat's jaws meet. The teeth should close together evenly when the bite is said to be "level."*

Blaze *a distinctive, contrasting mark running down the cat's face from forehead to nostrils. Usually found in tortoiseshell or particolored cats.*

Blotched *the term given to the tabby pattern, also known as "classic" or "marbled."*

Blowing-up *stud males are said to be showing this behavior when confronting another male or a female that smells of another male. The cat turns sideways to the animal it considers a threat, its coat becomes erect, and its jowls are puffed out. The ears are laid back and it growls deeply, with lip-smacking and some salivating. The cat is highly dangerous in this situation and will attack at the slightest provocation.*

Breech birth *when a kitten is presented with its rump first. When a kitten is presented with its hind feet first, it usually emerges without difficulty. A true breech birth may cause some difficulty in a young maiden queen.*

Brindling *is the effect caused when hairs of an incorrect color are interspersed in the coat. This effect is often seen after illness in some cats. For example, a Siamese may have many white hairs scattered among the colored hairs of its mask, and is then said to have a brindled face. Brindling is usually a temporary condition and is corrected at the next molt.*

Brush *the tail of a longhaired cat.*

Butterfly *the shape of the pattern of markings on the shoulders of blotched, classic, or marbled tabbies.*

CA *Cat Association of Britain*

CAC *Certificat d'Aptitude de Championnat.*

CACIB *Certificat d'Aptitude de Championnat International de Beaute.*

CACIP *Certificat d'Aptitude de Championnat International de Premier.*

Caesarean section *an operation performed to remove a queen's litter when she is unable to produce them in the normal way.*

Calico *an American name for the Tortie-and-White.*

Calling *the crying emitted by a female cat in estrus.*

Cameo *a series of cat varieties in which the orange and silver genes have been combined to give a beautiful two-layered "cameo" effect in the coat.*

Canker *usually refers to any inflammatory condition of the cat's ears, but most often associated with infestation by ear mites.*

Carrier (1) *any container used for the safe transport of a cat. It can be made of any suitable material such as mesh, wickerwork, fiberglass, wood, cardboard, or plastic.*

Carrier (2) *a cat that appears perfectly normal, but is able to infect other cats with disease, usually viral, e.g., cat flu. The animal may have contracted and recovered from the disease.*

Castration *the neutering or altering operation carried out on male cats.*

Catatonic state *a state of shock in which the cat is motionless and appears to be in a death-like trance.*

Cat door *a small hinged door made to allow a cat ready access to the yard or its run without opening the main door.*

Catnip *Nepeta cataria, or cat mint, contains a chemical substance that is attractive to cats. The dried leaves may be used as catnip to stuff small toys or to impregnate scratching posts.*

CC *an abbreviation for the Governing Council of the Cat Fancy's Challenge Certificate.*

CCA *Canadian Cat Association (Canada).*

CCFF *Crown Cat Fanciers Federation (U.S.A.) Now disbanded.*

CFA *Cat Fanciers Association (U.S.A.).*

CFF *Cat Fanciers Federation (U.S.A.).*

Champagne *the term given by some associations to a buff-cream coat.*

Champion *status earned by cats after completing a required number of specialized wins.*

Championship show *a show at which Championship points or certificates may be won.*

Chromosome *a structure within the nucleus of the cell, carrying genetic information. A cat has 19 pairs of chromosomes in each cell.*

CLA *Cat Lovers of America.*

Classic *a tabby pattern (see blotched).*

Cleft palate *a congenital abnormality in which the newborn kitten has a fissure in the roof of its mouth.*

Coarse *a term used to describe a cat that is larger or heavier than the ideal indicated by its breed standard.*

Cobby *the short-coupled, stocky effect as seen in American, British, Domestic, European, and Exotic Shorthairs.*

Colostrum *the first milk secreted by the cat after parturition, through which the kittens receive antibodies to protect them against infections.*

Colorpoints *Red, Tortie, and Tabby Pointed cats of Siamese type (U.S.A.)*

Colourpoints *Siamese or Himalayan patterned longhaired cats of (U.K.) Persian type.*

Cowhocked *a condition in which the cat's hocks turn in toward each other; a weakness.*

Cryptorchid *a male cat without descended testicles who cannot be used for breeding.*

Dam *mother cat.*

Dehydration *rapid loss of fluids from the body tissues during the course of some feline diseases.*

Dentition *the conformation of the cat's teeth.*

Dilution *a lighter color variation of standard feline color.*

Disinfectant *a substance used for cleaning; those used for catteries and in the home where cats are present must be carefully checked to ensure that they are nontoxic to the feline species.*

Dome *term given to the shape of certain cats' heads (see Burmese standard).*

Dominant factor *the member of an allelic gene pair which overrides the effects of the other (recessive) allele.*

Dominant genes in cats
Tabby is dominant to Non-Tabby.
Black is dominant to Chocolate.
Dense Color is dominant to Dilute Color.
Orange is dominant to Non-Orange.
White is dominant to Non-White.
Burmese is dominant to Siamese.
Self-Color is dominant to Himalayan.
Shorthair is dominant to Longhair.
Normal Coat is dominant to Rex Coat.
Manx is dominant to Normal Tail.

Double coat *having two thick coats in one, comprising a soft undercoat of thick, short hairs and another set of coarser, slightly longer hairs (Manx).*

Eclampsia *milk fever or lactational tetany.*

E. Coli *a bacterium which can cause gastro-enteritis.*

Entire *male or female cats that have not been altered or neutered.*

Estrus *the period of heat when the queen will mate. A queen in estrus is said to be "in heat," "on call," "calling," or "in season."*

Eumelanin *black or brown pigmentation.*

Experimental breeds *varieties being developed by breeders wishing to modify type or produce additional colors or coat patterns within existing breeds of cat.*

Fancier *one who breeds or exhibits cats as a serious hobby.*

Feral cat *a domestic cat that has reverted to the wild or has been born in the wild and is not domesticated.*

FeLV *Feline Leukemia Virus.*

FIE *Feline Infectious Enteritis/Parvovirus/Feline Panleucopenia.*

FIFE *Federation Internationale Feline d'Europe.*

FIP *Feline Infectious Peritonitis.*

FIV *Reline Immunodeficiency Virus (Cat AIDS).*

Flehmen reaction *seen when a cat savors an unusual or evocative scent. The head is raised and the mouth is held slightly open.*

FLUTD *Feline Lower Urinary Tract Disease.*

Flyer (1) *a cat that is an exceptional example of its breed, considered virtually unbeatable at shows.*

Flyer (2) *an announcement and full details of a cat show or other social event (U.S.A.).*

Foreign type *a cat with long, elegant lines and fine bones.*

Formalin *(formaldehyde solution B.P. 36%) is excellent for disinfecting in cases of viral and other disease; great care must be exercised in handling this substance. It must be diluted 1 part in 400 parts of water before use. It may also be used as a fumigant.*

FPL *Feline Panleucopenia (or Feline Infectious Enteritis).*

Frill *the fine hairs around the neck of a longhaired cat, forming a frame for the face and sometimes called the "ruff."*

Furball *fur swallowed by the cat during self-grooming that forms into a tightly packed ball in the stomach or bowels.*

FVR *Feline Viral Rhinotracheitis/ Herpesvirus.*

Gauntlets *the white glove-like markings on the legs of the Birman.*

GCACC *Governing Council of Associated Cat Clubs of South Africa.*

GCCF *Governing Council of the Cat Fancy (U.K.).*

Gene *each chromosome has many genes; each gene contributes a characteristic to the cat's makeup.*

Genotype *the genetic makeup of an individual cat.*

Gestation *the period of pregnancy from conception to birth, about 65 days in the cat.*

Ghost markings *the faint tabby markings that may be visible in the coats of young kittens of self-colored (solid-colored) breeds.*

Gingivitis *inflammation of the gums.*

Gloves *white feet as seen in Birman cats.*

Hairball *see furball.*

Haw *the nictitating membrane, or third eyelid of the cat. Seen as a membrane across the inner corner of the cat's eye during illness or in times of stress.*

Heat *period of estrus.*

Hematoma *a blood blister.*

Hepatic encepholopathy *Liver failure.*

Heterozygous *a condition in which any particular characteristic has been derived from only one parent.*

Homozygous *a condition in which any particular characteristic has been derived from both parents.*

Himalayan (U.S.A.) *a Persian cat of Siamese or Himalayan coloring (see Colourpoint).*

Hot *a term used to describe a cream cat with too much red in the coat.*

Incubation period *the time that elapses between the actual infection of the cat and the appearance of the first symptoms. Most diseases have specific incubation periods.*

Inoculation *see vaccination.*

Intranasal vaccines *vaccines in liquid form instilled into the cat's nostrils with a dropper. Currently the only such vaccines are those developed for cat flu.*

Jaundice *a yellowing of the tissues caused by absorption into the blood of bile pigments. A symptom of serious disease in the cat.*

Jaw pinch *indentation of the line of the muzzle, a fault in cats whose standard calls for a wedge-shaped head narrowing in perfectly straight lines to a fine muzzle.*

Jowls *the extra development of the cheeks seen in entire male cats.*

Kink *a bend or twist in the tail of a cat due to malformation of two or more vertebrae. Considered a fault in most breeds and heavily penalized in show specimens.*

Kitten *a young cat up to the age of 9 months under the rules of GCCF. Other Associations vary; some consider them as kittens up to the age of eight months, some up to the age of ten months.*

Lactation the production of milk by the queen.
Lavender the term given to the lilac coloration in cats by some Associations.
Lesion any change in an organ or tissue, but commonly taken to be a scar or scab on the skin of the cat.
Level bite see "bite."
Lilac the simple dilution of chocolate (see lavender).
Litter (1) a family of kittens born to one queen.
Litter (2) the substance used in a litter box.
Locket a white spot at the base of the cat's throat—a serious fault in most breeds.

Mackerel a pattern of tabby markings in which thin unbroken lines run vertically down from the spine line.
Marbled the tabby pattern, also known as blotched or classic.
Mask the darker-colored areas of the face as seen in Siamese or Himalayan cats.
Mats clumps of matted hair that form in a neglected coat and may need clipping away.
Mayor's chains the lines around the neck of the classic tabbies.
Melanin see eumelanin and phaenomelanin.
Melanistic a black variety of a cat normally of some other color.
Membrane a thin skin of connective tissue.
Midline incision used in some feline operations. Made along a central line straight down the belly.
Molt (U.S.A.), Moult (U.K.) the periodic or seasonal shedding of dead hair.
Monorchid a male cat with only one testicle descended.
Mutation a change that occurs spontaneously and gives rise to a new color, type, or species variation.
Muzzle the nose and jaws of the cat.
Muzzle-break indentation in the lines of the muzzle. This is desirable in some breeds but a serious fault in others.

Nephritis inflammation of the kidneys.
Neuter a castrated male or spayed female.
Nictitating membrane see haw.
Non-self (non-solid) a cat which has a coat of more than one color.
Nose leather the smooth area of skin to be found around the cat's nostrils.

Obesity overweight.
Odd-eyed having one eye of blue and the other one of orange or copper.
Oestrus see estrus.
Oriental a group of varieties derived from Siamese, with Siamese type and conformation but without either the blue eyes or restriction of color to the points of the body.
Out of coat refers mainly to longhaired breeds during molting, or following a hot summer when their coats are thin, short, or sparse. In other varieties, a cat is said to be out of coat when the coat condition leaves much to be desired and the animal is unfit for showing.
Ovario-hysterectomy the surgical removal of the uterus and ovaries following illness or infection, or to sterilize, neuter, or spay the female cat.
Overshot jaw the upper jaw is longer than the lower jaw, causing the upper teeth to overlap the lower teeth—a serious fault.
Ovulation the process by which the ovaries release ova. In the cat, this takes place after mating.

Pads the tough, hairless cushions on the soles of the cat's feet.
Particolored having a coat of more than one distinct color, such as the Bicolor.
Parturition the process of giving birth.
Patching the way in which colors are arranged in clearly defined areas on the coat, as seen in the Tortie-and-White.
Penciling the term given to the striking fine lines seen on the cheeks of tabby cats.
Phaenomelanin orange pigment.
Phenotype in heredity, this refers to individuals showing the same characteristics of appearance.
Pinch a break in the straight lines of the muzzle—a fault in many breeds.
Placenta the afterbirth—embryonic tissue to which each kitten is attached by its umbilical cord and from which it receives nourishment before birth. It is expelled soon after the kitten's birth.
Pneumonia inflammation of the lungs—very serious in the cat.
Points the extremities of the cat's body: the mask, ears, feet and legs, and tail. In Siamese these are variously colored, giving Seal-Point, Blue-Point etc.
Polydactyl having six toes or more on the forefeet and five toes or more on the hind feet.
Poisons chemicals that may result in illness or death if used incorrectly, indiscriminately, or contacted accidentally. These may be contained in the following:
agricultural sprays—arsenic, nicotine, nitrites.
disinfectants containing—cresol, phenol, chloroxylenol, iodine.
domestic dangers—anti-freeze, caustic soda, coal gas, creosote, oils, paint, paraffin (kerosene), slug bait, sump oil, tar, turpentine, waxes.
drugs prepared as painkillers for humans—aspirin, paracetamol.
food preservative—benzoic acid.
insecticides—Aldrin, benzyl benzoate, BHC (Gammexane), Chlordane, DDT, derris, Dieldrin, Malathion, Ronnel (Ectoral), TDE, toxaphene.
plants—dieffenbachia, common house plants, philodendron, laurel, toadstools, other fungi.
rodenticides—alphanaphylthiourea (Antu), sodium fluoracetate, strychnine, thallium, Warfarin.
To produce vomiting to bring up poisons use Universal Antidote (see below) or two teaspoons of either salt (dissolving 1 tablespoon in half a cup of water) or bicarbonate of soda (1 tablespoon to a quarter cup), or place half a teaspoon of salt on the back of the tongue. For alkalis (e.g., bleaches, cleaners, solvents) do not use emetics. Give vinegar or lemon juice mixed 1:4 with water or undiluted evaporated milk to neutralize. Antifreeze must be treated by injection. For petrol products give vegetable oil or medicinal paraffin. For phenols give vegetable oil or evaporated milk before giving an emetic.

Pot belly the typically distended belly of a kitten with a heavy worm burden or cats with dropsy.
Prefix a registered cattery name used at the beginning of the name of each cat bred and registered by that cattery.
Premier a title attained by neutered cats that is equivalent to the title of Champion for entire cats.
Pricked a term used to describe ears when held high and alert, a desired trait in some breeds but may be considered a fault in others.
Progeny the offspring of a particular cat.
Progesterone a sex hormone, most important in the breeding queen.
Pulse this normally rests at about 100 beats per minute.

Queen a female cat used for breeding.
Quick the sensitive area within the cat's claw.

Recessive factor the member of an allelic gene pair which is overridden or masked by the other dominant allele.
Recognition the official acceptance of a breed or variety by a governing body.
Registration details of each animal recorded by governing body.
Regurgitation the bringing back of recently eaten food or fluid, sometimes for re-eating or feeding to the kittens.

Rex *a curled effect of the coat caused by one of several genes that resulted from separate mutations.*

Ribbon (U.S.A.) *a colored ribbon, generally printed, presented to prize-winning cats.*

Ringed *a term used to describe the bands of darker colored hairs on legs and tails of tabbies.*

Rolling *the posturing and rolling-over of the queen in estrus, usually accompanied by strident cries. A stud owner, when contacted, may ask to be contacted again when the queen is "rolling and calling" and therefore considered ready for mating.*

Rosette *a gathered or pleated rose-shaped ribbon ornament awarded to prize winners.*

Ruff *the hair around the neck of a longhaired cat (see frill).*

Rumpy *a true Manx cat with a well-rounded rump and no detectable tail structure.*

Saline solution *made by boiling 1 pt. (550 ml) of water and using this to dissolve 1 tsp. (5 ml) salt (sodium chloride). Cooled and then stored in a sterilized, tightly corked bottle, this solution should be kept for emergency use in the feline First Aid cupboard.*

Salivation *excessive production of saliva. May be a symptom of respiratory disease, ulcerated mouth or tongue, dental pain or inflamed gums, a foreign body in the mouth or throat, or a sign of aggression or apprehension.*

Salmonella *a bacterium that can cause gastro-enteritis.*

Scarab *the distinctive marking found on the forehead of the Oriental Tabby cats.*

Schedule *a printed broadsheet or booklet announcing the classes and judges of a particular cat show (see flyer).*

Scruff *the loose skin at the nape of the cat's neck, taken up by the male when mating the female. May be held firmly in order to restrain a difficult or fractious cat.*

Self *a cat which is evenly covered in hair of one color.*

Shaded Silver *a striking cat with a silver undercoat heavily tipped with black.*

Shedding *see molting, moulting.*

Silver *a gene that is present in several breeds including the Cameo, Chinchilla, Silver Tabby, and Smoke.*

Sire *the male responsible for the production of a litter.*

Smoke *a variety in which there is a dark or colored top coat that is white or silver at the roots.*

Solid *see self.*

Spay *see ovario-hysterectomy.*

Spotted *a form of tabby in which the bands of color are broken into distinct spots that may be of any regular shape.*

Spraying *the habit of urinating (micturating) to mark out a territory.*

Standard of points *agreed lists of points laid down by governing bodies by which exhibition cats are judged and assessed.*

sternum *the breast bone. In some breeds, a projected sternum is found from time to time as a hard lump near the navel. This is an hereditary defect.*

Stools *feces.*

Stop *a break in the straight line of the profile. This is a desirable trait in some breeds but a serious fault in others.*

Stropping *the habit of sharpening the claws.*

Stud cat *an entire male kept for breeding purposes.*

Stud tail *a greasy condition of the sebaceous glands situated along the root end of the cat's tail; found in females as well as males, it should be cleaned regularly.*

Stumpy *a Manx cat with a short stump of a tail.*

Suffix *see affix.*

Tabby *a series of striped, blotched, spotted, or ticked patterns. Tabby varieties are found in longhaired, shorthaired, foreign, and Siamese breeds.*

Tangles *knots that form in the coat, especially in longhaired breeds, when grooming has been neglected (see also mats).*

Tapetum lucidum *the reflective layer at the back of the cat's eye.*

Tartar *a concretion that accumulates on the teeth of cats and should be removed from time to time as necessary.*

Teat *nipple.*

Temperature *the average normal temperature of the domestic cat is 101.5°F (38.6°C).*

Testes *the male generative glands; the testicles.*

Testosterone *male hormone secreted by the testes.*

Thumb-mark *also called thumb-print, is the distinctive mark on the back of each ear of Tabby-Point Siamese and some other tabby varieties.*

TICA *The International Cat Associaion*

Ticking *the two or three bands of color seen in the typical agouti coat.*

Tipping *the contrasting color seen at the tips of the hairs of some cats' coats. The tipping may be very slight as in the Chinchilla, or British Tipped, or extend further down the hairs to give a darker effect as in the Shaded Silver and Shaded Cameo.*

Tom *an entire male cat.*

Tourniquet *a band used above an injury on a limb in order to stop bleeding.*

Toxins *poisons.*

Transfer *on the change of ownership, a registered cat or kitten must have this registered with the governing body by the completion of the appropriate form and payment of a small fee.*

Tricolor *a cat of three distinct colors.*

Tufts *small clusters of hairs at the tips of some cats' ears. Fairly common in Abyssinian cats.*

Type *the essential characteristics distinguishing a breed. A cat of good type conforms closely to the official standard of points for its breed.*

UCF *United Cat Federation (U.S.A.).*

Umbilical cord *the cord through which the unborn kitten receives nourishment. After birth this is severed about 1 in. (25 mm) from the kitten's navel and after a few days it dries up completely and falls away.*

Undershot jaw *the lower jaw protrudes farther than the upper jaw and the front teeth do not meet—a serious fault in any breed.*

Universal Antidote *a useful component of the feline first aid kit. 1–2 tablespoons should be given by mouth to the poisoned cat or kitten.*
To Make: Mix together the following ingredients:
   2 parts powdered charcoal
   1 part Milk of Magnesia
   1 part tannic acid
   Store in a sterile, tightly closed bottle for
   emergency use.
In extreme emergency, burnt toast or charcoal dog biscuits may be crushed and used instead of the charcoal, and cold, strong tea may be used instead of the tannic acid.

Uterus *the womb.*

Vaccination *inoculation with a vaccine against infectious disease.*

Vibrissae *whiskers—long sensitive bristles protruding from the face of the cat and from back of the front legs.*

Wedge *describes the head shape of some breeds, notably the Siamese varieties.*

Whip *describes the desired long, thin tapering tail required in some varieties such as the Siamese.*

Whiskers *see vibrissae.*

INDEX

Page numbers in *italics* refer to picture captions; bold numbers refer to main entry for each breed

ACKNOWLEDGMENTS

AKG, London: National Acropolis Museum, Athens 16; Jean-Louis Nou 18 Bottom;

Bridgeman Art Library, London/New York: Ashmolean Museum 13 Top; British Museum 8–9; Louvre, Paris 12 Top, 12 Bottom; Museo Archeologico, Naples 17;

Chanan Photography: 41 Top, 41 Bottom, 47 Bottom, 55 Top, 55 Bottom, 57 Top, 57 Bottom, 59 Bottom, 86 Bottom Right, 87 Bottom Left, 87 Bottom Center, 87 Bottom Right, 161 Bottom, 162 Bottom Left;

Bruce Coleman Ltd.: 11 Bottom; Adriano Bacchella 28 Bottom Left; 38 Top, 62 Top, 62 Bottom, 86 Bottom Center, 99; Jane Burton 93 Bottom, 95 Center, 96, 98 Top, 100 Bottom, 101 Bottom, 102 left, 102 right, 103 left, 105 left, 105 right, 107 Top, 109 Bottom, 110, 112 Top, 113 Bottom, 116 Top, 126, 142 Bottom, 149 Top, 154 Center; Fritz Prenzel 53 Top, HPH Photography 2-3; Harald Lange 97 Bottom; Werner Layer 32, 37 Bottom, 63 Top; Robert Maier 116 Center Left; Luiz Claudio Marigo 10 Center; Hans Reinhard 73 Bottom, 142 Top; Kim Taylor 61 Top, 92-93,152 Top; Konrad Wothe 94 Top;

Corbis UK Ltd.: 24 left; Yann Arthus-Bertrand 15 Top; Asian Art & Archaeology Inc. 19 Bottom, 24 right, Graeme Buchan Photo Library 95 Top; Frank Lane Picture Agency 21 Bottom; Robert Holmes 25 right; Hulton-Deutsch Collection 21 Top, Francis G. Mayer/National Gallery of Art, Washington/"Woman with a cat" (1875) Pierre-Auguste Renoir 20 Bottom; Joe McDonald 6-7, 11 Top; Lynda Richards 116 Center Right; Walter Rohdich 114 left; Scott T. Smith 120-121; Karen Tweedy-Hol 18 Top; Corbis-Bettmann 23, 25 left;

Frank Lane Picture Agency: Foto Natura 158; Gerard Lacz 34 Top, 35 Bottom,39 Top, 40 Top, 42 Bottom,54 Top, 68 Top, 114 right;

Octopus Publishing Group Ltd.: 30-31, 34 Bottom, 38 Bottom, 36 Bottom, 44 Bottom, 74 Top, 80 Bottom, Ray Moller 91, 111 Bottom Right, 128, 160 Bottom, 164 right; Jane Burton 106, 108 Top, 108 Bottom, 111 Bottom Left, 112 Bottom, 113 Top, 124 left, 124 right, 125 Top, 125 Center Left, 125 Bottom, 127 Top Left, 127 Top Right, 127 Center, 131 Top Left, 131 Top Right, 131 Center, 131 Bottom, 132 Top, 132 Center, 133, 136 Bottom Left, 136 Bottom Right, 137 Bottom Left, 137 Bottom Right, 138, 144, 145 Center, 145 Bottom, 156 Top Left, 156 Top Right,156 Bottom, 157 Top; Nick Goodall 139 Bottom; Rosie Hyde/Stonehenge Veterinary Hospital 151; Peter Loughran 29 Top, 33 Top, 33 Bottom, 43 Bottom, 70-71, 75,76 Bottom, 88-89, 118 Right, 119 Top, 129, 134,140-141; John Moss 51 left; Ray Moller 29 Center, 36 Top, 45 Bottom, 46 Top, 51 right, 54 Bottom, 56 Top, 61 Bottom, 63 Bottom, 65 Top, 66 Top, 76 Top, 80 Top, 81, 82, 83 Top, 84; John Moss 48-49; George Taylor 139 Top, 146;

Gill Harris BVA: 152 Center, 155 Top, 155 Center;

Marc Henrie: 44 Top, 64 Bottom, 69 Top, 69 Bottom, 78 Top, 135 Top, 160 Top, 161 Top, 162 Bottom Right, 163, 164 left, 166 Bottom;

Image Bank: G.K. & Vikki Hart Front Cover;

Howard Loxton: 20 Top, 22 Bottom, 86 Bottom Left;

Alan Robinson: 28 Top, 37 Top, 39 Bottom, 40 Bottom, 45 Top, 46 Bottom, 47 Top, 52, 53 Bottom, 56 Bottom, 59 Top, 60 Bottom, 64 Top, 65 Bottom, 6768 Bottom, 74 Bottom, 77, 83 Bottom, 85, 162 Center, 165 Top, 166 Top, 167 Top, 167 Bottom;

Solitaire Photographic: Angela Rixon 15 Bottom, 42 Top, 50, 100 Top, 123, 143, 145 Top, 165 Bottom;

Dr. A. H. Sparkes: 148 Top Left, 148 Top Right, 149 Bottom, 150 Center;

Tony Stone Images: Back Cover; Claire Hayden 115; Pal Hermansen 117; Walter Hodges Back Endpaper, 4-5; Kathi Lamm 101 Top, John Livzey 1; Renee Lynn Front Endpaper; Thomas Peterson 26-27;

Warren Photographic: Jane Burton 28 Bottom Right, 29 Bottom, 92 Top, 92 Center, 92 Bottom, 93 Top, 94 Center, 97 Top, 98 Bottom, 103 right, 103 Center, 104 Top, 104 Bottom, 107 Bottom, 109 Top, 118 left, 119 Bottom, 122, 125 Center, Right, 130 Bottom, 135 Bottom, 147 Top, 147 Bottom, 150 Top, 154 Top, 157 Bottom;

Werner Forman Archive: British Museum 13 Bottom; National Palace Museum, Taipei 19 Top

With thanks to Michael Findlay, BVMS, MRCVS, Veterinary Consultant Editor